Beyond

The

Tomb

What Happens to Your
Soul After Death

H. M. Riggle

Author of The Sabbath and the Lord's Day; Roman
Catholicism in the Light of Their Own Scriptures and
Authorities; Christian Baptism, the Lord's Supper, and
Feet Washing; Christ's Kingdom and Reign; Christ's
Second Coming, and What Will Follow

Edited by R. John Anderson

TABLE OF CONTENTS

REPRINT FOREWORD

There are many opinions, speculations, superstitions and myths about what happens to the human soul after death. In this book, however, we look at truth; we look at what the Bible–the inerrant, inspired Word of God–has to say on the matter.

Beyond the Tomb was first published in 1909 by H. M. Riggle; it is just as Biblically accurate, timely, pertinent and desperately needed today. The world around us emits so much noise constantly, pressing in on us from all sides as it pursues its own fleeting worldly interests. It is preoccupied with itself–rushing along in never-ending commotion, activity and pursuit of selfish and fleshly entertainment, without even a passing thought of the eternity that lies before it, and indeed, before each of us.

I hope that by reprinting and distributing this book, we can help you to consider very thoughtfully where your eternal destiny will be: with God in heaven and paradise, or away and apart from God, with the devil and his angels who sinned in hell. I urge you to seriously contemplate the enormity of eternity. For we all are, each of us, rushing towards that great day of judgement, where we stand before the Lord to give an account of ourselves. We can be saved from judgement and condemnation by grace through faith in the Lord Jesus Christ, or be condemned to hell. It is a matter of choosing eternal life or eternal death. We each have that choice to make. Always remember that we serve a God of love, who is love (1 John 4:8), who desires that none is lost (2 Pet. 3:9) and doesn't take pleasure at the destruction of the wicked (Ezek. 18:32). It is God alone who is from eternity past to eternity future; you too can have the new life offered by the one true and living God, the Lord Jesus Christ. He offers it as a gift to all who come and are thirsty.

"Truly, truly, I say to you, he who hears My word, and believes Him who sent Me, has eternal life, and does not come into judgment, but has passed out of death into life. Truly, truly, I say to you, an hour is coming and now is, when the dead will hear the voice of the Son of God, and those who hear will live. For just as the Father has life in Himself, even so He gave to the Son also to have life in Himself; and He gave Him authority to execute judgment, because He is the Son of Man. Do not marvel at this; for an hour is coming, in which all who are in the tombs will hear His voice, and will come forth; those who did the good deeds to a resurrection of life, those who committed the evil deeds to a resurrection of judgment." (John 5:24-29)

"For God so loved the world, that He gave His only begotten Son, that whoever believes in Him shall not perish, but have eternal life. For God did not send the Son into the world to judge the world, but that the world might be saved through Him." (John 3:16-17)

In reprinting this book, some minor changes were made: 1) outdated words and phrases that appeared in the main text were either modernized with no change to the original meaning or some helpful notes were added in brackets to assist in understanding; 2) some punctuation was updated (adding a comma, etc.); 3) pronouns for God (he, his, him, etc.) were capitalized, except where they occurred in KJV verses or in embedded quotes from other writers or books, as I find that this style of capitalization helps me maintain reverence and focus on any mention of the Lord in the text; 4) editor's notes were added reflecting historical hindsight or other clarifications that are available to us now; 5) some wording was updated and a few sentences omitted, where I thought it provided additional clarity or avoided words or phrases of the time that carry different connotations today, and so could be misunderstood if left as they were; and 6) additional verse references were added throughout the book. The original book theology and doctrine remain unchanged. All Bible quotations are left exactly as they were in the original printing and are from the King James Version (KJV). When an uncommon or obscure word is used, a definition of the word is given in brackets to help the reader who may not have a dictionary or concordance handy.

Thank God we have these works of prior servants of God available to us today, so we may learn from, build on and stand upon them. May God bless Pastor Riggle with great heavenly rewards, for it is written:

"'Do not store up for yourselves treasures on earth, where moth and rust destroy, and where thieves break in and steal. But store up for yourselves treasures in heaven, where neither moth nor rust destroys, and where thieves do not break in or steal; for where your treasure is, there your heart will be also'" (Matt. 6:19-21).

"Those who are wise shall shine like the brightness of the sky above; and those who turn many to righteousness, like the stars forever and ever" (Dan. 12:3, ESV).

We are the most blessed generation in history from this standpoint, having come after many wonderful saints (and martyrs) before us. It is wise to learn from those who have gone before us.

The strange thing about eternity
is that it rushes at you very slowly at first,
almost imperceptibly,
and then suddenly.

All "Blessing and glory and wisdom and thanksgiving and honor and power and might, be to our God forever and ever. Amen." (Rev. 7:12)

May God richly bless you.

– In Jesus Christ, R. John Anderson

PREFACE

This is the door into a storehouse of truth that deals with a vital subject. I hope that every reader will find some treasures "new and old." The most interesting of all subjects should be *"Man, his Nature and Destiny"*.

"Man is more than constitutions."—*Whittier*

"Man is man, and master of his fate."—*Tennyson*

"Man is a piece of the universe made alive."—*Emerson*

"Men are earthen jugs with spirits in them."—*Hawthorne*

"God never made anything else so beautiful as man."—*Henry Ward Beecher*

"Man is the image and glory of God."—*Paul*

The Bible is the only book that clearly reveals our nature and unlocks the mysteries of eternity. It lifts the curtain and gives us a look beyond the tomb [grave, death]. In this work, I have appealed directly to its authentic testimony and endeavored to present facts. I have tried to be fair with those who hold opposite views. Their honesty and sincerity I do not question. All I ask is a careful perusal with unbiased mind. Let us reason together, that we may ascertain the truth. Whatever the future holds in store for us will not long be a question, for very soon all of us will experience its solemn realities. The subject of this book is of eternal moment [importance] to every human being. May our readers imbibe [soak up, take in] the spirit of deep interest and pleasure that the writer has enjoyed in its preparation.

—Herbert McClellan Riggle

ORIGIN OF MAN

The question was once asked, "What is man?" This is a subject which should occupy our minds and be considered with much careful study. We have acquired knowledge along nearly every line of study in God's vast creation; therefore, it is reasonable that we should know ourselves. Man's problems are of eternal moment, for he is destined to live long after this heavens and earth have passed away (Isa. 65:17; Isa. 66:22; 2 Pet. 3:12-13; Rev. 21:1-4). Eternal verities are his. It is not my purpose to undertake to solve this question from a scientific standpoint; I shall treat it purely from the Bible standpoint. The Word of God is the only Book that lifts the veil which separates this material world from the future and eternal state and gives us a clear view not only of the present but of the future. Its teaching is plain. It gives us a clear solution of what man is, and what his eternal destiny will be. Being a Divine revelation, its teachings can be relied upon and are perfectly safe to accept. Jesus said, "The Scriptures CANNOT BE BROKEN," and what He said is authentic.

King David said, "I am fearfully and wonderfully made" (Ps. 139:14). Man is the crowning work of God's creation. He stands upon the highest pedestal of all earthly creatures, on a much higher plane than the beasts which perish. "Thou hast crowned him with glory and honor. Thou madest him to have dominion over the works of thy hands" (Ps. 8:5-6).

Physically—we are "fearfully and wonderfully made." While the elements that compose the human body are practically the same as those found in the lower animals, man in his physical organism is far superior. Our body is a congeries [collection] of wonders and mysteries, so finely, delicately, and exquisitely made that its beauty, symmetry, utility, and form places us far above the other creatures about us. But man's superiority does not lie in this alone.

Mentally—we are "fearfully and wonderfully made." Man has the power to plan, think, reason, learn, and to know. This is the vital force back of every earthly achievement—the power of ideas, the might of reason. By it we have discovered the mysteries that surround us in earth and sky. A materialist once argued with me on this point and declared that he had absolutely no superior qualities above the other animals. I told him that if I believed as did he, I would go to the barn and take my place in a stall with the horses and cows. Or I would send the donkey to school and college, and invite my dog and jersey cow into the office to keep books and do business. Why not? A moment's reflection here should suffice.

[Editor's note: Materialists deny that we possess a spiritual, conscious entity (eternal soul) separate and distinct from the body. They claim our life here and now is all there is and that when we die, we become nothingness.]

Just stop and consider what the mind of man has accomplished. He ransacks [searches through] the galaxies above; tells us the number of the stars, and unlocks the mysteries of the heavens. He delves into the strata of the rocks and in the stone-book [geologic record] of nature he reads the history of the ages. He blasts the rocks unshaken by ages and hurls their ponderous masses into the air as easily as a child tosses up a tennis ball. He tunnels the mountains, bridges the mighty streams, builds great ships that plow the briny deep, and circumnavigates the globe. He flies around the world and over the top of the earth like an eagle. He girdles the earth with a belt of wire, and as swift as thought flashes his messages from pole to pole, and even without the wire on the waves of the ether [air, e.g. radio, satellite] he accomplishes all this. He discovers the forces of nature, harnesses them, and starts the wheels of machinery all over the world. He is capable of intermingling with all wisdom, and of receiving continuous supplies of advanced knowledge. All this positively differentiates us from the brutes [beasts or animals, the word is not derogatory, just the language of that time] and allies us with Deity. But above all this—

Morally and spiritually—we are "fearfully and wonderfully made" (Ps. 139:14). The first man Adam "was made a living soul" (1 Cor. 15:45). We are moral as well as physical beings. We stand associated with two worlds. Through our physical nature we take our place in the material world and we are affiliated with the things of earth, while through our moral and spiritual nature we are associated with the environments of the spiritual and eternal world.

Thus, we are beings accountable to God, who is the Creator of all things in heaven and in earth. These natures of ours are distinguished through a moral sense, a perception of right and wrong; and we shall never be divested of this to all eternity. We are capable of choosing the evil or the good, of understanding the difference, and this choice is our own act, making us wholly responsible. Our life here and our destiny hereafter are determined by a *choice* and a *course,* and the consequences. "To whom ye yield yourselves servants to obey, his servants ye are to whom you obey" (Rom. 6:16). We choose our master and the service we render. We are blessed with astounding possibilities for time and eternity, and this lays upon us a fearful responsibility.

These facts distinguish man from the other creatures of this lower world. And such a wonderful being could not possibly be the result of mere chance. He must be the work of an infinite, independent, all-wise Creator. Life cannot generate itself; it must come from pre-existing life. The Bible testimony on this point is clear: "Know ye not that the Lord he is God: it is he that hath made us, and not we ourselves; we are his people, and the sheep of his pasture" (Ps. 100:3). "For in him we live, and move, and have our being. ... For we are also his offspring" (Acts 17:28). "Have we not all one Father? Hath not one God created us?" (Mal. 2:10). "Let us kneel before the Lord our maker" (Ps. 95:6). "The rich and poor meet together: the Lord is the maker of them all." (Prov. 22:2). "For thy Maker is thine husband; the Lord of hosts is his name" (Isa. 54:5).

Now, the opposite of this reasonable truth is the modern materialistic teaching of [the theory of] evolution that links man to the lower forms of life and makes him a lineal descendent [direct line of ancestry] of the brute. These guessers who base their belief on what they themselves style a mere "hypothesis," would have man come up through hundreds of millions of years from a common ancestry or blood relationship with the spider, elephant, toad, horse, lizard, cow, worm, ape, hummingbird, cat, dog, snail, monkey, giraffe, and what not. It is a thousand times easier to believe the Bible account of creation that we are "THE OFFSPRING OF GOD." How plain and simple is the language! "So God created man in his own image, in the image of God created he him; male and female created he them" (Gen. 1:27).

LIFE AND TIME

Natural life is probably the greatest of earthly blessings. As to its value we read, "Is not the life more than meat, and the body than raiment [clothing]?" (Matt. 6:25) God has placed us in this world and surrounded us with blessings innumerable. He made the sun to shine upon us and give us light by day and the moon by night. He made the stars that twinkle in the sky and the clouds to send us the refreshing showers. He sends the sparkling dew-drops, and covers the earth with a carpet of verdant green. The beautiful hills and valleys, the sparkling streamlets that dash down the mountainside, the fields of golden grain, the beautiful flowers, the singing birds—yes, all nature abounds with tokens of God's love, and these are intended to point us to Him who is the giver of every good gift. The heavens, and all nature about us declare the handiwork of God:

"The heavens declare the glory of God; and the firmament sheweth his handywork. Day unto day uttereth speech, and night unto night sheweth knowledge. There is no speech nor language, where their voice is not heard. Their line is gone out through all the earth, and their words to the end of the world" (Ps. 19:1-4).

"For by him were all things created, that are in heaven, and that are in earth, visible and invisible, whether they be thrones, or dominions, or principalities, or powers: all things were created by him, and for him: And he is before all things, and by him all things consist" (Col. 1:16-17).

To us life is the greatest gift, for without this all other earthly blessings would profit us nothing. Our life was given us of God and is in His hand, for "in him we live and move and have our being" (Acts 17:28). There is a purpose in life. God placed us here to glorify Him: "I made man for my glory" (Isa. 43:7). This present life molds our future and eternal destiny; hence, every moment is laden with eternal responsibilities. All along life's pathway we are scattering seeds of good or bad, and "whatsoever a man soweth, that shall he also reap" (Gal. 6:7).

In the present life, we are the subjects of Time. With gigantic footsteps
Time bears us to the future. Time is measured by moments, hours, days,
weeks, months, years, centuries, and ages. Time to us is limited by our
short life here. Life's brevity is likened in the Scriptures to a hand-breadth,
a swift post [something which goes by quickly], a dream, a shadow, a
vapor, and an eagle hastening to the prey. It is soon cut down and we fly
away. Before us lies an eternal world, an unseen state, which will be the
portion of all of us [something each of us will have part in]. This life and
world is not our final destiny.

"Man is born for a higher destiny than that of earth.
There is a realm where the rainbow never fades;
Where the stars will be spread out before us
Like islands that slumber upon the ocean.
Where the beautiful beings that here pass before us like visions,
Will stay in our presence forever."

"Brighter than the glorious sunsets,
Which delight this earthly clime [climate];
Than the splendors of the dawnings [mornings],
Breaking o'er the hills of time,
Is the richness of the radiance,
Of that land beyond the sun;
Where the noble have their country,
When their work on earth is done."

THE NATURE OF MAN IN HIS PRESENT STATE

Compared to God, man is a very insignificant creature. Of God we read: "To whom then will ye liken God? Or what likeness will ye compare unto him?" (Isa. 40:18) "It is he that sitteth upon the circle of the earth, and the inhabitants thereof are as grasshoppers. ... Who hath measured the waters in the hollow of his hand, and meted out heaven with the span, and comprehended the dust of the earth in a measure, and weighed the mountains in scales, and the hills in a balance. ... Behold, the nations are as a drop of a bucket, and are counted as the small dust of the balance. ... All nations before him are as nothing; and they are counted to him less than nothing, and vanity" (Isa. 40:12-17). In the light of all this, no wonder the Psalmist asked, "What is man, that thou art mindful of him?" (Ps. 8:4).

Yet man is a wonderful creature. God made him for His glory. He possesses unlimited possibilities and is capable of wonderful development. God takes knowledge of him, and even the hairs of his head are numbered (Luke 12:7). Yes, "Thou art mindful of him, ... for thou hast made him" (Ps. 8:4-5). God pays special regard to His creature—man, who is an immortal intelligence possessing personality.

Man has a soul and is capable of religion, hence is quite unique in God's creation. The distance between the highest brute intelligence and the rational soul of the lowest man is so wide, so great, that the chasm can never be bridged. Man was created, not evolved. No lower animal gives evidence of the personality which man possesses. The reason is we are spiritual beings. Right here is where man's superiority is so clearly seen. It is this that lifts him above the brute creation [animal kingdom] and constitutes him an active, intelligent, responsible agent. This princely power to think places him upon the throne above all material beings: "In his hand is the scepter of dominion, and on his brow the crown of a possible and glorious destiny." "For thou hast made him a little lower than the angels, and hast crowned him with glory and honor. Thou madest him to have dominion over the works of thy hands: thou hast put all things under his feet: All sheep and oxen, yea, and the beasts of the field; The fowl of the air, and the fish of the sea, and whatsoever passeth through the paths of the sea" (Ps. 8:5-8).

This inspired scripture places man upon a distinct plane above the rest of earthly creation. He is divine in his origin and possesses kinship to God. In every man there is something that is akin to God, something which separates him from all other creatures on the face of the earth, so that he can comprehend, know, and love God. No animal possesses this capacity, this high endowment, this power to know and do his Maker's will. Thus, man in his moral and rational nature resembles God. Why, we ask? Because man, like God, is a spirit. His Creator made him just "a LITTLE LOWER THAN THE ANGELS."

What then, we may ask, is the nature of angels? Inspiration answers: "Who maketh his angels spirits. Are they not all ministering spirits?" (Heb. 1:7, 14). Angels are spirit beings, not mortal, not flesh and blood, but "SPIRITS." Jesus plainly declares that "a spirit hath not flesh and bones" (Luke 24:39). David assures us that "the angel of the Lord encampeth round about them that fear him, and delivereth them" (Ps. 34:7). The fact is in this dispensation [New Testament], we have come to "an innumerable company of angels" (Heb. 12:22). Unseen to the natural eye, there are ever present angelic beings who minister to and protect God's people. They are not material beings.

It is true that at different times angels have appeared to men in various forms, which it seems they have the power to do, but this does not disprove the fact that they are immortal spirits. In their nature, they stand wholly upon the plain of spirit beings. Man was created but a *"little"* lower. "There is a spirit in man" (Job 32:8). "Glorify God in your body, and in your spirit, which are God's" (1 Cor. 6:20). "Holy both in body and in spirit" (1 Cor. 7:34). These texts declare in so many words that we are compound beings, of both "body and *spirit*" The body is material, hence subject to death: "Your mortal bodies" (Rom. 8:11). But inside these mortal bodies their lives a spirit, for "there is a spirit in man" (Job 32:8), and "the body without the spirit is dead" (James 2:26).

God is a spirit (John 4:24), eternal and immortal (1 Tim. 1:17). The third person in the trinity is the Holy Spirit, the "eternal Spirit" (Heb. 9:14). Angels are spirits (Heb. 1:7, 14) not subject to natural death, but are immortal beings (Matt. 22:29-30; Luke 20:35-36). There is a spirit or soul in man (Job 32:8; 14:22; 1 Cor. 7:34), which is not subject to physical death (Matt. 10:28); hence is immortal. Here then we have man's nature clearly defined. The sense in which he stands a little lower than the angels, or as some [translations] render it, "a little *while* lower than the angels," is in that he now inhabits a mortal body which is subject to physical death whereas the angels are wholly spirit beings, wholly immortal. Man is both spirit and flesh, soul and body. In the resurrection when "that which is sown a natural body shall be raised a spiritual body" (1 Cor. 15:42-44), we shall be "equal unto the angels" (Luke 20:36).

The twofoldness of man's nature and being is clearly seen in his creation: "And God said, Let us make man in our image, after our likeness: and let them have dominion over the fish of the sea, and over the fowl of the air, and over the cattle, and over all the earth, and over every creeping thing that creepeth upon the earth. So, God created man in his own image, in the image of God created he him; male and female created he them" (Gen. 1:26-27). "And the Lord God formed man of the dust of the ground, and breathed into his nostrils the breath of life; and man became a living soul" (Gen. 2:7). The corporeal part, or physical being, was formed from the dust of the ground. This Paul terms the "outward man" (2 Cor. 4:16), our "earthly house," and "this tabernacle" in which we now dwell (2 Cor. 5:1). Inside this dust-born body there lives an "inward man" (2 Cor. 4:16), the "hidden man of the heart" (1 Pet. 3:4), the accountable part of our being. This God created in His own image and likeness, a "LIVING SOUL": "The first man Adam was made a living soul" (1 Cor. 15:45).

It is well to note the fact right here that nowhere in the Bible is it said that when God created the lower animals He ever breathed into them the "breath of life." No other creature was thus made in "the likeness and image of God." All this is said of man alone. On this point, I quote Dr. Adam Clarke— "What is here said refers to his soul. This was made in the *image* and *likeness* of God. Now, as the Divine Being is infinite…therefore he can have no corporeal image after which he made the body of man. ... His mind, his soul, must have been formed after the nature and perfections of his God. The human mind is still endowed with most extraordinary capacities; it was more so when issuing out of the hands of its Creator. God was now producing a spirit, and a spirit, too, formed after the perfections of his own nature. God is the fountain whence this spirit issued, hence the stream must resemble the spring which produced it" (*Comments on Gen.* 1:26-27). "In the most distinct manner God shows us that man is a compound being, having a body and soul distinctly and separately created; the body out of the dust of the earth, the soul immediately breathed from God himself. Does not this strongly mark that the soul and body are not the same thing?" (*Comments on Gen.* 2:7). This is sound reasoning and we believe it gives a true exegesis of these texts. The soul is separable from the body. The Chaldee [the Semitic language of the ancient Chaldeans, used in some portions of the Old Testament] translates Gen. 2:7: "And it was in man for a speaking spirit."

But what have the materialists to offer? In a work before me entitled *Here and Hereafter,* by Elder Uriah Smith, one of the ablest writers of the Seventh-day Adventist faith [which this book disagrees with in the strongest possible terms], I read that by "living soul" is simply meant "living creature." That is, as formed from the dust "he was a lifeless man," and after God blew breath into his nostrils he was "a living one." "The lungs began to expand, the heart to beat, the blood to flow, and the limbs to move." "When the breath of life was imparted, which, as we have seen, was given in common to all the animal creation, that simply was applied that set the machine in motion." He further enlarges on the word *"became,"* endeavoring to prove that the dust-created form simply became a living person. "He became a living soul. He was a soul before, but not a *living* soul" (pp. 42-44). Further he finds the same Hebrew words here translated "living soul"—*nephesh chaiyah*—applied to the lower order of animals in Gen. 1:20-21, 24, 30, and concludes that the souls of animals and man are the same in kind (p. 46).

We readily admit that the term "soul"—Hebrew *nephesh,* Greek *psuche*—is a general word and has more than one meaning. In a few scriptures, it is applied to the individual, as in 1 Pet. 3:20: "Eight souls were saved by water." The term is so used in our common language today, as "Poor souls, they need our sympathy." That the term is sometimes applied to lower animals we have always known and never denied. That is nothing new. But all this by no means destroys the fact so clearly taught in the Bible that man possesses a spiritual entity called the soul which is separate and distinct in substance from the body and continues to live after the body returns to dust. The following scriptures do most positively teach this fact: Job 14:22; 2 Cor. 4:16; Mic. 6:7; 3 John 2; Matt. 10:28; Gen. 35:18; Luke 12:20; 16:19-31; Rev. 6:9-10; 2 Cor. 5:1-9; and Phil. 1:21-25. The soul of man is the volitional part of his being; it sins against God and needs salvation through the precious blood of Jesus Christ: "Believe to the saving of the soul" (Heb. 10:39). "The salvation of your souls" (1 Pet. 1:9). "Ye have purified your souls" (1 Pet. 1:22). Such language is never applied to the brutes.

Elder Smith, on the image and likeness in which God created man, says that "God is a person, and so that man, though of course in an imperfect and finite degree, may be an image, or likeness, of him, *as to his bodily form*" (p. 34). He then quotes Phil. 2:5-6, and Heb. 1:1-3 to prove that Christ in human flesh was "in the *form* of God" and "in the *express image of his person*" (pp. 35, 36).

To all this we reply: That God is a person we always have taught. That in person He sits upon His throne in heaven the Bible clearly teaches; and that man was made "after the similitude of God" (James 3:9) we readily grant. But to claim that this is all that is meant in Gen. 1:26-27, we most emphatically deny. God is not a fleshly being, for "a spirit hath not flesh and bones" (Luke 24:39), and "GOD IS A SPIRIT" (John 4:24). He is "eternal, immortal, invisible" (1 Tim. 1:17), wholly spirit. Now, in our creation God "formeth the spirit of man within him" (Zech. 12:1), for "there IS A SPIRIT IN MAN" (Job 32:8). Thus, we are "both body and spirit" (1 Cor. 7:34). This spirit in man is invisible to the natural eye; it is "the *hidden man* of the heart" (1 Pet. 3:4). It survives the death of the body (Eccl. 12:7), hence is immortal.

Now, it was this inward spiritual man that God created in His own moral image and likeness: "Which after God is created in righteousness and true holiness" (Eph. 4:24). Through the fall, the human family became morally depraved; but through Jesus Christ, the soul is now restored to the likeness and image of the Creator again, and this is a state of "righteousness and true holiness." Thus "we all, with open face beholding as in a glass the glory of the Lord, are changed into the same image from glory to glory, even as by the Spirit of the Lord" (2 Cor. 3:18). You see in the work of redemption which brings us back into the image of the glory of God, it is not our fleshly body that is thus restored, but "he restoreth MY SOUL" (Ps. 23:3). This is absolute proof that man possesses a spiritual, immortal element, separate and distinct from the body, created in the image of God, defiled by sin, and again restored to a state of purity through the blood of Christ. It now inhabits a mortal body, which is simply the "earthly house of this tabernacle" (2 Cor. 5:1) which will return to dust again (Gen. 3:19), while the former will live forever.

SOUL AND SPIRIT

The term soul is from the Hebrew *nephesh* and from the Greek *psuche.* The word *nephesh* occurs 753 times in the Old Testament. It is translated "soul" 475 times, "life" and "lives" 118 times, "person" 29 times, "mind" 15 times, "heart" 15 times, "body" 8 times, "will" 4 times, "appetite" twice, "lust" twice, and "thing" twice [along with other miscellaneous translations]. *Psuche* appears in the New Testament 105 times. It is translated "soul" 58 times, "life" 40 times, "mind" 3 times, "heart" twice, "us" once, and "you" once. From this it will be seen that *soul* in both the Old and New Testament is a generic term. It has a variety of meanings. Then it follows that the signification of the word in any portion of the Scriptures must be determined by the sense in which it is used in the sacred record, and in the light of its context. To do otherwise is to do violence to the Scriptures. Materialists violate this principle by applying "animal life" and "breath of life" to the soul wherever it suits their theory. There are a host of texts, as this book will show, where these terms will not apply at all, but where soul means the real inner man, the moral and spiritual part of our being, the part that survives the death of the fleshly body.

The term spirit is from the Hebrew *ruach* and from the Greek *pneuma.* The word *ruach* occurs in the Old Testament 378 times. It is translated "spirit" 232 times, "wind" 92 times, "breath" 27 times, "smell" 8 times, "mind" 5 times, and "blast" 4 times [along with other miscellaneous translations]. *Pneuma* occurs in the New Testament 385 times. It is rendered "spirit" 288 times, "ghost" 89 times, "wind" once, and "life" once [along with other miscellaneous translations]. Spirit also, as well as soul, is a generic term, with more than one meaning. Its signification must also be determined by the sense in which it is used, and by the context. Materialists have three favorite terms they use for spirit and apply them in a way that makes many texts bend to their peculiar doctrine, namely, "wind," "breath," and "life." "God is a spirit" (John 4:24). It can hardly be said with consistency that the Almighty is a mere puff of wind, a breath, or a life. Angels are "spirits" (Heb. 1:7, 14). Are they not more than a breath, a wind, a life? I think so. And "there is A SPIRIT IN MAN" (Job 32:8). It is an intelligent entity that can be saved through Jesus Christ (1 Cor. 5:5) and survives the death of the body (Eccl. 12:7). Surely this is not our breath, or even the animal life we possess.

I shall now present a number of texts where the term soul does not mean animal life, breath of life, or the mere physical person. Isaac desired Esau to come before him "that my soul may bless thee before I die" (Gen. 27:4). "To make an atonement for your souls" (Exod. 30:15). "But if from thence thou shalt seek the Lord thy God, thou shalt find him, if thou seek him with all thy heart and with all thy soul" (Deut. 4:29). "Thou shalt love the Lord thy God with all thy heart, and with all thy soul" (Deut. 6:5). "But his flesh upon him shall have pain, and his soul within him shall mourn" (Job 14:22). Here is a clear distinction between our flesh and the soul. Note the language, "His soul WITHIN HIM." This soul is capable of bestowing blessing, of seeking and finding God, and of loving Him supremely.

"The law of the Lord is perfect, converting the soul" (Ps. 19:7). "He restoreth my soul" (Ps. 23:3). "Our soul waiteth for the Lord" (Ps. 33:20). "My soul shall make her boast in the Lord" (Ps. 34:2). "My soul shall be joyful in the Lord: it shall rejoice in his salvation" (Ps. 35:9). "As the hart [deer] panteth after the water brooks, so panteth my soul after thee, O God. My soul thirsteth for God, for the living God" (Ps. 42:1-2). "Truly my soul waiteth upon God: from him cometh my salvation" (Ps. 62:1). "He preserveth the souls of his saints" (Ps. 97:10). "Bless the Lord, O my soul: and all that is within me, bless his holy name" (Ps. 103:1). "For he satisfieth the longing soul, and filleth the hungry soul with goodness" (Ps. 107:9). How dark and meaningless are all these scriptures from the materialist's standpoint! But what a wreath of heavenly truth to those enlightened to know that we have a soul, a conscious entity within that stands associated with God and things eternal. Will such texts apply to the ox, donkey, or orangutan? Why not, if man has not a soul different from the brute's?

Man is "both soul and body" (Isa. 10:18). "Hear, and your soul shall live" (Isa. 55:3). "Ye shall find rest for your souls" (Jer. 6:16). "The fruit of my body for the sin of my soul" (Mic. 6:7). "Fear not them which kill the body, but are not able to kill the soul: but rather fear him which is able to destroy both soul and body in hell" (Matt. 10:28). "For what is a man profited, if he shall gain the whole world, and lose his own soul? or what shall a man give in exchange for his soul?" (Matt. 16:26). "But God said unto him, Thou fool, this night thy soul shall be required of thee" (Luke 12:20). "His soul was not left in hell [hades], neither his flesh did see corruption [decay]" (Acts 2:31). "Tribulation and anguish, upon every soul of man that doeth evil" (Rom. 2:9). "We have as an anchor of the soul" (Heb. 6:19). "Believe to the saving of the soul" (Heb. 10:39). "The salvation of your souls" (1 Pet. 1:9). "Ye have purified your souls" (1 Pet. 1:22). Some of these texts will be examined critically in other parts of this book, but I have here brought together these many references to show that man possesses more than animal life, breath, and his outer physical being. To apply these scriptures to the brutes would be ridiculous in the extreme. But why, we ask? Because man stands upon a higher and a spiritual plane. Materialism cannot be harmonized with these scriptures.

I shall now present a number of texts in which the term "spirit" does not mean animal life, breath, or wind. "My Spirit shall not always strive with man" (Gen. 6:3). "I have filled him with the spirit of God" (Exod. 31:3). "And the Spirit of the Lord came mightily upon him" (Judg. 14:6). "But the Spirit of the Lord departed from Saul" (1 Sam. 16:14). "I am full of power by the spirit of the Lord" (Mic. 3:8). "Then was Jesus led up of the spirit into the wilderness" (Matt. 4:1). "The Spirit like a dove descending upon him" (Mark 1:10). "And began to speak with other tongues, as the Spirit gave them utterance" (Acts 2:4). "How is it that ye have agreed together to tempt the Spirit of the Lord?" (Acts 5:9). "Then the Spirit said unto Philip, Go near, and join thyself to this chariot [carriage]" (Acts 8:29). "The Spirit of the Lord caught away Philip" (Acts 8:39).

These are but a few of a multitude of texts that could be given to show that a spirit is an intelligent Person. In every reference from the Old Testament the Hebrew word is *ruach,* and from the New Testament the Greek word is *pneuma.* All these texts refer to the Holy Spirit. He is a Person. Personal actions are ascribed to Him (John 16:7-8, 13-15; 14:16-17). He searches, speaks, makes intercession, distributes gifts, appoints overseers in the church, leads, guides, comforts, reproves, convicts, regenerates, sanctifies, and preserves. He may be resisted, grieved, insulted, lied to, quenched, and blasphemed. Here then is a spirit— *ruach—pneuma—*that means more than wind, breath, or animal life.

If spirit means no more than wind or breath, then to substitute these terms for "spirit" ought to make good, sensible reading. Let us try this rule: "It seemed good to the *wind* and to us" (Acts 15:28). "God anointed Jesus of Nazareth with the *wind* and with power" (Acts 10:38). "Be zealous of *windy* gifts" (1 Cor. 14:12). "The *breath* itself beareth witness with our *breath,* that we are the children of God" (Rom. 8:16). Anyone can see that this would be ridiculous, and yet the materialistic argument presents such inconsistencies.

Again— "And there came forth a spirit [*ruach*], and stood before the Lord, and said, I will persuade him" (1 Kings 22:21). "Then a spirit [*ruach*] passed before my face; the hair of my flesh stood up: It stood still, but I could not discern the form thereof: an image was before mine eyes, there was silence, and I heard a voice, saying, Shall mortal man be more just than God?" (Job 4:15-17). Who ever heard materialists talk like this? Who ever read such language in their literature? Their teachings do not fit these scriptures at all. Surely it was more than a breath, a puff of wind, or an animal life, that appeared before the Lord, stood there, and spoke. Did Eliphaz suppose he had seen a breath, and this breath actually spoke to him? Incredible, preposterous. The inspired writer of the Books of Kings and Chronicles believed in actual spirits that could speak. Eliphaz believed the same thing.

"When the unclean spirit [*pneuma*] is gone out of a man, he *walketh* through dry places, seeking rest, and finding none. Then *he saith,* I will return into my house from whence I came out; and when he is come, he findeth it empty, swept, and garnished [put in order]. Then goeth he, and taketh with himself seven other spirits more wicked than himself, and they enter in and dwell there: and the last state of that man is worse than the first" (Matt. 12:43-45). Is this merely wind and breath that Jesus is talking about?

Or is it a life? If a life, then Mary Magdalene was delivered from seven lives. There is no way under heaven to harmonize these scriptures with the doctrine of materialism. There are personal, intelligent spirits both good and bad. During the ministry of Christ and the apostles we read of unclean, deaf-and-dumb spirits being cast out of people. Sometimes these spirits cried out and spoke to Jesus. The inspired writers have told us so. They believed in spirits. When Jesus suddenly appeared in the midst of His disciples after His resurrection "they were terrified and affrighted, and supposed that they had seen a spirit [*pneuma*]" (Luke 24:37). But Jesus said to them, "Behold my hands and my feet, that it is I myself; handle me, and see; for a spirit hath not flesh and bones, as ye see me have" (Luke 24:37, 39). If the disciples did not believe in spirits, strange it is that they all thought one appeared visibly in their midst. The very fact that they thought they actually saw a spirit proves that they believed in them. And Jesus confirmed their belief in spirits by saying, "A spirit hath not flesh and bones, as ye see me have." Was Jesus here talking about the wind, or a breath?

God Himself, as we have seen, is a spirit (*pneuma*)—not a fleshly person with corporeal frame, but a being wholly spirit. And this eternal God, our Creator "formeth the spirit [*ruach*] of man within him" (Zech. 12:1). "For what man knoweth the things of a man, save the spirit [*pneuma*] of man which is in him?" (1 Cor. 2:11). Paul is not here talking about wind, breath, or animal life, but the real, intelligent inner man, the soul, or spirit. "That the spirit [*pneuma*] may be saved in the day of the Lord Jesus" (1 Cor. 5:5). "For I delight in the law of God after the *inward man;* But I see another law in my members [parts of my body]" (Rom. 7:22-23). Here the "inward man" is clearly contrasted and distinguished from the physical "members," or body. The redeemed inward man delights in God's law, because it is spiritual—saved.

Now this inner or hidden man of the heart is termed the soul, or spirit. It may be asked, "Why are two terms used to express the same thing?" I answer, for the same reason that the outward man, the physical part of our being, is expressed by "flesh" and "body," two words as different as "spirit" and "soul." "Flesh" denotes that the outer man, the "earthly house" and "tabernacle" in which we dwell, is of material substance, mortal and subject to death. "Body" denotes this fleshly substance in its organized form, the physical outward man. "Spirit" denotes that the inward man is not a material, fleshly being, but wholly of spirit substance like God and the angels in heaven. "Soul" denotes this spiritual substance in its organized form, a real inner man, separate and distinct in substance from the body, and yet in our present state living in union with it. While there is a distinction made in 1 Thess. 5:23 and Heb. 4:12 between the soul and spirit, which is accounted for in that both these terms have a variety of meanings, yet when referring to the inner, spiritual part of our being, the real inward man, the terms soul and spirit are used interchangeably and mean the same thing. In this book, I shall thus refer to them when treating on the immortal, spiritual nature of our being.

GOD, THE FATHER OF SPIRITS

"Furthermore we have had fathers of our flesh which corrected us, and we gave them reverence: shall we not much rather be in subjection unto the Father of spirits, and live?" (Heb. 12:9). The writer of this Epistle makes a clear distinction between "the fathers of our FLESH" and "the Father of SPIRITS." It is true that God is the creator of both body and soul, the physical as well as the spiritual; but it appears in a more direct sense He "*formeth* the spirit of man within him" (Zech. 12:1). We see this in the original creation. The fleshly body that comes through natural procreation was made from the dust of the ground; but that part that was created in the image and likeness of God He "breathed into man," and this is the "living soul." No doubt in the scripture just quoted the writer is referring back to the original creation. One thing the text clearly teaches—the spirit is not the same substance as the body, and it is a real inner being.

"Forasmuch then as we are the offspring of God, we ought not to think that the Godhead is like unto gold, or silver, or stone, graven by art and man's device" (Acts 17:29). Paul, standing on Mars' Hill in Athens, addresses those idolaters, first quoting from their own poets that "we are his offspring," and then himself affirming the fact. Paul's argument was very strong and conclusive. If we are the offspring of God, He cannot be like those images of gold, silver, and stone which are formed by the art and device of man, for the parent must resemble his offspring. As Dr. Adam Clarke has well said in his comments on this text: "Seeing therefore, that we are living intelligent beings, he from whom we have derived that being must be living and intelligent."

The fact that we are the offspring of God suggests resemblance to Him. It means more than simply to be God's creatures, but resemblance in essential attributes—as intellectual perception, moral sensibility, and spiritual personality. This constitutes man the highest natural reflection of God, yes, the brightest reflector of the Infinite. It is possible to see the sun in a ray of light, the ocean in a dew-drop, and God in man. Thus, unlike the brute, we form ideas of God our Father. We love Him, adore Him, worship Him. To the brute, God's existence is a blank; but not so with man. We are His direct offspring, know Him, can become intimately acquainted with Him, are under His government, and with David we can say, "Oh, how I love thy law" (Ps. 119:97).

The soul is vastly superior to the rational universe. Wherever the voice of man's nature is allowed to speak it declares that he is the offspring of God and that the Supreme Being is the Father of his spirit. The intellectual difference between the lowest human and the highest animal is so great that it can only be accounted for by this fact. Our marvelous powers are seen in the capacity we have of knowing God. I here quote F. Frazer, M.A.: "His religious nature. 1—His consciousness of guilt, everywhere demonstrated by sacrifice, shows his alienation from a Being with whom he was once in harmony. 2—His struggles after a purer and higher life are but the effort of God's child to recover a lost condition and relationship. 3—His restlessness and dissatisfaction till he finds rest in God is the culminating proof." **People talk about the "missing link" [from the false theory of evolution] between the highest brute and the lowest man. Friends, it is not a link that is missing, but the whole chain. There is no common relationship at all, for man is a moral and spiritual being, directly related to his Maker, "the Father of SPIRITS."** [Editor's Bold] "Behold all souls are mine; as the soul of father, so also the soul of the son is mine: the soul that sinneth, it shall die" (Ezek. 18:4). "O God, the God of the spirits of all flesh" (Num. 16:22; 27:16). "In whose hand is the soul of every living thing, and the breath [*ruach*—spirit] of all mankind" (Job 12:10). Dr. Clarke, commenting on Num. 16:22, says: "This address sufficiently proves that these holy men believed that man is a being compounded of flesh and spirit, and that these principles are perfectly distinct. Either the materiality of the human soul is a fable, or, if it be a true doctrine, these men did not pray under the influence of the divine Spirit." Then after quoting Job 12:10, Dr. Clarke remarks, "Are not these decisive proofs that the Old Testament teaches that there is an immortal spirit in man? But does not *ruach* signify wind or breath? Sometimes it does, but certainly not here; for how absurd would it be to say, 'O God, the God of the *breaths* of all flesh.'"

Since the Almighty declares Himself to be "the God of the spirits of all flesh," not of the decaying material bodies alone, but the *"spirits"* that live inside these earthly tabernacles, and He is said to be "the Father of spirits," and we are thus "the offspring of God," it is easy to understand why He declares "all *souls* are mine." **They belong to Him by creation right. He has the most absolute, unquestionable right to our souls. He created them to glorify Him, hence He has the only right; they are His property.** [Editor's bold] The indestructible elements and capacities of the human soul are His product. Then again all souls belong to God by redemption: "Ye are not your own. For ye are bought with a price; therefore, glorify God in your body, and in your spirit, which are God" (1 Cor. 6:19-20).

The lofty aspirations, unsatisfied desires, keen remorse, passionate affections, and the infinite, outspoken yearnings of the human soul in every man prove that we possess an immortal element akin to God, an inward conscious being whose life and personality is not bounded by the grave.

"All souls are mine" appears to imply a distinction and dignity as to their origin. The soul has personality akin to God. The soul came from God, not as a part of His substance, which is erroneous, but by a creative act of His will. This infusion of the soul puts man, "as distinguished from the brute, in a conscious relation to God" (Aubrey Moore), and this is the very root of religion. Souls, too, belong to God in a way the material creation does not—they are made in His image "and likeness"; they are a created copy of the divine life. They hold communion with Him, can be conscious of His presence and touch, and can respond to His love. The soul possesses faculties and moral qualities "which are shadows of the infinite perfections of God."

Thus far, I have not treated the subject of the *direct* origin of the human spirit as it relates to each individual. There are three distinct theories held: 1. The theory of preexistence [before-life, or that your soul existed long before you were ever born and was simply placed into your body]. 2. The theory of traducianism [the belief that the child inherits the material and immaterial (soul) aspects of the parents]. 3. The theory of creationism [which is where God creates a new body and soul for each person at conception]. The first is paganism, an unscriptural assumption, and has no support whatever in the Bible. The second was held anciently by such men as Tertullian and Augustine, and today is held by the Lutheran Church and some others. The principal objection to this theory is that it is apt to run into the materialistic view of the soul. The direct creationism view was held anciently by such leaders as Jerome and Pelagius, and in modern times is held by the Roman Catholics and a large number of Protestants.

Since the Bible deals with the *fact* of the human spirit and not so much with its direct origin in every individual, I do not believe this point of practical consequence and of much vital concern to us. [As you are in existence here and now, reading this book with a body and a soul already, and must choose what to do with your life, which is the focus of this book.]

THE HUMAN SPIRIT IN UNION WITH A PHYSICAL BODY, OR MAN A TWOFOLD BEING

The Bible clearly teaches three states of the human soul, or spirit: *First*—In union with a physical, material body. This is man's present state and it terminates at death. *Second*—A state in which the human spirit is separated from the body and remains conscious. This commences at death and terminates with the resurrection. *Third*—The reunion of soul and body. This takes place in the final resurrection, and continues ever after, which is the eternal state.

"For which cause we faint not; but tho our outward man perish, yet the inward man is renewed day by day" (2 Cor. 4:16). This text teaches that we are compound beings possessing an "outward man" [body] and an "inward man" [soul, spirit]. The one is visible, material, mortal, hence is subject to death and perishes, while the other is spirit and does not perish with the body, but "is renewed" day by day. The outward man is the part of us that can be seen, heard, and felt; and is subject to sickness and death; therefore, it decays and wastes away through disease and old age. It is the visible man. And "the things which *are seen are temporal*"—for a time only (2 Cor. 4:18). At the very time the outer, visible man is perishing the "inner man"—the soul or spirit, is daily being "renewed" by receiving "light and life from God." This Peter calls "the *hidden man* of the heart" (1 Pet. 3:4). It is the invisible man—and "things *which are not seen ARE ETERNAL*" (2 Cor. 4:18). These two parts of our being then are absolutely distinct in substance, and while the one is perishing the other is being renewed.

In mentioning the *outer man* and *inner man*, Paul shows that he was no materialist. He believed that we have both a body and a soul, that we are a compound of flesh and spirit. And so far was he from supposing that when the body dies the whole man is decomposed, and continues so until the resurrection, that he boldly asserts that as the body of the regenerated [one who is born again] decays the other is invigorated, that the very decomposition of the body itself in the saved person, leaves the soul in the state of renewed youth. The doctrine of materialism was not apostolic [taught by the original Twelve Apostles]. Paul was not a Sadducee—for they denied both angels and spirits (Acts 23:8). Paul originally was a Pharisee, and they confessed both. In fact, they believed that spirits are conscious intelligences capable of speaking (Acts 23:9). He here speaks of the *outward* and *inward* man as distinct, though in life wedded.

Let us examine his language carefully. This outer man is part of us, but not *us*. This body is mine, but not *me*. There is a real inner man, invisible to the eyes of sense [your senses], that believes in God, loves Him, has hope in Him, and is capable of accomplishing many acts which the physical man cannot do. This outer man will decay, while the inner spiritual man is being polished day by day, and is being fitted to shine in the Savior's crown "in that day when he makes up his jewels" (Mal. 3:17). Underneath this visible form is a conscious element at work, a secret element of life that does not grow old and decay, but survives. It is right here that "life and immortality are *brought to light* through the gospel" (2 Tim. 1:10). Not brought into existence, but that which already exists is clearly brought "to light." Day by day the soul's inner life grows stronger, richer, and deeper: "Strengthened with might by his Spirit *in the INNER MAN*" (Eph. 3:16).

This is the part of us that stands particularly with reference to God and eternity. The outward man feeds on material substances. The inner man feeds on God through the Spirit [and by reading God's Word (Matt. 4:4)]. It is renewed by spiritual and heavenly influences. Divine knowledge, love, joy, peace, holiness, grace, and glory are what the soul feeds on. These are all found in Christ, the bread of life that came from heaven. Thus the inner man is as truly fed and nourished as the outer man: but the two are clearly distinct. Right here materialism must fall. It cannot stand in the light of these facts. Praise God. The Christian cries— "Let my body perish: I can look calmly on the changes of my mortality, on my pains and infirmities, on the advance of age, on the flight of time, and on death itself, for this will but set the inward man free in an infinite and eternal liberty." This immortal fire gave the martyrs courage, and lights our way through the valley of the shadow of death (Ps. 23:4), and points to heaven where we have a "more enduring substance [possession]" (Heb. 10:34). Can all this apply to the brute? No! Why not? Because we alone possess this spiritual inner being that finds in Christ its seat of strength and spring of everlasting consolation.

Materialists make no distinction between soul and body. They usually argue that the soul simply means the whole man, including the body. In a debate I held with Elder C. W. Stephens of the Second Adventist faith, he boldly asserted that when he stepped on the scales and weighed 145 pounds, his soul weighed that amount. In a discussion with Elder J. W. Watt of the Seventh-day Adventist movement, he publicly took the same position. Here is a statement I distinctly remember— "The only spirit a man possesses is in his nostrils, and if you take a bad cold your soul is in danger." Such language is common in their literature. How dark and hopeless is this teaching in the light of the transplendent, illuminating influences of the Holy Spirit that shine upon the pages of Divine revelation and lift the veil and give us a true conception of spiritual things that are eternal.

All agree that the "outward man" is the body. Now let us ascertain what the "inner man" really is. The Bible testimony is clear. "But his flesh upon him shall have pain, and his soul *within him* shall mourn" (Job 14:22). Carefully note this language—soul *"within"* him, and flesh *"upon"* him. While the one suffers pain, the other mourns. While in union, they are however clearly distinct in substance. God "formeth the spirit of man *within* him" (Zech. 12:1). "There is a spirit in man" (Job 32:8). "Watch and pray, that ye enter not into temptation: the spirit indeed is willing, but the flesh is weak" (Matt. 26:41). Note the clear distinction between our flesh—the physical man, and the spirit, the inner man. "For what man knoweth the things of a man, save the spirit of man *which is in him*" (1 Cor. 2:11). "For ye are bought with a price: therefore glorify God in your body, and in your spirit, which are God's" (1 Cor. 6:20). "The unmarried woman careth for the things of the Lord, that she may be holy both in body and in spirit" (1 Cor. 7:34).

But why multiply texts? Man is not wholly a material, physical being, neither is he wholly a spiritual being. He is both "body and spirit," "flesh and soul," an "outer and inner man"; and the two are clearly distinct in substance, but in this life are in union together.

The members of the body are but the instruments of the soul: "Let not sin therefore reign in your mortal body, that ye should obey it in the lusts thereof. Neither yield ye your members as instruments of unrighteousness unto sin: but yield yourselves unto God, as those that are alive from the dead, and your members as instruments of righteousness unto God" (Rom. 6:12-13). Here "*your*-selves" and "your mortal body," or "members," are distinct. The real inner man rules the outward man. It is the soul that is saved (James 1:21), and when this great work of salvation is wrought [brought about] in the inward man, the outward man is brought in harmony with that inward condition. Paul says, "I bring under my body" (1 Cor. 9:27). When the soul is saved the feet no longer dance on the ballroom floor [seek not the things of this world (Col. 3:1-2)], the lips no longer lie and swear, the hands cease to steal, and by the grace of God we can glorify God in both body and spirit.

THE SOUL IS THE VOLITIONAL PART OF OUR BEING. IT IS A CONSCIOUS ENTITY, AND IS IMMORTAL

"Behold, all souls are mine; as the soul of the father, so also the soul of the son is mine: the soul that sinneth, it shall die" (Ezek. 18:4). "Will the Lord be pleased with thousands of rams, or with ten thousands of rivers of oil? shall I give my firstborn for my transgression, the fruit of my body for the sin of my soul?" (Mic. 6:7). Note carefully the distinction between the physical and spiritual— "The fruit of my *body* for the sin of my *soul.*" The "soul of the son," the "soul of the father," "the soul that sinneth *it* shall die." Materialists have no little difficulty with these and similar texts. Soul here cannot mean animal life, breath, or the physical man. "The *breath* that sinneth, it shall die." "For the sin of my *physical animal life.*" How would that sound? Remember, with materialists there is no other life in man but his natural, physical life. To admit spiritual life apart from our natural life would explode all their contention [prove their assertions false].

It is not the members of our body that are accountable to God. While the hand steals, the lips and tongue profane, the feet dance, and the eyes look on the opposite sex to lust after them, the real trouble is deeper. These members are but the external instruments of the soul. You might cut off the hand, pluck out the literal eye, and tear out the tongue, but the real trouble would still remain. **Sin is not a physical affair. It is a moral, spiritual evil.** [Editor's bold] It is not the breath, the animal life, the physical man that stands condemned before God. It is the soul of man. "The *soul* that sinneth, *it* shall die." "The sin of *my soul.*" Thus, the soul of man is vastly different from that of the brute.

There is another term that is frequently used in the Bible to denote the moral, spiritual part of us, and in a host of texts refers directly to the inward man. It is "heart." "Seeing ye have purified your souls in obeying the truth through the Spirit unto unfeigned [genuine, sincere] love of the brethren, see that ye love one another with a pure heart fervently" (1 Pet. 1:22). Here soul and heart mean the same thing. I shall now give a number of texts where the term "heart" cannot mean the muscle in our breast that pumps the blood through the body, but refers directly to the moral, spiritual man: "The law of his God is in his heart; none of his steps shall slide" (Ps. 37:31). "I will put my laws in their mind, and write them in their hearts" (Heb. 8:10). "Written not with ink, but with the Spirit of the living God; not in tables of stone, but in fleshly tables of the heart" (2 Cor. 3:3). "Thy word have I hid in mine heart, that I might not sin against thee" (Ps. 119:11). "Behold, thou desirest truth in the inward parts" (Ps. 51:6).

What sense would be attached to these texts if man were only flesh and blood and breath and intellect without a soul? These scriptures would be meaningless and nonsensical. Apply these texts to the hippopotamus and see how they would sound. Note also that in Heb. 8:10 God said, "I will put my laws into their mind, and write them in their hearts." Here heart means more than merely the mind. God's law was to be written in both the heart and mind. Thought and mind in man is more than a property of matter—it is a faculty of the soul, and continues active after death, as this book will show. A person might have the Word of God so stored away in his mind that he could repeat from memory the whole Book, but that would not effect for him what these scriptures declare. It is in our spiritual and moral being that God puts His law when He saves the soul from sin.

"Keep thy heart with all diligence; for out of it are the issues of life" (Prov. 4:23). "For from within, out of the heart of men, proceed evil thoughts, adulteries, fornications, murders, etc." (Mark 7:21). "A good man out of the good treasure of the heart bringeth forth good things; and an evil man out of the evil treasure bringeth forth evil things" (Matt. 12:35). The heart then is the treasure-house, the fountain and spring from which flows our outward life. If man were no more than an animal how could this be? Will such texts apply to the ape or giraffe? Heart here can only apply to the soul, the real inner man. "Man looketh on the outward

Beyond the Tomb37

appearance, but the Lord looketh on the heart" (1 Sam. 16:7). The Bible speaks of the heart as being "deceitful," "desperately wicked," etc. (Jer. 17:9; Mark 7:21)

And again, we read of a "clean heart," "perfect heart," "honest and good heart," and "pure heart." All such expressions can only apply to our spiritual and moral nature, the soul, or spirit, of man. "And God, which knoweth the hearts, bare them witness, giving them the Holy Ghost, even as he did unto us; and put no difference between us and them, purifying their hearts by faith" (Acts 15:8-9). On the disciples at Pentecost (Acts 2), and subsequently on the household of Cornelius (Acts 10), was poured out the Holy Ghost, at which time their hearts—souls—were purified.

In the great work of salvation, it is not the flesh, bones, or blood, nor is it the breath or mere animal life that is converted, regenerated, and changed from a sinful state to a righteous condition, but it is the heart, the soul, the real inner man. It is more than the mind. [Editor's bold] For a Jew or Mohammedan simply to see [intellectually] that his religion is wrong and the Christian faith and religion is right, and in belief accept Christ as the Son of God, will not change his moral nature. It takes more than that. [It takes the blood of Christ shed on the cross to restore the soul.] A man may with his mind endorse the whole truth and yet be a sinner. Salvation goes deeper than the mind. Now if man were wholly a material being and possessed no conscious spiritual entity he could not undergo a spiritual change. All the change that could be wrought upon him by his Creator would be material and physical or fleshly. The brute *cannot* undergo a moral or spiritual change.

The very fact that man has become MORALLY defiled by sin and can be MORALLY purified by the blood of Christ in salvation proves beyond all question that he is more than a physical being, that he has a spiritual nature, and that this spiritual nature is a conscious entity. This is what Paul meant in Rom. 7:22-23: "For I delight in the law of God after the inward man: But I see another law in my members [parts of the body]." The twofold nature is here clearly taught. The inward man delights in the law of God and at the same time the law of sin works in the members of the physical body. This was Paul's experience under the law before his conversion. In order for this inner man to delight in God's law he must first learn that law, get a knowledge of it. How could this be unless he is a conscious entity, an intelligent being? Yes, the soul is capable of knowing God, understanding His will and word, and delighting in His law. "For what man knoweth the things of a man, save the spirit of man which is in him?" (1 Cor. 2:11). The Spirit searches the deep things of God and reveals them to us, just as the human spirit knows all the things of a man and makes us conscious of them. That is exactly what this text and its context teaches. Therefore, the human spirit is a conscious entity.

As we have seen the soul is the volitional part that sins against God, becomes [morally] defiled and depraved, and feels the sting of guilt and condemnation. Therefore, it is the soul that needs to be saved. "Receive with meekness the engrafted [implanted] word, which is able to save your souls" (James 1:21). "The law of the Lord is perfect, converting the soul" (Ps. 19:7). "The salvation of your souls" (1 Pet. 1:9). "That the spirit may be saved" (1 Cor. 5:5). "Ye have purified your souls" (1 Pet. 1:22). "Purifying their hearts by faith" (Acts 15:9). "Blessed are the pure in heart: for they shall see God" (Matt. 5:8). What a beautiful wreath of heavenly truth!

In salvation, [by the blood of Christ,] the spiritual and moral nature of man is restored. "He restoreth my soul" (Ps. 23:3). All these scriptures teach the conscious existence of the human soul. God has promised "to give knowledge of salvation unto his people by the remission of their sins" (Luke 1:77). How is this given? "He that believeth on the Son of God hath the witness in himself" (1 John 5:10). "Knowing in yourselves that ye have in heaven a better and an enduring substance [possession]" (Heb. 10:34).

In what part of our inward being is this precious knowledge and witness given? Answer: "The Spirit itself beareth witness with OUR SPIRIT, that we are the children of God" (Rom. 8:16). It is by our spiritual nature that we are made conscious of God. The blessed Holy Ghost communicates to "our spirit" a sweet consciousness of our acceptance with Him. Materialism cannot stand in the light of this truth. Paul further explains this experience in Gal. 4:6: "God hath sent forth the Spirit of his Son into your hearts, crying, Abba, Father." Our "hearts" and our "spirit" here mean the same thing—another proof our heart, or spirit, is a conscious entity.

But our materialist friends say spirit means breath, wind. How would this sound? "His *wind* beareth witness with our *wind,* that we are the children of God." Our "God hath sent forth the *breath* of his Son into our *breath,* crying, Abba Father." No, friends, "there is a spirit in man," an intelligent, conscious entity, that can be saved through the blood of Jesus Christ and can receive from God through the Holy Spirit a sweet inward assurance and consciousness of it. This is the immortal part of our being.

"Your heart shall live forever" (Ps. 22:26). How much is implied in these words. This teaches the absolute indestructibility of the seat of our spiritual affections—the heart, or soul. There is one thing in this fleeting world that is immortal, the nature of which is undying, and that is the human soul. It "shall LIVE FOREVER." So positively teaches the Word of God.

How beautifully this text in Ps. 22:26 blends with that of 1 Pet. 3:3-4: "Whose adorning let it not be that outward adorning of plaiting the hair, and of wearing of gold, or of putting on of apparel; but let it be the hidden man of the heart, in that which is not corruptible [mortal, subject to decay], even the ornament of a meek and quiet spirit, which is in the sight of God of great price." Here again immortality is clearly brought to light. The subject is adornment, outward and inward beautifying. The embellishment of a true Christian is not external decorations, "not that *outward* adorning" of the body with costly apparel, gold, etc. Do not spend your time trying to adorn and beautify the outward man, the physical body, for it is corruptible and will soon decay and die. Your *"mortal* body," "mortal flesh" (Rom. 6:12; 8:11; 2 Cor. 4:11). How vain to spend valuable time hanging jewels on this poor "vile [morally defiled, wicked] body" of ours. What then shall we adorn? Answer: "Let it be the hidden man of the heart, in that which is not corruptible." How plain this statement. A "hidden man" which is "not corruptible" dwells inside this corruptible and decaying body. The adorning of this inner man—the soul—is not something that we put on, but is a state or condition of our spiritual being, a "meek and quiet SPIRIT" (1 Pet. 3:4). The hidden man of the heart is our spirit, and it is beautified by meekness and quietness in salvation. "He will beautify the meek with salvation" (Ps. 149:4). "The beauty of the Lord God is upon me" (Ps. 90:17). "Out of Zion, the perfection of beauty, God hath shined" (Ps. 50:2).

On this text Dr. Adam Clarke remarks— "*Hidden man of the heart.* This phrase is of the same import with that of St. Paul—Rom. 7:22 the *inner man;* that is the soul, with the whole system of affections and passions. Every part of the scripture treats man as a compound being: the body is the outward or visible man; the soul, the inward, hidden, or invisible man." ... "All the ornaments placed on the head and body of the most illustrious female are, in the sight of God, of no worth; but a meek and silent spirit are, in his sight, invaluable, because proceeding from and leading to himself, being incorruptible [immortal and everlasting, not subject to decay and death], surviving the ruins of the body and the ruins of time, and enduring eternally." This is sound. Man possesses both a corruptible and an incorruptible part. The outer man is corruptible— subject to natural decay, and as a result, death. It is the only part of us that will put on immortality and incorruption at the resurrection (Phil. 3:20-21; 1 Cor. 15:42, 44). The inner, or hidden man of the soul, the human spirit, "is not corruptible". It is spirit— "for there is a spirit in man." All spirits, now and all the time, and evermore, are incorruptible; and the human soul is spiritual. Materialists will argue that it is not the hidden man but the adornment that is incorruptible, the ornament the hidden man is to wear. But this ornament is not a trinket of some kind—it is a state, a condition of the soul when saved by grace. The inward man, being incorruptible, must be adorned with incorruptible, imperishable graces.

The words "not corruptible" in 1 Pet. 3:3-4 are derived from the Greek word *aphthartos*. This same word is found in the following texts: 1 Cor. 9:25, "incorruptible [*aphthartos*] crown"; 1 Cor. 15:52, "The dead shall be raised incorruptible [*aphthartos*]"; 1 Pet. 1:4, "Inheritance incorruptible [*aphthartos*]; and in 1 Tim. 1:17, "Now unto the King eternal, IMMORTAL, [*aphthartos*]." Here then we unmistakably have its true meaning. The Deity is *aphthartos*—immortal; and in the final resurrection the dead shall be raised *aphthartos*—incorruptible, and Paul defines this— "this mortal shall put on immortality" (1 Cor. 15:54). Immortality is from either of two Greek words—*aphthartos* or *aphtharsia,* which mean imperishable, incorruptible; or from *athanasia*—deathlessness. The words "not corruptible" in 1 Pet. 3:4 are rendered "imperishable" in Bible Union and Sawyers translations. "Imperishable—not subject to decay; indestructible"—*Webster.* So this text properly rendered reads, "The hidden man of the heart, is that which is immortal —imperishable." So, there is no evasion of the fact that inside our mortal flesh there lives a conscious entity, a soul or spirit, an intelligent being, the real inner, hidden man of the heart, and it is immortal, imperishable, and does not go down in decomposition with the body.

Jesus taught this truth in the clearest manner: "And fear not them which kill the body, but are not able to kill the soul: but rather fear him which is able to destroy both soul and body in hell" (Matt. 10:28). "And I say unto you my friends, Be not afraid of them that kill the body, and after that have no more that they can do. But I will forewarn you whom ye shall fear: Fear him, which after he hath killed hath power to cast into hell; yea, I say unto you, Fear him" (Luke 12:4-5). If the body were the soul men could kill that. If by soul is meant merely the physical man, men can kill him. If by soul is simply meant physical life, man can take that from us. But here Jesus plainly taught that the soul of man is indestructible by material forces. Man can kill the body, but "he CANNOT KILL THE SOUL." So, when the body dies the soul still lives. Then it is immortal.

This clear teaching of Christ's announcing the separability of the soul from the body and of the fact that the death of the body does not involve the extinction of the soul, has troubled and perplexed our materialistic friends not a little, and it is surprising how much time and space they devote in their writings to explain away the force of its meaning. But with all their labor, Matt. 10:28 stands unshaken and mocks their efforts. One of their own materialistic writers, J. P. Ham, in his work *Life and Death*, says, "Nothing more is implied than that the soul is distinct from the body." Good for Ham. While he denies its immortality, he admits what is fatal to the whole materialistic teaching— "the soul is *distinct* from the body." And, may I add, Matt. 10:28 as clearly teaches that the soul survives the death of the body. Uriah Smith in *Here and Hereafter* (pp. 109-116) argues that soul here means "the life which is to come." He quotes Matt. 16:25, "Whosoever will lose his life for my sake shall find it." That is, we may lose our present life in martyrdom or death for Christ's sake and gain it again in the resurrection. That would make Matt. 10:28 read, "Fear not them which kill the body, but are not able to kill the life which is to come in the resurrection." This is certainly a new definition of the term soul and does not at all give a correct exegesis of this scripture.

I quote Dr. Clarke: "We find that the body and the soul are distinct principles, for the body may be slain and the soul escape; and secondly, that the soul is immaterial [spirit], for the murderers of the body are not able, have it not in their power, to injure it." The import of Christ's words cannot be mistaken. He expressly asserts that man consists of both soul and body, and that the soul survives the death of the body and continues in a state of consciousness when separated from the body. The soul and body do not perish together at death. Jesus taught that all of us possess souls which come not under the power of men but are subject to the power of God alone. Fear him, who, when the body is killed, can cast the soul into hell, the God who has power to destroy both soul and body in hell. The term *kill* as it relates to the power of both man and God in both these texts has reference only to the body. For surely Christ did not teach that God will kill the soul and then cast it into hell. If so, why fear its being cast into hell? 'Fear him, which *after* he hath killed, hath power to cast into hell' (Luke 12:5). To cast a dead body into hell was not Christ's meaning, nor did He mean to cast a dead soul there either. This casting into hell as recorded in Luke 12:4-5 is after the body has been slain, hence *can refer only to the soul.* This proves that the soul is the conscious personality, and that after death the soul is susceptible of happiness and misery. After the death of the rich man, in Luke 16, he lifted up his eyes 'in hell' and cried, 'am tormented in this flame.'"

ANGELS ARE INTELLIGENT, IMMORTAL SPIRITS

The Bible teaches that there is a race of spiritual beings called angels. From the beginning of the world's history they have communicated with men at many times and appeared visibly in various forms. An angel appeared to Hagar on two occasions and made known to her God's will and decree (Gen. 16:7-13; 21:14-18).

These heavenly messengers visited Abraham and apprised him of the impending destruction of Sodom, and then two of them delivered Lot and his family out of the doomed city. In the Old Testament record are many instances where angels revealed themselves to people and declared God's will. An angel went before the armies of Israel and fought against their enemies. It was God's angel [possibly preincarnate Jesus Himself] that protected the three Hebrews in the fiery furnace (Dan. 3), and delivered Daniel from the lions (Dan. 6). The angel Gabriel revealed to Daniel the future history of his nation (Dan. 8-9).

When we come to the New Testament, Gabriel announced to Mary the conception and birth of Jesus (Luke 1:26-38). Angels proclaimed the birth of the Savior and sang the blessed paean [a song of praise and triumph] recorded in Luke (Luke 2:13-14). Angels ministered to Christ at the time of His temptation in the wilderness (Matt. 4:11), and again at the close of His agonies in the Garden of Gethsemane (Luke 22:43). One of these heavenly messengers delivered Peter from prison (Acts 12:6-10). The gospel history is replete with similar experiences. I believe it will well be worth the time of any of our readers to get a complete concordance and read all of the texts in the Bible on angels.

There are different orders of angels, as the archangel, named Michael. We have some of their names, as Gabriel and Raphael [from the apocryphal book of Tobias, which is not included in the Protestant Bible]. Some of them "excel in strength," we are told, and when the Lord descends from heaven to punish the wicked He will be accompanied "with his *mighty* angels," yes "all the holy angels with him." As to their number, the scriptures teach that there is "an *innumerable* company of angels" (Heb. 12:22). Jesus said in the Garden of Gethsemane that if He wished He could call "more than twelve legions of angels" (Matt. 26:53). [A legion represents a vast number, and was a unit of 3,000-6,000 men in the Roman army.] Lazarus "was carried by the angels" to Abraham's bosom, or the Paradise of God (Luke 16:22). Angels, then, are intelligent heavenly beings and minister to the people of God on earth. Like Jesus after His resurrection, these heavenly messengers have the power to appear in visible form and in various forms, which they have done.

Sometime, not clearly revealed to us, some "angels sinned," "kept not their first estate, but left their own habitation," and are reserved in "chains of darkness unto the judgment of the great day" (2 Pet. 2:4; Jude 6). It is generally believed that Satan and his hosts of demons are the ones referred to. Satan is called the "prince of devils" (Matt. 9:34), "prince of the power of the air" (Eph. 2:2), "ruler of the darkness of this world" (Eph. 6:12), and the "power of darkness" (Col 1:13; Eph. 6:12). He then has a kingdom, has a dominion, and reigns. From Matt. 25:41 we infer that hell was "prepared for the devil *and his angels*." Then demons are angels, and of course must be fallen angels [also called unclean spirits]. Knowing their final doom, James tells us they "believe and tremble" (James 2:19) This is evident from what the demons said to Jesus: "And, behold, they cried out, saying, What have we to do with thee, Jesus, thou Son of God? Art thou come hither to torment us before the time?" (Matt. 8:29). So there are good, holy angels in heaven, and there are evil, fallen angels in hell. The good are "sent forth to minister for them who shall be heirs of salvation" (Heb. 1:14). The evil ones are under the direction and rulership of Satan and are sent forth to destroy the souls of men.

We shall now consider the *nature* of angels. Of good angels we read: "Who maketh his angels *spirits,* and his ministers a flame of fire" (Heb. 1:7). "Are they not all ministering *spirits?*" (Heb. 1:14). Of the devil and his angels, we read: "When the even [evening] was come, they brought unto him many that were possessed with devils [demons]: and he cast out the *spirits* with his word" (Matt. 8:16). "He gave them power against unclean *spirits,* to cast them out" (Matt. 10:1). The demoniac [demon possessed person] mentioned in Mark 5:2-13 was possessed with a legion of devils, and at the command of Christ, "the unclean *spirits* went out." "For unclean *spirits,* crying with loud voice, came out of many that were possessed with them" (Acts 8:7). Angels, then, whether good or bad, are *"spirits."* They do not possess material, physical, fleshly bodies, as man in his present state does, yet they are real beings. "The angel of the Lord encampeth round about them that fear him, and delivereth them" (Ps. 34:7). "He shall give his angels charge over thee" (Ps. 91:11). Yes, invisible to the natural eye, there are ever present angelic beings ministering to and protecting the people of God. And just as surely evil angels, spirits of darkness, swarm the earth and prey upon the souls of men.

[Editor's note: As mentioned, angels can also take the form of men and appear at times (see Gen. 16:7; Gen. 18:2; Gen. 19:1-11; Gen. 32:1; Num. 22:22; Matt. 2:13; Matt. 28:5; Rev. 22:8-9; etc.). But be aware that Satan and his demons can also appear as angels (Gal. 1:8; 2 Cor. 11:14-15). Also, angels are not to be worshipped (Col. 2:18).]

In referring to "materialists" in this work, I mean only those religious bodies that hold materialistic views of theology including Adventists, Russelites, etc.

Before me lies a work entitled *Eternal Principles,* by Miles Grant, one of the ablest preachers and writers that the materialist cause ever produced. He first gives the definition of *material,* as follows: "'Consisting of matter, not spiritual, corporeal, physical; as physical substance, material bodies' (Webster). 'Consisting of matter; of physical nature, not spiritual' (Century Dictionary). Next *immaterial*— 'Not consisting of matter; incorporeal; spiritual; disembodied' (Webster). 'Not consisting of matter; not material' (Century Dictionary)." Now, after giving the definitions as found in the dictionaries, Mr. Grant says: "Whenever all that is immaterial is separated from that which is material, then both will become extinct. One cannot exist without the other" (page 10). "The existence of love, thought, joy, sorrow, life, consciousness, and intelligence, without a living *material* organism is inconceivable; and is most fully opposed to the facts of science, the eternal principles of pure reason, metaphysics, common sense, and the Bible" (p. 11). "The material and the immaterial are always correlated." "All immaterialities cease with the material objects in which they adhere." "An immaterial, organic living being is also a contradiction of terms" (p. 14). "All immaterial things are lifeless, unconscious, unintelligent, inorganic, formless, and absolutely destitute of any attributes." "That which is immaterial cannot be tormented or be happy." "All living beings are material" (p. 15). "It is impossible to have any form, likeness, image, or personality without materiality" (p. 21).

I have quoted a number of Grant's "principles" to show exactly what they believe and teach. Now, after all this Grant says: *"If there is even one fact to prove that there has been, is now, or ever will be, in heaven or on earth, a single case of life, consciousness, and intelligence, without materiality, then it must follow that there is not one fact to prove the position I have taken"* (pp. 23, 24). This is his conclusion because he admits that "whatever is opposed by one fact, is also opposed by all other facts relating to that subject" (p. 14). Now, on his own ground and premise I shall prove his so-called "principles" false and present some facts that completely overthrow his position. He says *"All* living beings are *material,"* and accepts the definition of the dictionaries that material means— "Consisting of matter, physical, not spiritual."

All right, friend Grant. First: What about God? Is He a living, conscious, intelligent being? If you answer yes, I ask you, Does the eternal, invisible, omnipresent Jehovah consist of matter? Is He a physical being, and "not spiritual"? The Bible answers this in a most positive manner and forever destroys your position: "God is a Spirit: and they that worship him must worship him in spirit and in truth" (John 4:24). Second:

What about the Holy Ghost? He is a Person, an intelligent Person. He speaks, guides, convicts, converts, sanctifies, and distributes gifts in the church. He is the third Person in the Trinity. You can grieve Him, sin against Him, and reject Him. I ask you, what about Him? Is He physical, material, consisting of matter, not spiritual? He is called the "eternal Spirit." It is said that Stephen was a man "full of the Holy Ghost" (Acts 6:5). Was he full of something material, physical, consisting of matter? Is the Holy Spirit material? Is He "not spiritual"? If spiritual, can He not think? Is He not intelligent? Does the Holy Ghost have a material body such as we have? You surely would be ashamed to say He is confined within the limits of a physical body. Then, since the Holy Ghost is not physical, made of matter, He is not material. Being wholly spiritual He possesses life, consciousness, intelligence, and many other attributes without being a physical being. In the light of this truth, in the face of real facts, your supposed principles fade into oblivion. Here is a "case of life, consciousness, and intelligence without materiality," the very thing that verifies that there is not "one fact to prove the position" of Mr. Grant.

Third: What about angels? Are they not spiritual? The Bible says that they are "spirits," "ministering spirits." They have life, consciousness, and intelligence.

Fourth: What about the legion of spirits that possessed the man who lived among the tombs of Gadara? You say "*all* living beings are *material.*" Were these demons material? Did they consist of matter, and were they physical? Was this poor man possessed of a legion of physical beings? If a spirit cannot live apart from matter, please tell us what happened to those demons in the intervening time between when Jesus cast them out of the man and when they then entered into the swine? From the time they came out of the man until they entered the swine were they dead or living? What happened to them after the herd was drowned in the sea? Did they die with the swine? This may sound ludicrous, but I desire to show the inconsistency of this materialistic doctrine.

Jesus said, "When the unclean spirit is gone out of a man, he walketh through dry places" (Matt. 12:43). Later "he saith, I will return unto my house whence I came out" (Matt. 12:44). Here is a spirit speaking and walking after it leaves a material body. It is a clear case of life, consciousness, and intelligence without materiality. "Then goeth he, and taketh to him seven other spirits more wicked than himself; and they "enter in, and dwell there: and the last state of that man is worse than the first" (Luke 11:24-26). Strange language this from the materialistic viewpoint. According to Elder Miles Grant, eight physical, corporeal, material bodies consisting of matter enter this one man and dwell there. Pray, tell us how this could be? Anyone can see at a glance that the whole materialistic contention and Grant's so-called principles are baseless, preposterous, incredible, and present an incomprehensible enigma that cannot be solved. Did Jesus cast seven physical, material beings out of Mary Magdalene? Who can accept such teaching?

I shall now show that angels are immortal beings. In order to uphold their doctrine, some materialists go so far as to deny the immortality of angels. If angels are not immortal, then they are mortal. If mortal, they are subject to death. If not subject to death, they are immortal. In Heb. 2:9, we read that Jesus "was made a little lower than the angels, *for the suffering of death.*" This clearly proves that angels are not subject to death. I shall now give Christ's own words on this point: "Ye do err, not knowing the scriptures, nor the power of God. For in the resurrection they neither marry, nor are given in marriage, but are as the angels of God in heaven" (Matt. 22:29-30). "But they which shall be accounted worthy to obtain that world, and the resurrection from the dead, neither marry, nor are given in marriage: *neither can they die any more: for they are equal unto the angels*" (Luke 20:35-36). In the resurrection, after the corruptible body has put on incorruption, and this mortal flesh has put on immortality, then we shall stand wholly upon the plane of immortal beings, being "equal unto the angels." The result of this equality is stated in these words: "Neither can they die any more." If these scriptures do not teach that angels stand wholly upon the plane of spiritual and immortal beings, then it would be difficult indeed to convey such an idea in our language.

WHAT PART OF MAN IS MORTAL?

Mortal is defined by Webster — "Subject to death; destined to die; as, man is mortal." *Mortality*— "Subjection to death, or the necessity of dying." That human beings are mortal but very few deny. "Shall mortal man be more just than God?" (Job 4:17). As a penalty for sin God decreed, "Dust thou art, and unto dust shalt thou return" (Gen. 3:19). "By man [Adam] came death" (1 Cor. 15:21). "It is appointed unto men once to die" (Heb. 9:27). That which was created from the dust of the ground—the body—the flesh—or what Paul terms "the outward man," will go back to dust again. "Then shall the dust return to the earth as it was: and the spirit shall return unto God who gave it" (Eccl. 12:7).

The physical man is subject to death, hence mortal: "Your mortal body" (Rom. 6:12). "Your mortal bodies" (Rom. 8:11). "Our mortal flesh" (2 Cor. 4:11). These texts need no comment. It is our fleshly body that is mortal. Only our bodies sleep in the dust of the ground (Eccl. 12:7; Matt. 27:52-53), and that which sleeps "in the dust of the earth shall awake" (Dan. 12:2). "We look for the Savior, the Lord Jesus Christ: who shall change our vile body, that it may be fashioned like unto his glorious body" (Phil. 3:20-21). It is not our soul, but our *body,* that will come forth and be changed in the final resurrection of the dead: "So also is the resurrection of the dead. ... It is sown a *natural body;* it is raised a *spiritual body*" (1 Cor. 15:42, 44). Only our bodies are mortal, and "this mortal must put on immortality" (1 Cor. 15:53).

THAT WHICH IS BORN OF THE SPIRIT IS SPIRIT

Materialism denies spiritual birth in this life. Jesus Himself positively taught that "Ye must be born again" (John 3:7). He also stated why: "Except a man be born again, he cannot see the kingdom of God. ... He cannot enter into the kingdom of God" (John 3:3, 5). The kingdom of God He referred to may apply to the kingdom of grace here on earth, or to the kingdom of glory in heaven above: or, as is most likely, it includes both. However, in any case, the new birth is absolutely necessary in order to enter into it. "Ye must be born again." This Jesus defined as being "born of the Spirit" (John 3:8). It is a spiritual birth.

Now if man were only a material being without any spiritual entity he could not undergo any spiritual change. In order for him to be born again he would have to, in the language of Nicodemus, "enter the second time into his mother's womb, and be born" (John 3:4). But Christ made this whole matter very clear, as follows: "That which is born of the flesh is flesh; and that which is born of the Spirit is spirit" (John 3:6). **Note well this language. That part of man which is born again is not our fleshly, physical being, but *is spirit.*** [Editor's bold] Right here materialism must fall. Man is both flesh and spirit. That which is born of the flesh is flesh, it is that which comes according to the course of nature—natural birth. But that which is born of the Holy Spirit is *spirit.* It is not our fleshly being, not our breath or merely our natural animal life, but our spirit. The Spirit of God operates upon our spirit and changes it from a defiled, sinful condition to a righteous state. This is regeneration. Thank God for the plain teaching of Scripture on this point.

Now, in order to evade the force of this truth, materialists usually hold and teach that spiritual birth does not take place in this life, not until the resurrection of the dead. They say *gennao,* the Greek word for *to be born,* only means to be begotten. So they argue that we are only in a begotten state until the resurrection of the dead, when we shall be born. With all boldness, we declare that this is but an evasion to deny the immortality of the human soul. Let us examine their argument. They say *gennao* simply means begotten, not really born. "Now when Jesus was born [Greek, *gennao*] in Bethlehem of Judea in the days of Herod the king, behold, there came wise men from the east to Jerusalem, saying, Where is he that is born [Greek, *gennao*] King of the Jews? ... And when they were come into the house, they saw the young child with Mary his mother and fell down, and worshiped him" (Matt. 2:1-11). Here the reader will observe that *gennao* means *to bring forth.* Jesus was actually born, and the wise men saw the young child. The Greek term, however, is *gennao.* Again, "A woman when she is in travail hath sorrow, because her hour is come: but as soon as she is delivered of the child, she remembereth no more the anguish, for joy that a man is born [*gennao*] into the world" (John 16:21). "I am verily a man which am a Jew, born [*gennao*] in Tarsus" (Acts 22:3). "Moses, when he was born [*gennao*], was hid three months of his parents" (Heb. 11:23). We could multiply proof-texts, but anyone can see that in the scriptures cited that *gennao* means actual birth, to bring forth.

Now I shall give other clear texts where the same word occurs in the original:

"But as many as received him, to them gave he power to become the sons of God, even to them that believe on his name: Which were born [*gennao*], not of blood, nor of the will of the flesh, nor of the will of man, but of God" (John 1:12-13). "Ye must be born [*gennao*] again" (John 3:7). "Every one that doeth righteousness is *born* of him" (1 John 2:29). "Whosoever is *born* of God doth not commit sin; ... because he is *born* of God" (1 John 3:9). "Every one that loveth is *born* of God, and knoweth God" (1 John 4:7). "Whosoever believeth that Jesus is the Christ is *born* of God" (1 John 5:1). In all these texts the word *born* is from *gennao,* which we already have proved means actual birth—to bring forth.

There are many other clear texts which prove that the new birth is effected in this life: "Seeing ye have purified your souls in obeying the truth through the Spirit unto unfeigned [genuine, sincere] love of the brethren, see that ye love one another with a pure heart fervently: being born again, not of corruptible seed, but of incorruptible, by the word of God, which liveth and abideth for ever" (1 Pet. 1:22-23). "As newborn babes, desire the sincere milk of the word, that ye may grow thereby" (1 Pet. 2:2). The Father does not record the names of His children on the family record until after they are born: "Rejoice, because your names are written in heaven" (Luke 10:20). "And of Zion it shall be said, This and that man was born in her. ... The Lord shall count, when he writeth up the people, that this man was born there" (Ps. 87:5-6).

God is our spiritual Father. The church is the bride, or wife, of Christ (Eph. 5:23-32). She is our mother (Gal. 4:26). "For as soon as Zion travailed, she brought forth her children. ... That ye may suck, and be satisfied with the breasts of her consolations; that ye may milk out [drink deeply], and be delighted with the abundance of her glory. ... Then shall ye suck, ye shall be borne upon her sides, and be dandled upon her knees [held or bounced in her lap]" (Isa. 66:8-12). Thus, having a spiritual Father and mother we become "sons of God" by being "born of God" (John 1:12-13). This is not effected in the resurrection, but, "beloved, *now* are we the sons of God" (1 John 3:2); "babes in Christ" (1 Cor. 3:1); "newborn babes" (1 Pet. 2:2); not by natural birth, for "that which is born of the Spirit is spirit."

A PRESENT STATE OF SPIRITUAL DEATH AND SPIRITUAL LIFE PROVES THAT THE SPIRIT OF MAN IS DISTINCT FROM THE BODY

Those religious bodies who deny the immortality of the human soul teach that we are now only under the sentence of death and will not actually die as the result of sin until after the resurrection. They also teach that when we come to Christ and accept Him, the sentence of death is lifted and that we now receive the promise of eternal life; but that this life in actual experience will not be realized until this mortal shall have put on immortality in the resurrection. We only now have it by promise, an object of hope, something not yet fully received. Of course, they are driven to this point in order to support their position; for if man were only a corporeal being he could die only a natural death and could enjoy and possess only natural life.

But the Bible plainly teaches both spiritual death and spiritual life. God said to our fore parents in the Garden of Eden, "But of the tree of the knowledge of good and evil, thou shalt not eat of it: for in the day that thou eatest thereof thou shalt surely die" (Gen. 2:17). The serpent told the woman, "Ye shall not surely die" (Gen. 3:4). Here the issue is clearly drawn. Materialists take their stand in this controversy on the side of the serpent! God said in unmistakable words, "In *the day* that thou eatest thereof thou shalt surely die." The Septuagint Version [the translation of the Old Testament from Hebrew into Greek, also referred to as LXX] renders this text as follows: "In whatsoever day ye eat of it, ye shall surely die." Our materialist friends say that man did not die that day, but that just the seed of death was implanted in his being. So did the serpent say, "Ye shall not surely die." But mark you God said, "In the *day*" that man would eat of the forbidden fruit he would "surely die." In this discussion, we take our stand with God on the side of truth and declare that man did die on the very day that he transgressed God's command. Of course he did not die a physical death at that time, but he did die a spiritual death.

Sin separates the soul from union with God: "But your iniquities have separated between you and your God, and your sins have hid his face from you, that he will not hear" (Isa. 59:2). As soon as the soul is cut off from union and fellowship with God it is in a state of death. This death is not a cessation of the soul's conscious existence and being, but is an alienation from God, in whose favor is the normal sphere of the soul's happiness. So when Adam and Eve transgressed the command of the Lord they still had a conscious existence but were alienated from their Creator, cut off from Divine favor; hence in a state of spiritual death. This was the immediate result of sin. But the effects of the fall were far-reaching: "By one man [Adam] sin entered into the world, and death by sin; and so death passed upon all men, for that all have sinned" (Rom. 5:12). Again, we read that "death reigned from Adam to Moses" (Rom. 5:14). The word *death* in these texts clearly refers to spiritual death in trespasses and sins, for Paul in this chapter uses it interchangeably with the word sin (Rom. 5:12-21).

So, every sinner is now actually dead, spiritually dead, and yet he has a conscious existence. This fact stands in square opposition to the entire doctrine of materialism. It proves beyond any question that the spirit of man is separate and distinct in substance from his fleshly body. Every unregenerate person is now "dead in trespasses and sins" (Eph. 2:1-5). Before our conversion "we were dead in sins" (Eph. 2:1-2). "You, being dead in your sins" (Col. 2:13). "To be carnally minded is death" (Rom. 8:6). "She that liveth in pleasure is dead while she liveth" (1 Tim. 5:6). "The soul that sinneth, it shall die" (Ezek. 18:4). These scriptures plainly show that the spiritual part of man's being is in an unsaved, unregenerate state, is dead to God. And yet this does not imply the destruction of the soul's conscious being, but the forfeiture of the bliss of Divine favor. "Dead while she liveth"—that is, the carnally minded are dead, dead in sin, yet they desire, hope, and fear; in fact, they are still conscious of a moral and spiritual existence but are also conscious of the fact that their spirit is not in its proper attitude toward God nor in its normal state of righteousness. Paul says that when he came to the years [age] of accountability and got a knowledge of God's law, "sin revived, and I died" (Rom. 7:9). Paul did not die a physical death when he sinned against God's law. So Paul was more than a physical being. Neither did he simply pass under the sentence of death. But he actually declares, "I died." And he remained dead until the time of his conversion. But, it may be asked, what part of Paul's being suffered death? We answer, that part which sinned against God. "Shall I give my firstborn for my transgression, the fruit of my body for the *sin of my soul?*" (Mic. 6:7).

Now, to all such thus dead in trespasses and sin, the voice of Jesus says, "I am come that they might have life" (John 10:10). This could not be natural, physical life, for sinners already have that. Neither can it refer to the natural sleep of the body, nor to men in the grave; but Jesus was addressing people in this world who are dead in sin. This is an experience of the soul, not of the body: "Incline your ear, and come unto me: hear, and your *soul shall live*" (Isa. 55:3).

But is this quickening of [restoring or giving life to] the soul into life a present experience? Do men actually possess eternal life in Christ right after conversion? Yes, thank God: "We know that WE HAVE PASSED from death unto life" (1 John 3:14). "Verily, verily, I say unto you, he that heareth my word, and believeth on him that sent me, hath everlasting life, and shall not come into condemnation; but IS PASSED from death unto life" (John 5:24). "And you *hath* he quickened, who WERE dead" (Eph. 2:1). A present experience, you see. [Editor's caps]

This life is received by faith, not through the resurrection of the dead: "He that *believeth* on me hath everlasting life" (John 6:47). The apostles and early Christians actually possessed this spiritual life, and it is eternal life, as John testifies. "God hath given to us eternal life. ... He that hath the Son hath life" (1 John 5:11-12). Neither was this mere conjecture or speculation, but the apostle confirms them in this truth by saying, "These things have I written unto you that believe on the name of the Son of God; that ye may know that ye have eternal life" (1 John 5:13). Is it true that the mission of Christ is not accomplished, and the apostles and early Christians were mistaken when they believed the testimony of the Spirit in their hearts, and then by Divine inspiration testified that they were made alive in Christ and possessed eternal life as a present, blessed experience of the soul?

If the Bible is of any weight, eternal, spiritual life is a present experience: "And this is life eternal, that they might know thee the only true God, and Jesus Christ, whom thou hast sent" (John 17:3). The doctrine of materialism cannot stand in the light of these scriptures. Spiritual death and spiritual life, being present conditions of the human family, prove that man possesses a spiritual, conscious entity that is separate and distinct from the body.

DEATH A SEPARATION

Death is a solemn event through which we all must pass. There have been but two exceptions in the history of mankind—in the cases of Enoch (Gen. 5:24) and Elijah (2 Kings 2:1-11), who were translated.

Paul shows a mystery, as recorded in 1 Cor. 15: "We shall not all sleep." Those who are left alive unto the arrival of the Lord in His second advent [coming] will be exempt from death and "changed, in a moment, in the twinkling of an eye, at the last trump [trumpet]" (1 Cor. 15:52). With these exceptions, all must taste the pangs of death. "It is appointed unto men once to die" (Heb. 9:27). Our short life here is but a shadow, a dream. "It is soon cut off, and we fly away" (Ps. 90:10). Amidst the hurry and whirl of this fast age, the rumbling and rattling of commercial, social, and political life, men are apt to forget this solemn fact, but still, in kindness, we would remind the reader that in the midst of the busiest scenes of life, we are also in the midst of death.

This truth is depicted in nature. In the springtime, the trees put forth their leaves and during sweet summer days furnish protection to the singing birds in their leafy bowers [a pleasant shady place]. But autumn frosts and winds turn the leaves to a golden hue, they fall to earth, and while winter snows cover the earth with a white carpet they molder [slowly decay and disintegrate] back to the dust of the earth. The flowers fade, the grass withers, the sturdy oak decays, the monuments crumble, and, in fact wherever we look we can see the end of all—death. O man, you must die! Death is no respecter of persons. He cuts off the young as well as the old. He comes in childhood's happy hours and plucks the fairest buds. He comes in the bloom of youth and with his sickle cuts down the noble son and daughter. He summons man in his busy days, while his bark of life is dashing through mad breakers and stormy billows, while cares of life are pressing around him. He enters the home, and man must obey the summons. He comes to the few who reach hoary [old, grayish] age, and tottering forward, they fall into the grave. Yes, we are all bending toward the tomb. Death enters alike the palace of the rich and the hovel [small, simple dwelling] of the poor. His silent tread is felt all over the earth, where homes are left with vacancies and hearts are saddened. The hour of death will be the most solemn hour of all our life.

But we cannot linger here. As we pass down through death's valley (Ps. 23:4) eternity's scenes loom up before us. The curtain is now lifted and we take a look into the unseen world. As I grasp my pen, solemn thoughts flash through my mind. Thank God for the unerring guide of truth (Ps. 23:3), a lamp to our feet, a light to our pathway (Ps. 119:105).

But what is death?

Death is a separation. "And it came to pass, as her soul was in departing, (for she died) that she called his name Benoni: but his father called him Benjamin" (Gen. 35:18). How plain this declaration from heaven! Death is simply the separation of soul and body. The soul departs when the body dies. Our materialist friends tell us that it is simply the breath, or physical life, that leaves the body when we die. It seems to me that there is more implied in this scripture than that. Surely the inspired writer was speaking of more than the mere exhaling from the lungs. "For as the body without the spirit is dead, so faith without works is dead also" (James 2:26). Here we see that it is the body that goes down into decomposition in death. "The body without the spirit is dead." So, when the spirit leaves the body the latter is dead. Death, then, is a separation.

"Then shall the dust return to the earth as it was: and the spirit shall return unto God who gave it" (Eccl. 12:7). It is impossible to mistake the import of this passage. The returning to the dust is not the same thing as returning to God. And mark the fact that in death it is only the dust—the fleshly body—that returns to dust again. The spirit does not go down into decomposition with the body, but is separable from it, survives the stroke of death, and returns to God. Our materialist friends tell us that *spirit* here means the breath of life, which of course means the exhaling from the lungs of a puff of wind. Let us examine their position just a moment. Their exposition that the breath returns to God who gave it robs the text of its great meaning and importance. The breath is simply the air we breathe. In what sense could the air we breathe return to God at death? It is surely a waste of time to press such matters. All these scriptures teach in the clearest language that the human spirit survives the stroke of death and still lives, understands, and feels either the favor or displeasure of God. The soul of the righteous enters into the immediate presence of the Lord, where there "is fullness of joy," while the soul of the wicked is forced out from beneath the clay covering [our earthly body (2 Cor. 4:7; Job 4:19)] into the immediate presence of the Almighty, conscious of His displeasure, to await punishment in the final resurrection.

"But God said unto him, Thou fool, this night thy soul shall be required of thee" (Luke 12:20). This man had spent all his time and talents in accumulating wealth. Probably without one thought of God or eternity intruding upon his visions of anticipated bliss, he plodded onward toward the goal of wealth. Finally, he reached the summit of his worldly ambitions. He had all the earthly goods that heart could wish. He thought to himself, I have labored hard all through life to accumulate this. Now I shall take my ease. "Soul, thou hast much goods laid up for many years." I will "eat, drink, and be merry." What a wretched portion for an immortal soul! God said, "Thou fool!" Oh, foolish man! He had neglected to lay up treasures in heaven. He overlooked the one thing above all things needful.

As the evening shadows gather fast a horror takes hold of him. The whole scene begins to change. Death, like a grim monster, enters his palace and seizes his mortal frame. The night winds moan and howl without, while wafted upon the breezes from the eternal world comes an awful summons: "This night *thy soul* shall be required of thee."

"He looked all aghast at the sound of that voice,
     Then gazed on his rich earthly store;
But it melted away; he had made a sad choice,
     He was poverty's slave evermore."

How awful was this saying! He had just made the necessary
arrangements for the gratification of his sensual appetites; and in the very
night in which he had finally settled all his plans, his soul was called into
the presence of his Maker. None of his worldly goods could accompany
him, and he had not a particle of heavenly treasure!

"Out, out from his mansion he wandered away,
     To the depths of eternity's night,
To beg for relief and to long for the day
     Which shall gladden—no, never—his sight."

THE SPIRIT SURVIVES THE DEATH OF THE BODY

"Then shall the dust return to the earth as it was; and the spirit shall return unto God who gave it" (Eccl. 12:7). We have already referred to this text, but I desire to use it here, for it is a clear proof that the human spirit does not die with the body. Immediately after death it appears before God to be consigned to a state of blessedness or misery in another world.

Then, the spirit is immortal. The inspired penman [the writer of Ecclesiastes] gives us a graphic description of death and what lies beyond it. To us is disclosed the fact of the separation of the soul from the body and its continued existence in another sphere. It retains a consciousness of its individual existence and of its personal identity, and there is no suspension of this state of being. Moses, Lazarus, and Dives [the rich man] are the same persons after death that they were before, and they knew it. It is very evident that after death the spirit of man is fully awake to a constant sense of the presence of God. It is awake to the memory of the past. Being brought before God for a judicial purpose, of the unsaved, all the sins of the past will come vividly to mind, because the faculty of memory will be quickened into new activity and power.

The spirit will also awake to the awful certainty of the near approach of final judgment and reward or punishment. This in itself proves a state after death of happiness or misery. Death dissolves the union of man's complex being, the soul and body, the spirit and flesh. The one goes to dust, and the other takes a different course, namely, "man goeth to his long home" (Eccl. 12:5). "Man has gone to his eternal home" (Septuagint Version). How different the teaching of the "soul-sleepers," who say that the whole man—body and soul—goes down into the grave and remains in unconscious slumber until the resurrection! In this they squarely contradict the Bible. The spirit returns to its source, it being an immortal entity beyond the reach of that disintegration which death produces in our "house of clay." In the present life, we simply "*dwell* in houses of clay"

(Job 4:19). In death, we "put off this…tabernacle" of clay (2 Pet. 1:13-15) and, go to our own place (Acts 1:25).

The spirit possesses properties that do not belong to matter, such as reflection, intelligence, and volition. It possesses qualities that are eternal in their nature, hence the human soul must from its very nature survive the death of the body. This truth is taught all through the Bible. Physical death does not involve the spirit in its ruin, but separates the "inner man" (soul) from the "outer man" (body). Nowhere in the Bible is it taught that the soul, or spirit, goes down in decomposition with the earthly house. All scripture teaches directly the opposite: "Tho our outward man perish, yet the inward man is renewed day by day" (2 Cor. 4:16). Here Paul teaches that as the Christian's body grows old and decays, his soul grows young and is invigorated. The very decomposition of the body itself in the normal spiritual man leaves the soul in the state of renewed youth. "Fear not them which kill the body, but are not able to kill the soul" (Matt. 10:28). Here Jesus taught that the soul and body are distinct entities, and when the body is slain, the soul escapes. It follows that the soul is immortal; hence the murderers of the body are not able to injure it.

"Oh, that I had wings like a dove! for then would I fly away, and be at rest" (Ps. 55:6). "The days of our years are three score years and ten; and if by reason of strength they be four score years, yet is there strength, labor and sorrows; for it is soon cut off [when the body dies] and we [the real inner man] fly away." "And Isaac gave up the ghost, and died, and was gathered unto his people, being old and full of days: and his sons Esau and Jacob buried him" (Gen. 35:29). "And when Jacob had made an end of commanding his sons, he gathered up his feet into the bed, and yielded up the ghost, and was gathered unto his people" (Gen. 49:33). At death both Isaac and Jacob were gathered to their people. This could not apply to the laying away of the body, for it is declared that *at death* they were gathered to their people, while their bodies were not buried until after this. At the very time Jacob yielded up the ghost [died] he was gathered to his people, and long after this his sons carried his body back to Canaan and buried it in the cave of Machpelah (Gen. 49:33; 50:1-13). Of course, this gathering relates to the soul; he was gathered to the assembly of the blessed. Job, speaking of the ungodly rich man, says: "The rich man shall lie down [that is, in the grave], but *he shall not be gathered*" (Job 27:19).

"And they stoned Stephen, [with Stephen] calling upon God, and saying, Lord Jesus, receive my spirit" (Acts 7:59). There is no possible way under heaven successfully to deny the testimony of this plain text of scripture. It is a strong and full proof of the immortality of the soul. Stephen would not have commended his spirit to Christ had he believed he had no spirit; or in other words, that his body and soul were one and the same thing. Allowing this most eminent saint to have had a correct notion of theology; and that, being full of the Holy Ghost, as he was at this time, he could make no mistake in matters of such vast importance, Stephen in his dying hour believed that the soul was immortal, for he commended his departing spirit into the hands of Christ.

One minister in our presence tried to escape the strong testimony of this text by saying that it was not Stephen but the mocking Jews that uttered this language. Shame on such twisting in order to uphold a false doctrine! "And they stoned Stephen, as he was invoking and saying, Lord Jesus receive my spirit" (Emphatic Diaglott). "And they stoned Stephen, as he was invoking and saying—Lord Jesus! give welcome unto my spirit" (Rotherham). It is clear to any mind not entirely befogged in the darkness of materialism that it was Stephen who said, "Lord Jesus, receive my spirit." And has not the dying testimony of Stephen been that of millions of saints? This fact alone ought to have some weight upon those who advocate the soul-sleeping doctrine. Can anyone suppose that Stephen committed his *breath* into the hands of the Lord Jesus, commended to God the last portion of the air he breathed? No serious mind could so trifle with such a solemn expression. Materialists deny that man possesses any other than the natural, physical life. Was it this that passed into nonentity at death? And can anyone suppose that Stephen would have commended to

God a nonentity? This would be a shameless trifling with sacred things. There is, therefore, but one answer to the question: he commended to God just what he expressed, *his spirit.*

In His dying hour Christ addressed His Father thus: "Father, into thy hands I commend [commit] my spirit" (Luke 23:46). This is absolute proof of the spirit's separate existence when the body is dead. But a few moments before this, the dying thief [on a cross next to Christ] made the following request: "Lord, remember me," "And Jesus said unto him, Verily I say unto thee, Today shalt thou be with me in paradise" (Luke 23:43). Paradise is a general term denoting a place of rest, delight, and happiness. It is spoken of as a heavenly realm (2 Cor. 12:1-4). In fact, it is the place where the righteous are comforted until the resurrection. This text most clearly teaches that the very day of their death both Christ and the penitent thief entered paradise: "Today shalt thou be with me in paradise."

"But," say our materialist [and soul-sleeper] friends, "one day is with the Lord as a thousand years. So, a thousand years from now, or at Christ's second advent, the thief will be with Christ: but he was not at his death." This is entirely too flimsy for fully enlightened people to accept. "Today" in this text is from the Greek *semeron,* the same word which occurs in Matt. 6:11: "Give us *this* day our daily bread." According to the foregoing argument, when we ask God to give us this day our daily bread we mean a thousand or two years in the future.

When driven from this position these preachers have another argument to present. They say that a simple change of the comma placed after the word today puts the answer of Christ to the penitent thief in the form of a question: "Verily I say unto thee today [to give emphasis]," as if the thief might be led to believe He had spoken it yesterday, or might survive and speak it tomorrow. They put it in the form of a question, as if that would answer the thief's request.

I here insert the following from Dr. Adam Clarke's commentary: "This saying of our Lord is justly considered as a strong proof of the immateriality of the soul; and it is no wonder that those who have embraced the contrary opinion should endeavor to explain away this meaning. In order to do this, a comma is placed after today, and then our Lord is supposed to have meant, 'Thou shalt be with me after the resurrection: I tell thee this today.' I am sorry to find men of great learning and abilities attempting to support this most feeble and worthless criticism. Such support a *good* cause cannot need, and in my opinion, even a *bad cause* must be discredited by it."

To this we can say amen. "Verily I say to you, That this day thou shalt be with me in paradise" (Syriac Version). So it is clear that the very day of their death Christ and the penitent thief entered the paradise of God.

"Yea, I think it meet, as long as I am in this tabernacle, to stir you up by putting you in remembrance; knowing that shortly I must put off this my tabernacle, even as our Lord Jesus Christ hath showed me. Moreover, I will endeavor that ye may be able after my decease to have these things always in remembrance" (2 Pet. 1:13-15).

Peter describes his sojourn upon earth in these words: "As long as I am in this tabernacle." By "this tabernacle" he means his mortal body. Several versions so render it. The body was not Peter, but Peter dwelt in the body. This proves that Peter understood that the soul is distinct from the body. As a man's house is the place where he dwells, so the body is the house where the soul dwells. His decease (death), he describes as the time when "I must *put off* this *my tabernacle.*" Here we have the testimony of an inspired apostle that at death we put off this earthly tabernacle, which is dissolved—goes back to the dust of the earth, while the soul, the inner man, departs and is in a more sacred nearness to Christ, which is "far better." "Absent from the body and present with the Lord" (2 Cor. 5:8). This testimony concurs with all Scripture.

Only the bodies of men, that part which returns to dust, sleep in the grave: "And many *bodies* of the saints which slept arose, and *came out of the graves"* (Matt. 27:52-53). "And many of them that sleep in the dust of the earth shall awake" (Dan. 12:2). "The dead know not anything" (Eccl. 9:5). This last text refers to participation in things of earth. They know nothing of what is being "done under the sun" (Eccl. 9:6).

Our spirit returns to God (Eccl. 12: 7), and continues to exist "absent from the body" (2 Cor. 5:8), which, to the righteous, is "far better than to abide in the flesh" (Phil. 1:24), "Whether we wake [are alive and remain in the body] or sleep [our body dies], we should live together with him" (1 Thess. 5:10). "Your heart shall live forever" (Ps. 22:26).

"Yea, tho I walk through the valley of the shadow of death, I will fear no evil: for thou art with me; thy rod and thy staff they comfort me. ... and I will dwell in the house of the Lord forever" (Ps. 23:4, 6). Death is here described as a valley, a shadow. Do we stop in this valley and remain there in an unconscious state till the resurrection? Absolutely not! David says, "I walk *through* the valley ... I will abide in the house of the Lord forever." Death, then, is but a dark shadow through which we pass to the realm of light beyond.

"There was a certain rich man, which was clothed in purple and fine linen, and fared sumptuously every day: and there was a certain beggar named Lazarus, which was laid at his gate, full of sores, and desiring to be fed with the crumbs which fell from the rich man's table: moreover the dogs came and licked his sores. And it came to pass, that the beggar died, and was carried by the angels into Abraham's bosom [the place of comfort in Biblical Sheol]: the rich man also died, and was buried; and in hell he lift up his eyes, being in torments, and seeth Abraham afar off, and Lazarus in his bosom. And he cried and said, Father Abraham, have mercy on me, and send Lazarus, that he may dip the tip of his finger in water, and cool my tongue; for I am tormented in this flame.

"But Abraham said, Son, remember that thou in thy lifetime receivest thy good things, and likewise Lazarus evil things: but now he is comforted, and thou art tormented. And beside all this, between us and you there is a great gulf fixed: so that they which pass from hence to you cannot, neither can they pass to us, that would come from thence. Then he said, I pray thee therefore, father, that thou wouldest send him to my father's house: for I have five brethren; that he may testify unto them, lest they also come into this place of torment. Abraham saith unto him, They have Moses and the prophets; let them hear them. And he said, Nay, father Abraham: but if one went unto them from the dead, they will repent. And he said unto him, If they hear not Moses and the prophets, neither will they be persuaded, tho one rose from the dead" (Luke 16:19-31).

The words of Christ emphatically teach the conscious state of the soul after death. The account of the rich man and Lazarus is either a parable or real history. If a parable, Christ chose either a falsehood or truth for the base of His parable. Mark that thought. I repeat: the basis of the parable is either a positive falsehood or a positive truth. If such a state of things does not exist after the death of the body, then Christ falsified. Every pious soul cries out, "Let God be true, tho every man a liar" (Rom. 3:4).

"There was a certain rich man, which was clothed in purple and fine linen, and fared sumptuously every day." Here we have a man rich in this world's goods. He had all that heart could wish for. He fared sumptuously. But one thing he neglected—salvation; he neglected to lay up treasures in heaven—eternal riches. A poor beggar lay at his gate full of sores. If this rich man had been a child of God, he would have taken this poor man in and dressed his sores and fed him from his bountiful table. But he was too proud and selfish. The starving beggar desired simply the crumbs which fell from the rich man's table: moreover, the dogs came and licked his sores. Oh, how sinful and haughty was that rich man!

But the time came when "the rich man died, and was buried." His mortal body returned back to dust. But did that end his existence? Was his soul buried in the grave, too? No. "In hell [hades] he lift up his eyes, being in torments." While his body was buried his soul was in torment.

Now let us glance briefly at the other side: "And it came to pass, that the beggar died." Did that end his existence? No. He "was carried by the angels into Abraham's bosom." At death, the real inner man departed. He did not go down with the decomposing body but was carried by the angels into Abraham's bosom, the paradise of God. Here he was "comforted," while the rich man "afar off" was in a state of torment. This narrative of the Savior's perfectly concurs with the multiplied scriptures already cited which so clearly teach the conscious state of the soul after death.

"And when he had opened the fifth seal, I saw under the altar the souls of them that were slain for the word of God, and for the testimony which they held: and they cried with a loud voice, saying, How long, O Lord, holy and true, dost thou not judge and avenge our blood on them that dwell on the earth? And white robes were given unto every one of them; and it was said unto them that they should rest yet for a little season, until their fellow servants also and their brethren, that should be killed as they were, should be fulfilled" (Rev. 6:9-11).

Here the souls of that great multitude who were slain under the second and fourth seals are brought to view, viz., the millions who were slain for the Word of God and for the testimony which they held during the reign of heathen Rome and papal Rome. They were the disembodied spirits of the host who laid down their lives for the gospel. They were conscious. "Upon the altar" would signify labor, sacrifice, and service, but "under the altar" signifies that their labors were done. "And it was said unto them, that they should *rest* yet for a little season. "They were at rest." "Blessed are the dead which die in the Lord...that they may rest from their labors" (Rev. 14:13). In that home of the soul "the wicked cease from troubling; and there the weary be at rest." Yes, they "rest together; they hear not the voice of the oppressor. The small and great are there; and the servant is free from his master" (Job 3:17-19). Oh, how comforting these scriptures, when we believe the truth, since life and immortality are brought to light in the gospel. These souls were not on the earth, for they spoke of them "that dwell on the earth." Their bodies had been slain on the earth. But their murderers could not kill the soul (Matt. 10:28). Their souls still lived and were conscious.

While thus reigning with the Lord (Rev. 20:6), these souls desired of Him to know when He would avenge their blood on them that dwell upon the earth. They were told that they should rest a "little season" until their fellow servants also and their brethren that should be killed as they were should be fulfilled. This, of course, referred to a second bloody martyrdom that would take place. This no doubt was fulfilled after the sixteenth century reformation when tens of thousands of Protestants laid down their lives before the papal power was broken. This may also include the putting to death of some of God's saints just before the end. God will avenge the blood of the martyrs by casting the beast into the burning flame or lake of fire (Dan. 7:11; Rev. 19:20; 20:10).

But the point to which we call the reader's attention is that those souls whose bodies had been slain *were alive,* under the altar of God, and they conversed with the Lord. So, while the body is dead and moldering [slowly decaying, decomposing] in the tomb, the soul still continues to live.

"I knew a man in Christ above [who] fourteen years ago (whether in the body, I cannot tell; or whether out of the body, I cannot tell: God knoweth); such an one caught up to the third heaven. And I knew such a man (whether in the body, or out of the body, I cannot tell: God knoweth); How that he was caught up into paradise, and heard unspeakable words, which it is not lawful for a man to utter" (2 Cor. 12:2-4). It is generally believed by all the commentators I have consulted that Paul here refers to himself. Some of these hold that he refers back to his experience at Lystra recorded in Acts 14:19-20. It is said there that the people, "having stoned Paul, drew him out of the city, supposing he had been dead" (Acts 14:19). In any case this passage expresses a full belief in the separability of the soul or spirit from the corporeal body. A materialist *never* uses language such as this. It does not fit their doctrine. The apostle clearly asserts that he was caught up into paradise, into the third heaven. While there in this state of rapture [being caught up into heaven] or transportation, he heard unspeakable words, which plainly shows a full consciousness on his part while this rapture continued. These words that he heard while in paradise were not "lawful for a man to utter": and this shows that he still retained those unspeakable words in his memory.

There is one particular point I wish the reader to note. When all this took place, Paul was not certain whether he was "in the body" or "out of the body." Then Paul believed in the possibility of being "out of the body" and still being conscious, yes, and in heaven, or paradise. There is no evasion of the fact that this text positively teaches that the spirit—the real inner man—may exist separately from the body, and that in this state it may retain its capacity to witness and enjoy celestial things. The apostle was a firm believer and advocate of the conscious state of man after death.

ABSENT FROM THE BODY AND
PRESENT WITH THE LORD

"For we know that if our earthly house of this tabernacle were dissolved, we have a building of God, an house not made with hands, eternal in the heavens. For in this we groan, earnestly desiring to be clothed upon with our house which is from heaven: if so be that being clothed we shall not be found naked. For we that are in this tabernacle do groan, being burdened: not for that we would be unclothed, but clothed upon, that mortality might be swallowed up of life. Now he that hath wrought [prepared] us for the selfsame [this very] thing is God, who also hath given unto us the earnest of the Spirit. Therefore we are always confident, knowing that, whilst we are at home in the body, we are absent from the Lord (*we walk by faith, not by sight*): we are confident, I say, and willing rather to be absent from the body, and to be present with the Lord. Wherefore we labor, that, whether present or absent, we may be accepted of him" (2 Cor. 5:1-9).

Paul here speaks of a time when we shall be "absent from the body" and "present with the Lord." This cannot apply before death for, as observed in a previous chapter, the spirit lives in union with the body until natural death. Neither can this text apply after the resurrection, for then shall these bodies be raised immortal and we shall inhabit them forever. So, the only time we can be absent from our bodies and present with the Lord is between natural death and the resurrection.

How clearly man's twofold nature is seen in this scripture! We are "in this tabernacle," "at home in the body," "our earthly house," etc., showing that the real man, the *inner man or spirit,* dwells in the body, which is its earthly house, till death dissolves the clay house, and the spirit returns to God, when we are absent from the body and present with the Lord. By "earthly house" the apostle most evidently means the body in which the soul is represented as dwelling or sojourning for a time, and from which it is to be liberated at death: for after death dissolves the tabernacle it can be no habitation for the soul.

Heaven is the home of every genuine Christian (Heb. 10:34; 1 Pet. 1:4-5; 2 Cor. 5:1). While here below on earth, the body is the proper home of the soul; but the soul is made for eternal glory, and that glory is its country [eternal home, place of eternal citizenship] (Heb. 11:16). Therefore, the soul is considered as being away from its proper home [heaven] while below [here on earth] in the body. All human souls are made for this glory; therefore, all are considered while here to be absent from their own country.

It is not merely the glory world that they have in view, but the Lord Himself. Without Him, paradise would not even be a place of rest for a spirit possessed of infinite desires. The apostle gives no intimation of an intermediate state of unconscious slumber between being at home in the body and being present with the Lord. There is not the slightest intimation here that the soul sleeps or, rather, that there is no soul, and when the body is decomposed no more of the man till the resurrection—the sentiment of those who condescend to allow us a resurrection, though they deny us a soul. This no-soul animalism is a philosophy in which St. Paul took no lessons, either from Gamaliel (Acts 5:34-39), Jesus Christ, or the Holy Ghost. Paul clearly teaches that when the earthly house dissolves, the inner man is not involved in its ruin and does not go down with its decomposing house into the grave, but into another building, another mode of existence, a house not made with hands. And being clothed with this new house, "mortality is swallowed up of life." The inner man is relieved from all connections with mortal elements and is now swallowed up in purely spiritual and immortal conditions.

The fact that dwelling in the body is comparative absence from the Lord, and to be "absent from the body" is to be more fully "present with the Lord," proves positively that the soul remains conscious after removal from the body. Otherwise this presence of the Lord could not be enjoyed.

The voice of inspiration leaves no possible chance to bring in a period of unconscious slumber between the dissolution of the "earthly house" and the possession of the building of God, for "to be absent from the body" is "to be present with the Lord." "Wherefore we labor that, whether present or absent, we may be accepted of him." This is clear proof of the consciousness of the soul after death, the knowledge of its acceptance with God whether in the body or out of the body.

"For to me to live is Christ, and to die is gain. But if I live in the flesh, this is the fruit of my labor: yet what I will choose I wot not [don't know]. For I am in a strait betwixt two, having a desire to depart, and to be with Christ; which is far better: nevertheless, to abide in the flesh is more needful for you" (Phil. 1:21-24).

What possible gain is there in death if it postpones to an indefinite period all the enjoyment of God's presence and blessings, yea, and existence itself? Nay, "to live is Christ," promotes his cause on earth, but *"to die is gain"* promotion to a higher plane of bliss and spiritual blessedness. And, mark you, that living here is described as "living *in the flesh*" to "abide in the flesh," and to "continue with you"; and "to die" is described as a *"departure"* to "be *with Christ*." And the apostle tells us that he was in a strait [a small narrow difficult passage] between the two; namely, whether to choose a longer sojourn in the flesh or "to depart and be with Christ, which is far better." Now it must be plain to all reasonable minds that if natural death involved the soul in an unconscious state until the resurrection, Paul could not gain that desired presence with the Lord until that great day, whether he died soon or lived long in the flesh. Hence, from the standpoint of non-immortality there could be no possible occasion for his indecision for a time whether to choose a longer stay on earth or to yield to the fervent desire to depart and be with Christ which is far better. But the apostle did not stand on the Sadduceean creed. Nothing can be more positive and clear than the fact that the inspired Apostle understood and believed that the natural death of the body was the instant of the soul's departure into a higher and far more glorious plane of conscious presence with the Lord.

In the verse preceding this passage of scripture, Paul expressed his earnest hope that Christ should be magnified by him whether through life or through death. Then follows this statement: "for to me to live is Christ, and to die is gain." The Geneva Bible [the primary Protestant English Bible in the late 1500s and early 1600s] renders the text, "For Christ is to me, both in life and in death, an advantage." The thought is, Christ is gain to me while I live; and this is the fruit of my labor. For if I live, what else is my life but Christ, that I may hope in Him, preach Him, honor Him, serve, and worship Him; in other words, show forth Christ in all my actions, and say and do all things for the glory of His name. He will be gain also to me when I die, for then I shall be absent from the body and present with Him. So, I have a deep desire in my heart to depart and be with Him, which for me is far better. But for the sake of the church, I am willing to remain here to abide in the flesh and labor for Christ to do you good. I am willing to forego the bliss of heaven for a season in order that I may be a benefit to you. This is clearly Paul's meaning.

It might be of interest to the reader to know what our materialist friends do with this text. The position taken by Elder Uriah Smith, Henry Grew, and J. P. Ham, leading materialist writers, is as follows: "The apostle does not affirm that he expected to be with Christ immediately on his departure, though such would be a fair construction of his words, if it were not a violation of the general tenor of divine truth on the subject." Then they all conclude that Paul was referring to the time he would be with the Lord beyond the final resurrection.

To all this I simply remark that Paul's present strait was a choice of the existing alternatives. He was certainly not speaking of being with Christ after the resurrection, when the resurrection was yet thousands of years in the future. It is absurd to say that he had in mind an intervening unconscious, joyless nothingness. He clearly places living "in the flesh," abiding "in the flesh," in sharp contrast with the expression "to depart AND BE WITH CHRIST; which is far better." The whole language clearly implies an *immediate* departure at death to be with Christ, and even our materialist friends are forced to admit that this is *"a fair construction of his words."*

DYING TESTIMONIES AND CONFIRMING WORDS

It will no doubt be edifying to the reader to add a few of the many clear testimonies of eminent saints and dying men.

"Lord, now lettest thou thy servant depart in peace."—*Simeon*

"Father, into thy hands I commend my spirit."—*Christ Jesus*

"Lord Jesus, receive my spirit."—*Stephen*

"I am now ready to be offered, and the time of my departure is at hand."—*Paul*

"Paul, when he had borne his testimony before rulers, departed from the world and went into the holy place."—*Clement of Rome (in his Epistle to the Corinthians)*

"There was Peter who, having borne his testimony, went to his appointed place in glory."—*Clement of Rome (Apostolic Fathers)*

"All the generations from Adam unto this day have passed away; but they that by God's grace were perfect in love, dwell in the abode of the pious."—*Clement of Rome (Apostolic Fathers)*

"For this reason art thou both of the flesh and spirit."—*Ignatius*

"They are gone to a place which was due to them in the presence of the Lord, with whom also they suffered."—*Polycarp* (speaking of the apostles)

"It is our doctrine that the souls of the wicked will be punished and are in a state of sensation after death, while those of the righteous are freed from torment and remain in bliss."—*Justin* (second century)

"This soul in flames I offer, Christ, to thee."—*Jerome of Prague*

"Lord Jesus, receive my spirit."—*Archbishop Cranmer* (in the flames)

"This day let me see the Lord Jesus."—*Jewel, of England*

"They can slay only the body, not the soul."—*Zwingli of Zurich*

"I am going from weeping friends to congratulate angels and rejoicing saints."—*Risden Darracott*

"Nothing but heaven."—Dying words of *Philip Melancthon*

"What glory! The angels are waiting for me."—*Dr. Bateman*

"I am going to glory."—*Robert Newton*

"Oh, let me be gone, I long to be at home."—*Samuel Spring*

"I am sweeping through the gates, washed in the blood of the Lamb."—*Alfred Cookman*

"Oh, how this soul of mine longs to be gone, like a bird out of his cage, to the realms of bliss."—*John Fletcher*

"I am drawing near to glory."—*Mrs. Fletcher*

"All my possessions for a moment of time."—*Queen Elizabeth*

"It is well."—*George Washington*

"I resign my soul to God."—*Thomas Jefferson*

"I am going home."—*David Livingstone*

"O my poor soul, whither wilt thou go?"—*Cardinal Mazarin*

"I am taking a fearful leap in the dark."—*Hobbes* (infidel)

The following is an account of a soul-sleeper, from *Touching Incidents and Remarkable Answers to Prayer:*

"Mrs. Mattie Campbell relates the happy death of her sister, a soul-sleeper, which occurred last May. In Sabbath-school [see editor's note at chapter end] this afternoon a message came: 'Emma is dying. Come quickly if you want to see her alive.' My dear sister! We had played together, and more than all, we dreamed dreams of the fairy future, wherein we saw everything but care and temptation crowning the golden pathway of our jubilant feet. She was plump and rosy, full of laughter and frolic, which life's stern realities had not subdued. Strong and well I had seen her but five days before. Yet, ah! 'In such an hour as ye think not the Son of man cometh' (Matt. 24:44). On our way, the sad face of the family physician confirmed the truth. 'She may linger until sundown,' he said, and all the way I prayed, and felt it would be answered: 'Lord, dear Lord, only let me have one word to know how it is with her soul.' Mother met me at the door. This was a heavy grief. 'Ask how it is with her soul,' said she. I entered the room filled with weeping friends. I pressed the damp, cold brow. She knew me and spoke in the old, sweet way. Soon I commenced slowly and low the hymn we used to sing together, 'Jesus lover of my soul,' while I anxiously watched to catch a mark of grace upon her fast changing features. A happy, peaceful smile broke over her face. I bent down and she spoke: 'God has always been good to me, Sister. He has not given me one harsh word since I came down to my bed.' How the promise rushed to my lips, 'He giveth, and upbraideth not.' Glory to His name! Divinely assured that she was dying she spoke of a long, sweet sleep, the sleep of the soul and body, until the resurrection, for that was her belief. With mind clear and composed she then lay, waiting to pass into an unconscious slumber, only to awaken at the last trump [trumpet]. 'Hark,' she said, listening intently; 'I hear music. Don't you hear it? And, Mother, I see a door. ... It is open. I see inside. It is a beautiful place. It is heaven. I see forms clothed in white, many, yea, a multitude of beautiful beings, their hands upraised, while they are waving something in their hands.' And then in wonder and astonishment, 'Why, there is pa.' Then she very intelligently gave orders for her burial. Good-byes were said and in childlike, pleading tones she called, 'Come, dear Lord, I am ready.' An effort on her part to close the dear eyes and mouth, a few more agonizing moments, and the open door received her gentle spirit."

Thus, we could multiply testimonies of dying men and women that the soul leaves the body at death. The reader perhaps has witnessed such death-bed scenes as just described. Millions in their last breath have testified to the world that they were then going to the Lord, to the realms of light, or to regions of dark despair. While penning these lines, memory goes back nearly forty years to the death-bed of my own sainted mother. Just before she expired she looked up and said, "I see heaven opened and the glory of God descending." She testified she was "going to dwell with Christ." Among her last words she said, "Tell my boy (referring to myself, her only child, who was then in the far West) to be true to God at the point of the bayonet." This charge I expect, by God's grace, to keep.

While these departing souls had control of the organs of speech they spoke audibly, to testify that existence was still real, and when the voice was stifled in the cold stream, some of them held up their hands in token of their yet conscious being. If the soul of man were only a breath, if life were only a spark which expires when the heart ceases to beat, would there not have been an experience of the waning flame? Would there not have been at least one testimony, in six thousand years, among the millions of dying men, to prove a conscious nearness to oblivion? But there is not one such, not one. On the contrary, millions have in their last breath testified to future conscious existence while absent from the body.

If the soul-sleeping doctrine be true then the Creator put it in the hearts of His creatures, in the most solemn hour of their existence, to testify to a falsehood. Men who would disdain a lie are made to speak an unconscious one in the hour of death—men filled with the Holy Ghost. Can this be so? Is it possible that the good men of all ages—men whom God has used to effect mighty reformations in the earth, testified to a lie in the hour of death? Was Stephen mistaken when he "looked up steadfastly into heaven, and saw the glory of God, and Jesus standing on the right hand of God" (Acts 7:55-56) and a little later addressed his Savior thus, "Lord Jesus, receive my spirit" (Acts 7:59)? Was the apostle Paul mistaken when he said, "We know" that when this earthly house, this mortal body, dissolves in death we shall "depart and be with Christ"—be "absent from the body, and present with the Lord" (2 Cor. 5:8)?

If all these witnesses were mistaken, and men do not have any existence after death, then we have a shadow more enduring than the substance, for Stephen, Paul, Luther, Wesley, and others of great moral natures have, in their names and histories, an earthly immortality while they themselves, going into eternity, conscious to the last, and expecting to live forever, have ceased to be. In a universe of harmony there cannot be such discord; in a world of truth there cannot be such contradiction.

Enoch was translated "for God took him" (Gen. 5:24). Moses lies down upon the mountainside and dies (Deut. 34:1-6). God Himself buries the dust. Elijah steps into a chariot of fire, and by a whirlwind is carried to the skies (2 Kings 2:11). Almost a thousand years after that, Jesus with three of His disciples goes to a mountain-top where He is transfigured before them (Matt. 17:1-7). Instantly there appear Moses and Elijah talking with Him. These men were still living. Abraham, Isaac, and Jacob had long since died, and their bodies were moldering in the dust, but God said, "I am the God of Abraham, Isaac, and Jacob, not the God of the dead, but of the *living*" (Matt. 22:32). Amen, and amen.

[Editor's note: Sabbath keeping and "legalism" (forcing all Christians back under the law of Moses) is (unfortunately) becoming popular today. It is a false teaching of groups who insist that the Old Testament Mosaic law given only to the ancient Jews of Israel on Mount Sinai is still in force today, and that all Christians are under obligation to keep it, and in particular, the fourth commandment about the Jewish Sabbath. But the Mosaic law was intended specifically for those ancient Jews of Israel, and was "nailed to the cross" (Col. 2:14) with Christ. We now live only by and under the grace of Christ, and we are to follow the commandments of Christ (His words). To return to the law which was abolished (by Christ, who FULFILLED the law) is to once again re-crucify Christ! The book of Galatians covers this subject in detail. The author of this book also wrote a great book on this subject called *The Sabbath and the Lord's Day*. I highly recommend it.]

CONDITIONAL IMMORTALITY

Among the theories extant [prominent] today is conditional immortality. They say there is no immortality out of Christ, that Christians are the only ones that possess it, and they only by promise. For several reasons this is an error. It is nowhere hinted in the Bible that when God saves us through Jesus Christ that He transmits to us an immortal existence. Salvation simply changes the soul from a sinful and defiled condition to a righteous state. Every sinner has a spirit, a soul, which must be saved; "For what is a man profited, if he shall gain the whole world, and lose his own soul? or what shall a man give in exchange for his soul?" (Matt. 16:26). "Wherefore lay apart all filthiness and superfluity of naughtiness [rampant wickedness], and receive with meekness the engrafted [implanted] word, which is able to save your souls" (James 1:21). "That the spirit may be saved" (1 Cor. 5:5). How clear these texts!

Man's spiritual and moral nature became defiled by sin, cut off from union with God—from Divine favor. If he continues in that state and dies unsaved, his soul is eternally lost. But if such a one comes to Christ, his soul is saved from eternal ruin.

Those who have assimilated this doctrine err in confounding the *experience* of spiritual life with *eternal existence*. They confound a *condition* of the soul with its *nature*. This is confusion and error. The following are some of the scriptures they use: "The gift of God is eternal life through Jesus Christ our Lord" (Rom. 6:23). "He that believeth on the Son hath everlasting life: and he that believeth not the Son shall not see life" (John 3:36). "That whosoever believeth in him should not perish, but have eternal life" (John 3:15). "My sheep hear my voice, and I know them, and they follow me: and I give unto them eternal life" (John 10:27-28). "God hath given to us eternal life, and this life is in his Son" (1 John 5:11).

"Eternal life" implies eternal conscious existence without intermission, and "God *hath given* to us eternal life." This utterly refutes the soul-sleeping theory. Jesus said, "Whosoever liveth and believeth in me shall never die" (John 11:26). The body will die but the soul shall "never die." On the solid Word of God we stand. But let us repeat: While the terms "eternal life," "everlasting life," etc., imply eternal existence, this is not the principal idea they convey. Sin separates the soul from God (Isa. 59:1-2). As soon as it is cut off from union with God it dies (Gen. 2:17; John 15:2, 6; Rom. 7:9). This death is not a cessation of the soul's conscious existence but an alienation from God, whose favor is the normal sphere of the soul's happiness. So every sinner is dead and yet has a conscious existence— "Dead while he lives." This is the sad state of the entire world out of Christ (Rom. 5:12, 14; Eph. 2:1-5; Rom. 8:6; 7:9; 1 John 3:14; 1 Tim. 5:6).

Sinners are now commanded to awaken out of sleep and arise from the dead (Eph. 5:14). When they meet the Bible requirements for salvation they "pass from death unto life" (1 John 3:14). "And this is life eternal, that they might know thee the only true God, and Jesus Christ, whom thou hast sent" (John 17:3). Thus, the sinner who has been cut off from union with God and abides in spiritual death is quickened into life, inducted into Christ, who is our life. This eternal life through Christ is union with God. Oh, the blessed state of the soul thus united to God! This union with Christ, this eternal life, is here enjoyed by the Christian (John 3:36; 1 John 3:14; 5:11), and if we prove faithful unto death we have the promise of enjoying the same blessed union and eternal life in the future (Mark 10:30). So instead of eternal life simply signifying eternal existence, it rather signifies eternal union with God, a blissful enjoyment of His favor, love, grace, peace, etc., upon our souls. And all this is granted to us through Jesus Christ. Christ is our life, our light, "the bright and morning star" (Rev. 22:16), which illuminates our rugged pathway through this dark world of sin; the "lily of the valley" (Song. 2:1), "the rose of Sharon" (Song. 2:1), blooming in our souls, sending a sweet fragrance to all around until the desert is made to "blossom as the rose"; "the one altogether lovely, the fairest among ten thousand" (Song. 5:10), living in us (John 14:20; Rom.

8:10; 1 John 4:15; Gal. 2:20), comforting our hearts (Ps. 51:10; Ps. 23), renewing our strength (Isa. 40:28-31; Phil. 4:13); our refuge (Ps. 91; Prov. 18:10; Ps. 61:3); "our all in all" (1 Cor. 15:28). Reader, "this is eternal life," a blessed condition of the soul.

"Who hath saved us, and called us with an holy calling, not according to our works, but according to his own purpose and grace, which was given to us in Christ Jesus before the world began, but is now made manifest by the appearing of our Savior Jesus Christ, who hath abolished death, and hath brought life and immortality to light through the gospel" (2 Tim. 1:9-10). He has abolished spiritual death by giving life to the soul; life which is freedom from sin, the cause of death; and the possession of Divine favor and peace, which is life—yea, the very indwelling of Christ, who is our life. And He has abolished the sting of death. The fact that the real inner man does not perish with the body but enjoys a more glorious presence with the Lord after the earthly house is dissolved, mitigates the terrors of death. "The sting of death is sin" (1 Cor. 15:56). But the blood of Christ cleanses us from all sin and the Holy Spirit quickens the soul into such a precious knowledge of our eternal life, and the spirit's immortality, that death, so much dreaded before, becomes the gateway to realms of glory beyond. Of course, death still remains an enemy, and there is a natural shrinking away from it, but the sting and terror caused by sin have been alleviated. Praise God!

Through the gospel, salvation, and illumination of the Spirit of God, there has been brought to light that which was always true, viz., that the soul is immortal. But, like many other great truths, it was not as clearly revealed in the Old Testament as in the New. We maintain that this is positive proof of man's immortal spirit. If man, in his spiritual nature, were not immortal, there would be no immortality to bring to light in him. If immortality be conditional and only imparted by Divine grace, the Word would read that God gave immortality. But the testimony of heaven is that He brought to light that which already existed.

Mr. Wilson, the translator of the *Emphatic Diaglott,* was a First-day Adventist, hence he believed in soul-sleeping. He translated 2 Tim. 1:9-10: "Who hath illustrated life and incorruptibility." But in the direct transliteration of the Greek he renders the word correctly, "hath illuminated." Could Christ illuminate a thing that does not exist? That this is correct we can make plain by an appeal to the original word. It is *photisantos.* Its root is *phos*, which means light, which word occurs in such texts as Matt. 4:16; 15:14, 16; John 1:4-5, 7-9. That *photisantos* means to cause something to come to light will be made plain by examining its use, "Will bring to light [*photisei*] the hidden things of darkness" (1 Cor. 4:5). "The bright shining of a candle doth give thee light [*photizei*]" (Luke 11:36). "The glory of God did lighten [*photisen*] it" (Rev. 21:23). *Photizo*, the verb, is clearly seen to mean to lighten, and as surely *photisantos,* a derivation, means to cause something to come to light and become clear to all: "hath brought immortality to light."

Most people who hold that the soul is only conditionally immortal, that it is imparted to it in salvation or in the resurrection, etc., confound a condition of the soul with its nature; namely, they see transition from death unto life by the grace of God, and with this life they identify the soul's immortality. But this is confusion and error. Spiritual death incurred by sin is only a condition of the soul. The soul still lives, as we have proved by the Word. The sinner is still conscious of the moral law written in man's being; is conscious that all actions are good or bad; and since, as we have stated, it is the soul that sins, he yet has a conscious soul.

Spiritual death is a forfeiture of righteousness and God's favor and peace, not a destruction of the conscious moral being or of the soul of man. It is only a consciousness of the wretched condition of the soul. So, spiritual life in Christ Jesus is not the impartation of an indestructible nature to the spirit, or soul, of man; for that essentially is already the nature of the spirit of man. But it is a change of the condition of that immortal element in man: its restoration to Divine favor, righteousness, and peace.

Death, the fruit of the soul's sin, is so called because it separates man from the enjoyment and glory of God. He is dead to the object of his creation. Life, given by the Word and Spirit of God, reunites the soul to God and makes it alive to His glory.

Immortality is the inherent and inseparable nature or property of spirit. So there is a vast difference between *zoe*—life, motion, activity, the ability to act in harmony with the Divine will—and *athanasia*—deathlessness, immortality. The former, when applied to the soul, is a moral condition; the latter describes an endless condition, that which is in its nature imperishable.

That the soul does not pass a period of unconscious slumber between death and the resurrection is also positively proved by such scriptures as the following: "Verily, verily, I say unto you, he that believeth on me hath everlasting life. I am that bread of life. Your fathers did eat manna in the wilderness, and are dead. This is the bread which cometh down from heaven, that a man may eat thereof, and not die. I am the living bread which came down from heaven: if any man eat of this bread, he shall live forever, and the bread that I will give is my flesh, which I will give for the life of the world" (John 6:47-51).

"Whoso eateth my flesh, and drinketh my blood, hath eternal life; and I will raise him up at the last day" (John 6:54). "Whosoever liveth and believeth in me *shall never die*" (John 11:26).

Eternal life signifies life, action, and conscious enjoyment in the service and favor of God, without end or termination. We here possess this life (1 John 5:11; 3:14), and if we hold out faithful (Matt. 24:13; Matt. 10:22; Heb. 3:14; 2 Tim. 4:7-8), we "shall never die," "but live forever." This implies that there shall be no interruption of this spiritual enjoyment. Yet the death of the body is clearly implied in John 6:54, for, says the Lord, "I will raise him up at the last day." How do we reconcile the two facts— he shall "live forever," shall "never die," and yet shall die and go to the grave, if we do not recognize the fact that man is "both spirit and body" (1 Cor. 7:34)? On any other basis, the Word of God contradicts itself. But, all taken together, there is no conflict. To "live forever" and "never die" are true of the inner man, the soul, while death and the resurrection pertain to the body, the outer man.

Nothing but a misconception of the teachings of the inspired Book can give countenance to the gloomy [soul-sleeping] doctrine that all of man goes into the grave and remains unconscious until the resurrection. In fact, to assert it is to squarely contradict the Teacher who came from heaven.

To live forever and yet the body dies, proves that man is something more than an animal body. The same thing is expressed in these words: "Who died for us, that, whether we wake or sleep [are dead or alive when he returns], we should live together with him" (1 Thess. 5:10). That is, our souls will live right on in a glorious presence with the Lord. The fact is we live forever though our bodies decompose in the grave. So teaches the Word of God. Thank God for life and immortality so clearly brought to light by the gospel.

THE INTERMEDIATE STATE

The fact of the continued existence of the soul after death, the clear Bible teaching of a future resurrection of these mortal bodies followed by the general judgment and the reward of the righteous and punishment of the wicked, clearly implies an intermediate state. On this particular point a number of views are held by both Jews and Christians. All these can be summed up under four headings.

First—The materialistic opinion held by such bodies as the Second Adventists, Seventh-day Adventists, and followers of Pastor Russell, the teaching that there is an unconscious state between death and the resurrection, the soul asleep [soul-sleeping] in the grave with the body. This we have treated in the preceding chapters. The ancient Sadducees denied the future resurrection of the dead and held the fundamental error that the soul, or spirit, expires when the body dies. Jesus struck at the very root of their teaching error and silenced them by quoting the words of God to Moses at the burning bush: "I am the God of Abraham, and the God of Isaac, and the God of Jacob. God is not the God of the dead, but of the living" (Matt. 22:32). "For he is not a God of the dead, but of the living: for *all live unto him*" (Luke 20:38).

Our Savior quoted this positive statement to disprove their erroneous position, and it utterly refutes the modern soul-sleeping contention. It clearly shows that Abraham, Isaac, and Jacob were still alive, though their bodies had been buried for hundreds of years in the cave of Machpelah. After the death of the bodies of these patriarchs the Lord was still their God—not the God of these dead bodies, but "of THE LIVING," for "ALL LIVE UNTO HIM." This proves that the souls of all men are immortal and conscious between death and the resurrection.

Second—The intermediate *world* theory. It is held that the terms *sheol* in the Old Testament and *hades* in the New Testament denote the *world* of spirits after death, the *place* where the souls of all men go. This is supposed to be divided into two parts—paradise, the abode of the righteous, and *tartarus,* or the lowest hades, the abode of the wicked. Some who hold this theory claim that *sheol* and *hades* in every text refer to the world of spirits and never to the grave. This is the extreme opposite of the materialist contention that *sheol* and *hades* always mean the grave.

Third—The intermediate *state* idea, that *sheol* and *hades* mean "the unseen state" or condition of the soul after death, separated from the physical body. Those who hold this position admit that these terms may apply also to the grave, hence have more than one meaning, and the signification in any particular text must be determined by its setting and by its context. There are a number of scriptures where these terms cannot mean the grave, and then again there are other texts where they seem to apply there rather than to the state of the soul.

Fourth—There are still others who deny the intermediate state and claim that immediately at death the righteous receive their eternal reward and the wicked enter upon their final, eternal punishment.

It is not our purpose in this work to commit ourselves to any particular theory, but to present some plain scriptural facts that bear directly upon our future both between death and the resurrection and beyond the judgment of the great day. One fact stands out most clearly in the Scriptures—the full reward of the righteous and the final, eternal punishment of the wicked will be rendered at the judgment. If man received this at death there would certainly be no need of a future resurrection and day of judgment: "Christ, who shall judge the quick [living] and the dead *at his appearing* and his kingdom" (2 Tim. 4:1). "Behold, I come quickly; and my reward is with me, to give every man according as his work shall be" (Rev. 22:12). In 2 Thess. 1:7-10, we read that it is "*when* the Lord Jesus shall be revealed from heaven with his mighty angels" that He will punish the wicked and "be glorified in his saints." "The Son of man shall come in the glory of his Father with his angels; and THEN he shall reward every man according to his works" (Matt. 16:27). In Matt. 25:31-46 we have a description of the final judgment. It is then that the righteous shall be received into the everlasting kingdom and the wicked will be sentenced and enter into their everlasting punishment in hell. In Rev. 11:18 we read that it is at "the time of the dead, that they should be judged" that the Lord will "give reward unto thy servants the prophets, and to the saints, and them that fear thy name, small and great." In Rev. 20:11-15 is a description of the final judgment [the Great White Throne judgment]. It is then that whosoever is not found in the book of life will be "cast into the lake of fire," and beyond this appears the new heaven and new earth (Rev. 21) which will be the eternal home of the redeemed. Then it is a clearly established fact that full reward and punishment does not immediately follow at death but will be administered beyond the general resurrection at the judgment. Paul says, "Henceforth there is laid up for me a crown of righteousness, which the Lord, the righteous judge, shall give me at THAT DAY: and not to me only, but unto all them also that love his appearing" (2 Tim. 4:8).

Peter declares that God has reserved "the unjust unto the day of judgment to be punished" (2 Pet. 2:9). In Jude 6 we read, "The angels which kept not their first estate, but left their own habitation, he hath reserved in everlasting chains under darkness unto the judgment of the great day." "God spared not the angels that sinned, but cast them down to hell [Greek *tartarosas,* Tartarus], and delivered them into chains of darkness, to be reserved unto judgment" (2 Pet. 2:4). By reference to Matt. 25:41, it will be seen that at the judgment the wicked will be cast into the same hell of torment as that into which "the devil and his angels" are cast.

It is very reasonable then to suppose that at death the souls of the impenitent [the unsaved, unrepentant, not feeling shame or regret about one's sins or actions] go to the same place where these fallen angels or demons are reserved in chains of darkness unto the judgment, when all together will receive their eternal damnation. This harmonizes with the dying testimonies of multitudes of unsaved people. How often such in their last moments have said, "I am taking an awful leap in the dark," and "The demons have come to take my soul into hell." From the account given in Luke 16 of the rich man after death, we are informed that "he lift up his eyes, being in torment," and cried, "I am tormented in this flame" (Luke 16:24).

Of the state of the righteous after death the Bible speaks explicitly. Jesus said to the dying thief, "Today shalt thou be with me in paradise" (Luke 23:43). In 2 Cor. 12:2-4, Paul tells us that paradise is the same as the "third heaven." At His ascension, Christ went up "into heaven" (1 Pet. 3:22). Stephen just before his death saw Christ there at the right hand of God (Acts 7:55-56, 59). Dying saints depart "to be with Christ" (2 Cor. 5:1-8; Phil. 1:23; 1 Thess. 5:10). They "live and reign with Christ" (Rev. 6:9-11; 20:4). Since Christ is in heaven, the righteous go there at death. They are "comforted" (Luke 16:25) and "rest from their labors" (Rev. 14:13), awaiting their future and eternal reward which will be given in the resurrection morning.

MATERIALISTS' ARGUMENTS CONSIDERED

Materialism denies that man possesses a spiritual, conscious entity, separate and distinct in substance from the body, and affirms that man is only a material being composed of flesh and blood and breath and intellect. Strictly speaking a hippopotamus or an orangutan possesses all that materialists claim for man. Of course, they admit that these qualities in man are somewhat of a higher order than that found in the brutes. Eccl. 3:19-20 is a favorite text in their preaching and writing.

Solomon here mentions a few things in which man "hath no preeminence above a beast." "They have all one breath"—that is, man breathes the same atmosphere that the beasts of the field breathe. "As the one dieth, so dieth the other." Just as all creatures die and return to dust, so does mortal man's dust "return to the earth as it was"— "all turn to dust again"— "all go unto one place"—the grave.

Now, the wise man [Solomon] was simply speaking of man's physical being, and this is only true of the fleshly outer man. But in the same chapter (Eccl. 3:21) the inspired writer makes a clear distinction: "Who knoweth the spirit of man that goeth upward, and the spirit of the beast that goeth downward *the earth?*" This is so plain it would seem that no one could mistake the meaning. The spirit of the beast goes downward. Where? "To the earth." It dies with the body. But the spirit of man is different. It does not go down into the earth—it "goeth upward." And the same writer tells us exactly where the spirit of man goes at death— "the spirit shall return unto God who gave it" (Eccl. 12:7).

If man were wholly a material being, he could only feed on material substance. Mark this thought. The brute creation cannot feed on or derive nourishment from spiritual food, for they are only material beings. But man is both flesh and spirit. He is classified with two worlds. By his fleshly nature he takes his place in the animal kingdom, and by the extreme abuse and subversion of his appetites and passions he renders himself scarcely fit for the companionship of the brutes. Yet by his spiritual nature and existence he is placed where, when his soul is saved from sin, he is fit for heaven's society.

Because he is a physical being man feeds on material substances. He has appetite for natural food. His body requires it. Materialism stops here. But, as before stated, the Bible teaches that man is a spiritual as well as a physical being. Therefore, he can feed on and derive nourishment from spiritual food—life, peace, and happiness from God. "Thy words were found, and I did eat them; and thy word was unto me the joy and rejoicing of mine heart" (Jer. 15:16).

"Man shall not live by bread alone, but by every word that proceedeth out of the mouth of God" (Matt. 4:4).

"As newborn babes, desire the sincere milk of the word, that ye may grow thereby" (1 Pet. 2:2). "O taste and see that the Lord is good" (Ps. 34:8). Jesus said, "I am that bread of life. ... I am the living bread which came down from heaven: if any man eat of this bread, he shall live forever" (John 6:48-51). "But whosoever drinketh of the water that I shall give him shall never thirst" (John 4:14). "There is a river, the streams whereof shall make glad the city of God" (Ps. 46:4). Its crystal waters which come rippling down from the glory world in mighty streams are love, grace, joy, peace, and righteousness. "I will extend peace to her like a river" (Isa. 66:12). "They shall be abundantly satisfied with the fatness of thy house; and thou shalt make them drink of the river of thy pleasure" (Ps. 36:8). "My soul thirsteth for God, for the living God" (Ps. 42:2).

All these are expressive of the experiences of the soul. "For he satisfieth the longing soul, and filleth the hungry soul with goodness" (Ps. 107:9). "Hearken diligently unto me, and eat ye that which is good, and let *your soul* delight itself in fatness" (Isa. 55:2).

Could the multiplied texts cited apply to the brute creation? Never. If man were only a material being how could he eat God's Word and live upon it—yes, by the sincere milk of the Word grow thereby? How could he taste of the Lord, eat of the living bread which came down from heaven, drink of the river of peace, love, and joy, and as a result his soul be "fat and flourishing"?

How plain these scriptures are to those who know that they are not beasts but spiritual beings as well as physical. And what is still grander is the actual experience taught in these scriptures.

I think it only fair to our materialist friends, and also to our readers generally, to present some of the leading arguments that are made in defense of soul-sleeping and against the fact of the immortality of the human spirit.

1. — "In 1 Tim. 6:16 it is applied to God, and the sweeping declaration is made that *He alone has it:* 'Who only hath immortality, dwelling in the light which no man can approach unto; whom no man hath seen, nor can see; to whom be honor and power everlasting. Amen.'" *Uriah Smith* (*Here and Hereafter,* p. 54). It is argued that if God *only* has immortality then man does not possess it.

The incorrectness of this inference appears when we carefully examine this passage of scripture. The Greek word for immortality in this particular text is *athanasia*, which means deathlessness—underived and eternal existence. The text therefore proves nothing but what we all believe—that God alone possesses inherent, underived, and eternal immortality. This text is to be understood in the same light as Rev. 15:4: "O Lord ... thou only art holy." There are abundant scriptures to prove that through salvation God's people are holy and can live holy lives here on earth. To take 1 Tim. 6:16 and apply it as the materialists do would deny the immortality of Enoch and Elijah. Of course, even materialists admit the immortality of these two men, which admission overthrows their argument to deny the immortality of the human soul. As they apply it, it would also deny the immortality of angels and all the hosts of heaven. So, when properly understood, this text has not a featherweight of evidence against the immortality of the human soul.

You will observe that I have used the text as applied to the eternal Father. Many scholars hold that this scripture refers to the glorified Christ.

"Our Lord Jesus Christ; ... who is the blessed and only Potentate, the King of kings, and Lord of lords; *who* only hath immortality" (1 Tim. 6:15-16). If this be correct it may then be asked, in what sense hath Christ "only" immortality? The Word answers: "But now is Christ risen from the dead, and become the first fruits of them that slept" (1 Cor. 15:20). "Knowing that Christ being raised from the dead dieth no more; death hath no more dominion over him" (Rom. 6:9). We all are yet mortal in body. We inhabit mortal flesh, which is subject to death. But Christ has already received His immortal and glorified body. He, being already "raised from the dead, dieth no more; death hath no more dominion over him" (Rom. 6:9). In this sense, He only hath immortality at this time. Our vile body will not be changed in the likeness of His glorious body until the final resurrection. So, since we yet inhabit a mortal body, decaying flesh, and Christ the "first-fruits" has already received His glorified body, He only can be said to be wholly immortal.

2.— "In Rom. 2:7 it is set forth as something for which we are to seek by patient continuance in welldoing [doing good]: 'To them who by patient continuance in welldoing *seek* for glory and honor and *immortality* (God will render) eternal life.' This shows that we do not possess immortality here; for if we do, how can we be exhorted to seek for it?" *Uriah Smith* (*Here and Hereafter*, p. 54).

Immortality in this particular text is not *athanasia*—deathlessness, but *aphtharsia*—incorruption. This makes the matter clear and does not in the least conflict with the multitude of scriptures already cited that man possesses a spiritual conscious entity—a soul, or spirit—which continues to live after the decease of the body. The apostle is speaking of the future resurrection to eternal life. In the final and universal resurrection of the dead there will be two classes, "they that have done good, unto the resurrection of life; and they that have done evil, unto the resurrection of damnation" (John 5:29).

The incorruption to be put on in the future is only for the body, for, "It is sown a natural *body;* it is raised a spiritual *body.* ... For this corruptible must put on incorruption, and this mortal must put immortality" (1 Cor. 15:44, 53). Now, to "seek for immortality" is to live so that we may have a glorious resurrection unto eternal life in an immortal and glorified body. A resurrection to eternal rewards, to eternal bliss, instead of one "to shame, and everlasting contempt" (Dan. 12:2). This very thing that the apostle instructed us to seek, for he himself was seeking: "If by any means I might attain unto the resurrection of the dead. Not as tho I had already attained, either were already perfect: but I follow after, if that I may apprehend that for which also I am apprehended of Christ Jesus" (Phil. 3:11-12).

There is not one text in the Bible where it is declared that our soul, or spirit, shall put on immortality. Have you ever read in the scriptures that— your mortal soul, your corruptible spirit, shall put on immortality? [Answer: no.] Our materialist friends frequently ask us to produce in scripture the words "immortal souls," "immortal spirit." With as good grace we kindly ask them to produce the words "mortal soul," and "mortal spirit." It would certainly be superfluity to say "cold ice," or "warm fire." Ice is cold and fire is hot in the very nature of these things. Spirits are immortal in their nature, and soul expresses this immortal part in its organized form—the real inner, intelligent, spiritual man. In the resurrection, it is only "*our* vile *body,* that it may be fashioned like unto his glorious body" (Phil. 3:21). This is an object to be sought for by a humble, godly walk in this world.

3.—The spirit of man simply means his breath. Proof: "All the while my breath is in me, and the spirit of God is in my nostrils" (Job 27:3).

This text comes far from proving that the spirit of man is the breath he breathes. In fact, it does not say so at all. But let us examine this argument. If spirit always means "breath," then to substitute "breath" for "spirit" would make good, sensible reading: "Father, into thy hands I commend my *breath*" (Luke 23:46). "Then was Jesus led up of the *breath* into the wilderness" (Matt. 4:1). "But there is a *breath* in man" (Job 32:8). "The unmarried woman careth for the things of the Lord, that she may be holy in body and in *breath*" (1 Cor. 7:34). "The *breath* itself beareth witness with our *breath,* that we are the children of God" (Rom. 8:16).

How ridiculous this position. When driven from it our friends usually shift to another, namely, that spirit means life. Then Jesus was led of the *life* to be tempted of the *life.* Out of Mary Magdalene would have been cast seven *lives.* A legion of *lives* would have possessed the man in the tombs.

"A *life* hath not flesh and bones, as ye see me have" (Luke 24:39). Anyone can see that the human spirit as well as other intelligent spirits are more than breath and life. Admitting that Job 27:3 does mean breath proves nothing against the consciousness of the human soul in man, since spirit is a generic term with a variety of meanings.

4.—The Bible teaches that "the dead know not anything" (Eccl. 9:5). If this be true they are in an unconscious slumber.

This can only apply to the outer, physical man which sleeps in the dust of the earth. It is only that part of our being that is declared to be *"dead"*— the mortal body, that is said to know not anything. At the same time the same writer tells us that the soul, or spirit, the real inner man, goes to God (Eccl. 12:7). It there remains conscious (2 Cor. 5:1-9; Phil. 1:21-25; Luke 16:19-31). But let us examine their proof text a little closer. In what sense does the wise man [the writer of the Book of Ecclesiastes] declare that the dead know not anything? In the very next verse he fully explains his meaning— "Neither have they any more a portion for ever in anything that is done under the sun" (Eccl. 9:6). Ah! He is talking about things here on earth, *"under the sun."* The idea is, at death people pass out of this world into another sphere [realm] and no longer have a part in anything that is being done here on earth. This is the true meaning of the text and has no bearing whatever on the conscious state of the soul after death.

5.—In the very day a man dies "his thoughts perish" (Ps. 146:4). Does this not prove that memory is destroyed in death?

Not by any means. A person's thoughts, insofar as they are actively concerned in the things of earth, perish in death's hour. "Their thoughts are thoughts of iniquity" (Isa. 59:7). The wicked have thousands of thoughts, schemes, and lusts which they expect to carry out, but they are all cut off by death. Their thoughts of iniquity are all defeated and perish. But the overthrow of their thoughts and plans in death does not destroy their memory. Abraham said to the rich man, "Son, *remember*," and he did remember that he had five brothers whom he did not desire to come to that place of torment.

6.—The Bible teaches that the soul will be redeemed "from the grave." Proof: Ps. 30:3, 49:15, 89:48. If this be true the soul sleeps in the grave with the body.

The regular Hebrew word for grave is *qeber,* and in none of the texts just cited is the original word *qeber,* but in every text it is *sheol,* "the unseen state." This usually expresses the intermediate state of departed spirits between this probationary life and the final judgment, while *qeber* represents the dwelling-place of the body. We shall give the rendering of the Septuagint Version of these texts: "Thou hast brought up my soul from Hades" (Ps. 30:3). "Deliver my soul from the power of Hades" (Ps. 49:15). "Deliver my soul from the hand of Hades" (Ps. 89:48).

So when these texts are understood in their true light, they perfectly harmonize with the host of scriptures which clearly teach that the soul does not go down into decomposition with the body.

THE PRESENT LIFE A PROBATIONARY DAY

"For he saith, I have heard thee in a time accepted, and in the day of salvation have I succored [helped] thee: behold, now is the accepted time; behold, now is the day of salvation" (2 Cor. 6:2).

Paul is here quoting the language of the evangelistic prophet Isaiah, who foretold the glories of the Christian era as the most propitious age of salvation that the world should ever see. Then Paul makes the application to every individual soul: *"Now* **is the accepted time" to be saved, "Now" is man's "day of salvation." God has placed us all under law [His moral law, not the Mosaic law], whether heathen or enlightened, the former under the law of conscience, the latter under revealed, written truth; therefore, all men are on probation, on trial, "so that they are without excuse" (Rom. 1:20). Man has the power of choice. He can choose the evil or the good, hence he stands responsible to God for his present state and his eternal destiny.** [Editor's bold]

"Wherefore (as the Holy Ghost saith, Today if ye will hear his voice, harden not your hearts" (Heb. 3:7-8). Yes, today is held out to this lost world as their only time to be saved. The gospel invitation says, "Come; for all things are now ready" (Luke 14:17). This is the age of grace and salvation, the dispensation of the Holy Spirit. Our natural life is the time allotted to man to appropriate these redemption blessings and avail ourselves of the blessed opportunity to be saved. Christianity now applies to all nations, all classes, and to every individual. Religion finds in the gospel of Christ a final and complete readiness for human use. The infinite wisdom of God devised the plan of salvation; His infinite love provided it; a great Savior brought it to earth; and the power of God through the Holy Spirit makes it effectual to every soul of man who will come with a thorough "repentance towards God, and faith in our Lord Jesus Christ" (Acts 20:21).

The free bounty of God, His generosity, unsolicited willingness, make Him our Benefactor. He who is "rich over all" with unlimited supplies of grace, takes an interest in our happiness and offers to make us partakers of His rich enjoyments. All this is fully prepared. A great variety of blessings are set before us, all the treasures and riches of heaven, and the offer of a free access to the very throne of grace. All the soul's desires are found in this. It is suited to the soul's tastes, to its lofty capacities, and is capable of eternally satisfying. To lost, sinful man it is like an oasis in the desert, like an ark in a deluge.

Salvation is ready for *you*. The Father waits to embrace each returning prodigal. Christ is waiting to speak forgiveness. At what cost He prepared this feast without any solicitation or desert [contribution or action deserving merit] on our part! He opens the way and offers to do us good before we inquire after it. He forbears His wrath when we justly deserve it. He lingers after we slam our heart's door in His face. Surely "the kindness and love of God our Savior has appeared" (Titus 3:4). The Holy Spirit now knocks at the door of your *heart,* ready to come in and lead you to eternal life. Angels are ready to rejoice over your conversion. Reader, your knowledge, your better reason, your conscience, all tell you that you ought to be saved. Sin and vice have revealed to you the wretchedness of their indulgence, and you have found sinful society empty, filled with pride, slavery, dishonor, and disappointment. Your heart is beating, like a muffled drum, a death march to the grave. All are invited to be saved, to "all the ends of the earth" (Acts 1:8; Mark 16:15). [Editor's bold]

This invitation is universal, free, generous, and direct. The Lord communes with souls familiarly (Isa. 1:18), commands by way of authority (Acts 17:30), beseeches [urges] by entreaty ("All day long have I held out my hand" (Isa. 65:2). "Turn ye, turn ye, for why will ye die" (Ezek. 33:11)), and He warns of the severe consequences, disaster and punishment for sin (Prov. 1:20-31). God calls through innumerable tokens of His love, through the gospel, and by direct warnings and providences.

His gospel is not only a thing of beauty and enjoyment but of power, a living, moving, working force. This power is seen in the effects produced. It attracts, awakens, convicts, converts, and changes the whole course of the individual life. Domestically it makes homes happier, makes better husbands, wives, parents, and children. It works a miracle in society and helps man socially; and politically it lays the foundation of liberty among the nations of earth.

The gospel of Christ "is the power of God" (Rom. 1:16). It is great in its theme, provisions, inspirations, rewards, and penalties. Its truth is incontrovertible, and its excellence incomparable. Wherever it goes it conquers, because it is the most potent force the world has ever known. It has a message for all classes—for the rich, as it offers them "true riches"; for the poor, who can be "rich in faith"; for the learned, as it is intended for thoughtful minds and awakens ideas that are sublime; for the unlearned, as it is simplicity in itself. It appeals to everyone, the best as well as the worst. As Joseph's sheaf [a bundle of grain stalks] stood up amid his brethren's, so the gospel of salvation is [stands] supreme among the powers of earth.

In the face of all these facts of life, who can deny that man is now on probation during this life? With all the provision for his salvation complete, with proffered mercies daily poured upon him, with tender invitations ringing in his ears, with solemn warnings of impending judgment hanging over him, if people are foolish enough in the face of all this to close their probationary state in rebellion against God's throne, they must suffer the consequence and will be wholly to blame. "*None* of those men which were bidden [invited] shall taste of my supper" (Luke 14:24). That means to be rejected forever. And remember, the rejected ones were warmly invited and had every opportunity to partake of the provision that was made. They loved the world more than Christ and refused to give Him place in their hearts and lives. Love long slighted turns to wrath and man stubbornly refuses until mercy ceases to be a virtue. It means death without hope, and beyond death's portals the "great gulf" that separates the sinner from God is "fixed" forever; it is an impassable chasm (Luke 16:26). There will be no hope beyond this life. To every human soul, "Now is the day of salvation."

CHRIST, THE SINNER'S ONLY HOPE

"Jesus Christ of Nazareth, whom ye crucified, whom God raised from the dead. ... Neither is there salvation in any other; for there is none [no] other name under heaven given among men, whereby we must be saved" (Acts 4:10, 12).

I love to think of Jesus as the Creator of all things, the great Upholder of the universe, the Lawgiver, King, Sovereign of earth and sky, and future Judge; but above all else the world's Redeemer and Savior. The name of Jesus shines with increasing luster as the ages roll on, and eclipses all others who have ever lived. Jesus saves by His blood virtually, by His Spirit vitally, by His gospel instrumentally, by His grace constantly, and by His power eternally. He saves from the guilt and stain of sin, from the love of sin, from the power and dominion of sin, from the curse and penalty of sin, from the habit and practice of sin, and from the painful remembrance of sin. He is a suitable, willing, perfect, all-sufficient, unchangeable, and infinite Savior.

There is no salvation outside of Him. His death paid our penalty. His blood is our atonement. His resurrection secured for us eternal life. His mediation at the right hand of God extends to us infinite Divine mercy. The Holy Spirit delegates to us all that Christ provided. His gospel extends to us our only hope. "Neither is there salvation in any other." The cross of Christ is the world's magnet: "And I, if I be lifted up from the earth, will draw all men unto me" (John 12:32). By sin man is ruined for time and eternity, disqualified to fulfill life's purpose, represented as a foreigner, alien, outcast, rebel, and lost.

Christ is the one remedy for the world's sin and misery: "God forbid that I should glory, save in the cross of Christ" (Gal. 6:14). This is the hub of Christianity. Remove the cross and the whole fabric of Christian religion will fall, for it is robbed of its life, power, and saving efficacy. The cross does not coerce, drive, force, nor scare, but it *"draws."* The great sacrifice of Christ in that "he laid down his life" for us (John 3:16), and thus displayed His love, adorns the rugged cross with sunshine, radiant light, glory, and beauty. It makes the crown of thorns look better than a golden diadem [jeweled crown of royalty] set with pearls and jewels.

Earthly crowns have faded, kings and queens have died and are forgotten, empires have fallen, but the cross of Jesus Christ grows more lustrous as the ages roll on. The cross means forgiveness, deliverance, reconciliation, adoption, sanctification, holiness, unity, and heaven forever. We can have none of this without the blood of Jesus.

Christ is the theme of the entire gospel. "Whom we preach." "Jesus, whom Paul preacheth." "Preached Christ unto them." "Preached unto him Jesus." "Straightway preached Christ." "We preach Christ crucified." These are familiar expressions found in all parts of the primitive [basic, core, simple] gospel message. This is the golden thread that makes up the fabric of Christian doctrine and experience. Christ is the glory, light, beauty, attractiveness, inspiration, and drawing power in every true gospel sermon. The foundation is the most important and essential part of a building, and the keystone in an arch holds the whole building in security. Every system has its main principles, its cardinal points. Christ is all this to the whole structure of Christianity.

Jesus only is all we need to preach. He alone can save. No empty dogmas, no wearisome rites, not even church ordinances, nor the preacher, nor the virgin Mary, nor your mother, nor the church, can save; no one or nothing can save but Jesus. He is offered to man as the only hope. To reject Him as your Savior is to forfeit eternal life and be lost eternally. To accept Him into your heart and soul is to be saved forevermore. [Editor's bold]

Here again the responsibility for our present condition and for our future, eternal state is seen to rest wholly with us.

"HOW SHALL WE ESCAPE IF WE NEGLECT
SO GREAT A SALVATION?"

"For if the word spoken by angels was stedfast, and every transgression and disobedience received a just recompence of reward; how shall we escape, if we neglect so great [a] salvation?" (Heb. 2:2-3).

The word spoken by angels here referred to no doubt applies to the [Mosaic] law. Paul tells us in Gal. 3:19 that it "was ordained by angels in the hand of a mediator," and Stephen told the Jews that they had received "the law by the disposition of angels" (Acts 7:53). Some authorities hold that since God spoke to men through angels in the patriarchal age, the statement quoted covers God's revealed will to man under the entire Old Testament Dispensation. No doubt this is correct. The writer of Hebrews calls attention to the fact that under that dispensation "every transgression and disobedience received a just recompense of reward." People never escaped punishment. The flood upon the world of the ungodly, the destruction of Sodom and Gomorrah, and the visitations of God's wrath upon Israel at different times, all confirm this fact. Peter tells us that the flood, and destruction of those ancient wicked cities were "an ensample [example] unto those that after should live ungodly" (2 Pet. 2:5-6). All the punishments meted out to transgressors of those times were a "just recompense of reward."

Now, "how shall we escape" wrath to the uttermost if we neglect the salvation provided for us and proclaimed in the gospel of the Son of God? Their [the antediluvian (pre-flood) wicked, and Sodom and Gomorrah's] offense was great, and they suffered here and will meet their sins at the day of judgment. But Jesus said it will be "more tolerable" for them there than for us who live under the transplendent glory of the gospel and then "neglect so great [a] salvation" freely offered. There are those who openly oppose and reject the gospel, but to *neglect* it is to incur the same awful penalty.

Suppose a man returns home at night and by mistake or otherwise takes poison. His good wife apprizes him of his danger and pleads with him to take at once an antidote she has secured that will counteract all the effects of the poison. But in bitterness and with curses he drives her away and absolutely refuses to apply the remedy. He dies because he opposed and rejected the only cure. Another scoffs and jeers at the antidote, makes light of it, and dies because he derided the only thing that would have saved him. But a third believes in the remedy. He knows it is a good thing and is a perfect antidote; but he simply neglects to take it. He tells his good wife that there is plenty of time, no immediate danger, and puts off taking the medicine until in the agonies of death he discovers it is too late.

Just so it is with salvation. Most great catastrophes come through neglect, and to neglect the soul is the greatest calamity that could befall any man. A great storm of wrath is gathering. Mercy has provided a shelter. But if we neglect to enter the refuge God has made the thunderbolts of eternal fury will burst upon us and there will be no escape. [Editor's bold]

"How shall we escape?" Here is the answer: "For yourselves know perfectly that the day of the Lord so cometh as a thief in the night. For when they shall say, Peace and safety; then *sudden destruction cometh upon them,* as travail upon a woman with child; and they shall not escape" (1 Thess. 5:2-3). "When the Lord Jesus shall be revealed from heaven with his mighty angels, in flaming fire taking vengeance on them that know not God, and that obey not the gospel of our Lord Jesus Christ: who shall be punished with everlasting destruction [away] from the presence of the Lord, and from the glory of his power." (2 Thess. 1:7-9).

TWO WAYS, TWO CLASSES, TWO DESTINIES—
HEAVEN AND HELL

I here quote from Rev. J. H. Potts, A.M.: "In the present dispensation we are the subjects of Time. With gigantic footsteps he bears us to our future. There is no escape from his course. Sometimes in the midst of extensive enterprises and important engagements he summons us, and we must obey. Prepared, or unprepared, we are compelled to do him service—the only service we can render him—yield up our life." The poet had this thought in mind:

> Remorseless Time!
> Fierce spirit of the glass and scythe—what power
> Can stay him in his silent course, or melt
> His iron heart to pity!
> On, still on he presses, and forever.

Few are the human hearts so hardened but that at some period or other they are melted into pity. But were the whole universe in tears over the rapid sweep of Time, his silent course would not be stayed nor his iron heart be moved. On, still on, he would press, and forever? No, not forever. The period comes on apace [quickly] when his own death-knell shall ring. He defeats himself by his reckless flight. "And the angel which I saw stand upon the sea and upon the earth lifted up his hand to heaven, and sware by him that liveth forever and ever ... that there should be time no longer" (Rev. 10:5-6). Swallowed up in eternity his iron heart shall yet be melted to pity; nay, shall feel the sting of death. The iron barriers of the tombs which he has built shall be broken asunder, and the numberless risen dead shall gather the scattered fragments to build an eternal sepulcher [burial chamber, grave, crypt] to him who has laid so many in their last repose, but who shall then be wrapped in the unending sleep of eternity. His funeral dirge shall be chanted by the saints, when "God shall wipe away all tears from their eyes; and there shall be no more death, neither sorrow, nor crying, neither shall there be any more pain: for the former things are passed away" (Rev. 21:4).

Man is born for a higher destiny than earth. This is not our eternal home. "For here have we no continuing city, but we seek one to come" (Heb. 13:14). The patriarchs and saints of old "confessed that they were strangers and pilgrims on the earth" (Heb. 11:13). They understood that this was not their final abode, but that they were sojourning here for a time. Peter denominates the New Testament church "strangers and pilgrims" who are merely "sojourning here" (1 Pet. 2:11; 1:17). We are all travelers to eternity. Every moment, hour, day, week, month, and year, carries us onward at a rapid rate to our destiny. Death is the gateway through which we all must pass. There we all meet on a common level, the rich, poor, young and old, saved and lost, all reach a common end—death. But this does not end all.

The question of the ages is— "If a man die, shall he live again?" (Job 14:14). This has been asked in every dispensation of time, in every nation of the world, by every individual who has ever lived, whether saint or sinner, priest or prophet, poet or philosopher. It is a profound question, greater than all the questions of life and time, because it concerns our future. It is a reasonable question from the fact that it affects our life here and hereafter, and because of our capacity to suffer and enjoy. But from where shall we expect and receive an answer? Go to the atheist and there is no answer. The evolutionist and the world's greatest scientists are silent. Go to the valley of death, to the grave, and to the cemetery, but no answer is heard. The materialist's answer enshrouds us with a pall of gloom. We turn from all these, and the future looks dark, unfathomable, impenetrable, locked in deep mystery.

At last we open the Book of Divine revelation—the Bible, and the mystery is solved. Its testimony is clear. It lifts the veil and gives us a look into the great beyond and reveals the realities of eternity. Elijah steps into a chariot of fire and is carried by a whirlwind into heaven (2 Kings 2:11). Moses is buried by the mountainside and his sepulcher is unknown (Deut. 34:1-6). More than a thousand years later these two men appear with Jesus on the holy mount of transfiguration and talk with Him (Matt. 17:1-7). They are both alive. Abraham, Isaac, and Jacob die and their bodies molder in the cave of Machpelah at Hebron, but God is still their God, "not the God of the dead, but of the living, for all live unto him" (Luke 20:38). With rocks crashing about his head Stephen looks up and testifies, "I see heaven opened, and the Son of man standing at the right hand of God" (Acts 7:56), and just as he passes away he cries, "Lord Jesus, receive my spirit" (Acts 7:59). Man lives beyond the tomb. And this is proof of a final resurrection of all the dead.

There are but two roads that lead from this time world out into eternity. Jesus described them thus: "Wide is the gate, and broad is the way, that leadeth to destruction, and many there be which go in thereat: Because strait [a narrow, difficult passage] is the gate, and narrow is the way, which leadeth unto life, and few there be that find it" (Matt. 7:13-14). These roads lead in opposite directions. The one to eternal destruction has a "wide gate" and is a "broad way." The other has a "strait"—difficult gate and is a "narrow" way, but it ends in life. On these two roads, all the human family are traveling. The "many"—multitudes—are on the broad way. Comparatively "few" find the strait gate and travel the narrow way. There is a reason. The gate to the way of destruction being *wide* is easily accessible and admits all types and manner of sin. Nothing to give up, just go in with all carnal lusts and desires; and people of all descriptions travel this *broad* road. It is the most agreeable way to the corrupt nature and blindness of the human mind. But it is a deceitful way, an unprofitable way, a trifling way, a disappointing way, a way that is hard to get off (and the longer you travel on it the harder), and a way that ends in eternal death.

The other gate is *strait*. It will not admit of any sin. People must forsake all to enter it. It has a narrow door that requires real struggle and effort to enter. "*Strive* to enter in," said Jesus, "for many will seek to enter, and shall not be able" (Luke 13:24). The reason is they are unwilling to give up all for Christ. The way is *narrow*. No unclean person can walk on this way. "The redeemed shall walk there, the ransomed of the Lord" (Isa. 35:10). It is the way of truth, holiness, humility, love, life, and salvation.

While the people of this world are divided into many and various classes and castes, the Bible recognizes but two distinct groups—the saved and the lost, the righteous and wicked, the Christian and the sinner. There is no neutral ground. We all belong to one or the other. "Then shall ye return, and discern between the *righteous* and the *wicked,* between him that serveth God and him that serveth him not" (Mal. 3:18). "He that committeth sin is of the devil. ... Whosoever is born of God doth not commit sin. ... *In this* the children of God are manifest, and the children of the devil" (1 John 3:8-10). Just two classes, and the line is drawn so clearly that we cannot misunderstand it. Two ways leading to the great future, and just two classes traveling thereon.

These roads lead somewhere, and the travelers will reach a destination, their destiny. As to that destiny the Bible is very explicit. Of the wicked who travel the broad way we read: "The wicked shall be turned into hell" (Ps. 9:17). "How can ye escape the damnation of *hell?*" (Matt. 23:33). "To be cast into *hell fire*" (Matt. 18:9). "Cast into *everlasting fire*" (Matt. 18:8). "Shall have their part in the lake which burneth with fire and brimstone" (Rev. 21:8). This is the "destruction" Jesus said lies at the end of the broad way. It will be "everlasting destruction [away] from the presence of the Lord" (2 Thess. 1:9). Banishment from Him forever.

Of the righteous who travel the narrow way we read, "Ye have *in heaven* a better and an enduring substance [possession]" (Heb. 10:34). "An inheritance incorruptible, and undefiled, and that fadeth not away, reserved *in heaven* for you" (1 Pet. 1:4). "Your reward is great *in heaven*" (Luke 6:23). This is "life," eternal life with Christ at the right hand of God.

WE CHOOSE OUR DESTINY

Man is not a mere machine, the creature of uncertain destiny. He has a will and can choose the right or wrong. When responsible years come upon us [at the age of accountability], we choose the road we travel, either the broad way of sin or the narrow way of righteousness. I am what I am today, not by a sovereign eternal decree independent of my own will, but by a personal choice of my own. Through Jesus Christ, God made such a choice possible, and I selected the way of life. If I am faithful until death, I shall receive a crown of life (James 1:12; 1 Pet. 5:4; 2 Tim. 4:8). It is up to me to make good. If through unfaithfulness I forfeit my crown, who but myself is responsible?

"I call heaven and earth to record this day against you, that I have set before you life and death, blessing and cursing: therefore choose life, that both thou and thy seed may live" (Deut. 30:19). Whatsoever else this meant to Israel, it shows that they were responsible. "Choose you this day whom ye will serve. ... As for me and my house, we will serve the Lord" (Josh. 24:15). "I have *chosen* the way of truth" (Ps. 119:30). "Refuse the evil, and *choose* the good" (Isa. 7:15). "Mary hath *chosen* that good part" (Luke 10:42). Life, then, is the result of a choice, and we ourselves make it.

But suppose people reject the good and choose the evil. Will not certain punishment fall upon them? Here is the Bible answer: "Therefore will I number you to the sword, and ye shall all bow down to the slaughter: because when I called, ye did not answer; when I spake, ye did not hear; but did evil before mine eyes, and did *choose* that wherein I delighted not" (Isa. 65:12). They brought judgment upon their own heads. "How long, ye simple ones, will ye love simplicity? and the scorners delight in their scorning, and fools hate knowledge? Turn you at my reproof: behold, I will pour out my spirit unto you, I will make known my words unto you. Because I have called, and ye refused; I have stretched out my hand, and no man regarded; but ye have set at nought all my counsel, and would none of my reproof: I also will laugh at your calamity; I will mock when your fear cometh; When your fear cometh as desolation, and your destruction cometh as a whirlwind; when distress and anguish cometh upon you. Then shall they call upon me, but I will not answer; they shall seek me early, but they shall not find me: For that they hated knowledge, and did not *choose* the fear of the Lord: They would none of my counsel: they despised all my reproof. Therefore, shall they eat of the fruit of their own way, and he filled with their own devices" (Prov. 1:22-31). Comment could not make stronger the fact expressed in this scripture that we choose our destiny, and when unmitigated wrath and judgment fall in awful severity we are simply eating the fruits of OUR OWN WAY. It is our selection, the result of our own devices.

"Judas by transgression fell, that he might go *to his own place*" (Acts 1:25).

First.—Every person has his own place here and hereafter. There is a place that God intends us all to fill, and there is room for all, room and place in the covenant of promise, in the great plan of salvation, in the provisions of Divine grace, in the kingdom of heaven, in the church of God, in the great harvest-field of work and endeavor, and at the Lord's rich table. We differ in talents and opportunities yet all can find a place of usefulness and efficiency. There is a place of responsibility in every home, community, and in the world at large. No one can fill *our* place, so we should be satisfied and faithfully fill it. But many, like Judas Iscariot, forfeit their place, and deliberately choose another.

Second.—Every person makes his own place here and hereafter. Ours is a self-made destiny. Men, by hard work, self-sacrificing, and sterling character have created for themselves a place in government, in inventive and commercial fields, and in the religious realm. It is in the power of every one of us to make a place for himself among the noble and pure, or among the low, vile, and wicked—to be a real success, or a miserable failure. And just as truly we are making our own destiny in heaven or hell.

Third.—Every person finds his place here and hereafter. You will notice some rushing to the racetrack, the card-table, the gambling-dens and casinos, the bar, the red-light district, the loafers' corner, the dance hall [nightclub], and the theater. They are simply finding their place. Others go to the place of honest business, the library, the study-room, the family circle, and the church. Question.—Where may those who know you best most reasonably expect to find you? The answer is an index to your character. The place does not make the man; he just finds his proper place, that is all, the place best suited to him.

Some people's place in the local, visible church seems to be that of grumblers, pickers, gossipers, fault-finders, and retarders of spiritual progress. Such individuals easily and quickly find their company—folks just like them. And the deeply spiritual, devoted, and hard workers among the Lord's people naturally flow together. Judas felt more at home with a band of murderers that night than with Jesus and His true disciples. "He went out quickly, and it was dark" (John 13:30). This will be true hereafter. Judas committed suicide and died in disgrace, "that he might *go to his own place*" (Acts 1:25), a place best suited and fitted for one who betrayed and sold his Christ. At death, he found "his place." "He which is filthy [here, in this life], let him be filthy STILL [in the eternal world after resurrection]" (Rev. 22:11). Righteous Noah and the wicked antediluvians [pre-flood] could not go to the same place. Neither Lot and the Sodomites, King Saul and David, Judas Iscariot and the beloved disciple John, Herod and James, nor Nero and Paul. It is the law of spiritual gravitation.

Fourth.—Every person will feel that it is his place when he gets there. This is true now. A gambler or sensualist [one who constantly pursues sex] feels perfectly at home in the company of like characters, and such people certainly feel out of place in a red-hot, Holy Ghost religious service. And a devout saint of God feels at home in a spiritual meeting and enjoys spiritual work. Such a one feels clear out of place in a modern dance hall [nightclub] or red-light district. In such a place and with such company he is like a bird in the water or a fish in the treetop, clear out of his element, away from his true environment. Thus, we all *make* our place, *find* our place, and feel at home when we get there. This will be true also in eternity. Judas went to "his own place." He feels it is his place, the abode he deserves. He could not feel at home in heaven with Christ and the faithful apostles. At death Lazarus was carried by the angels to his place—paradise—where he is "comforted." The rich man who lifted up his eyes in hell and was tormented knew it was his place. He was concerned that the rest of his folks on earth be warned not to come to that awful place of torment.

THE WORLD IN AWFUL SLEEP

"Wherefore he saith, Awake thou that sleepest, and arise from the dead, and Christ shall give thee light" (Eph. 5:14).

This describes the spiritual state and terrible condition of the whole unregenerate world. Various similitudes are employed in the Scriptures to represent the condition of the unsaved, as aliens, captives, prisoners, rebels, outcasts, diseased, blind, poor, naked, wretched, deceived, perishing, and lost. But here we have a deadly sleep. Fast asleep amid the darkness of a spiritual night, sleeping the dreadful sleep of death. Drifting out towards the "blackness of darkness forever" (Jude 13). Nearing the vortex of eternal perdition [a state of eternal punishment and damnation], rushing on to hell, and yet sound asleep, apparently unconscious of impending judgment and danger. How dark the night of sin, and they that sleep "sleep in the light" (Eph. 5:14).

Sin acts on the soul as deadly drugs do on the body. Opium, cocaine, morphine, alcohol and chloroform deaden and numb the sense of feeling. People under the influence of these drugs are not conscious of pain and are dead to the things about them. Just so, sin hardens the heart and turns it to stone. "But after thy *hardness* and impenitent heart treasurest up unto thyself wrath against the day of wrath" (Rom. 2:5). "They have made their hearts like an adamant stone" (Zech. 7:12). We read of some whose conscience is "seared as with a hot iron" (1 Tim. 4:2), and who are "past feeling." This well describes the condition of multitudes all about us, unawakened and impenitent. The solemn exhortation to the church is: "Let us not sleep as do others, but let us watch and be sober" (1 Thess. 5:6).

Satan, like "a strong man armed keepeth his palace [the unregenerate soul of man]" (Luke 11:21). He is a "prince of this world" (John 14:30), "ruler of the darkness of this world" (Eph. 6:12), the "god of this world" (2 Cor. 4:4), and holds dominion over countless millions of human beings. He reigns in their hearts and lives, controls, holds fast, destroys, ruins, blights, disqualifies, and throws over them his hellish opiates and lulls them to sleep in carnal security. He hangs up the curtains of deception and delusion decorated with unclean visions, and fills the affections with worldliness, pride, and vanity. Here in the human heart is his throne, and here he is exalted, served, and yielded to, so that he sways his scepter over the mind, heart, and life.

He keeps possession by blinding folks so they do not see themselves. He pulls down the blinds and shuts out the light so that his subjects are insensible to the gracious things of God and to their own danger. "For the heart of this people is waxed gross, and their ears are dull of hearing, and their eyes have they closed" (Acts 28:27). Such folks are very much alive and active in worldly affairs and in the business of sin but they are dead to God. God speaks in thunder-tones, but they hear not. He swings red lights of warning across their pathway, but their eyes are closed. A thousand blessings fall around them, but they have no taste nor desire for these, unconscious to the "things that belong to their peace." With the transplendent light of the gospel shining all about them they "sit in the valley and shadow of death" (Ps. 23:4). [Editor's note: We are to walk THROUGH the valley of the shadow of death, not sit and stay and dwell there!]

This is a state of great danger and of grave peril. A person sound asleep cannot defend himself against the thief or assassin. In a burning building, unless awakened, he is sure to perish. Every lost sinner is in a worse condition than a sleeping man in a structure all in flames. He is blind to eternal dangers. Deaf to the Spirit's voice, deaf to the roar of approaching storm, deaf to the rumblings of hell beneath. The thunder and lightning grows more loud and vivid. Death is at the door. Satan, the murderer of souls, is ready to strike a dagger at his heart. The casket in which he will be buried is now in the undertaker's rooms, and the tools that will dig his grave are waiting; and yet he slumbers on. Great God, awaken the slumbering souls of men.

The sleep here described is not the natural, restful slumber, but is an abnormal state, a diseased condition, the effect of moral depravity and volitional sin against God. The picture places one out in the cemetery of the dead. The most powerful sermon is lost on a sleeping or dead man. The only hope of such is a real Bible awakening. Until awakened, people will put forth no effort to be saved. As in the case of the publican [tax collector] and prodigal, when people are truly awakened by the Word and Spirit of God, it will lead to deep and thorough repentance and sound conversion of the soul.

Again, sleep is often a state of illusion, a season of dreams, when things appear real, and then on awakening it is found to be only a fancy or empty dream. So, with the unsaved: "It shall be even as when an hungry man dreameth, and, behold, he eateth; but he awaketh, and his soul is empty: or as when a thirsty man dreameth, and, behold, he drinketh; but he awaketh, and, behold, he is faint, and his soul hath appetite: so shall the multitude of all the nations be that fight against Mount Zion. Stay yourselves, and wonder; cry ye out, and cry: they are drunken, but not with wine; they stagger, but not with strong drink. For the Lord hath poured out upon you the spirit of deep sleep, and hath closed your eyes: the prophets and your rulers, the seers hath he covered" (Isa. 29:8-10). What a picture! A man is in the desert dying for food and water. He falls asleep and dreams that he is feasting on rich food and is drinking refreshing, cool water. But he then awakes out of his slumber to find it was all a dream and he dies in despair.

So it is also with the nations of the world that fight against God and Zion. Some go so far in their opposition to the truth that God sends them "strong delusion … that they all might be damned who believed not the truth, but had pleasure in unrighteousness" (2 Thess. 2:11-12). In the language of the prophet, the Lord pours out upon them the "spirit of deep sleep," and closes their eyes. "They shall sleep a *perpetual sleep*" (Jer. 51:57). Thus, while people sleep on in sin and rebellion there is one thing certain— *"their damnation slumbereth not."* Such will have a terrible awakening on the other side of death.

"What awful darkness shrouds all the earth.
Hearts sealed in hardness grope on in death.

"Hell's breathing stupor is now over all.
Who'll break the subtle, infernal pall?

"Awake, O sleeper, God help you hear,
Death coils about you, your doom is near.

"O world of sinners, if not too late,
While hope yet glimmers, flee from your fate.

"O hear the thunder, sinner in slumber,
Will you determine to break the spell,
And not abandon your soul in hell?"

PREPARE TO MEET GOD

"Prepare to meet thy God, O Israel" (Amos 4:12).

This is an age of preparedness. In every department of life, whether business, educational, governmental, or national, the requirement of the times is efficiency and thorough preparedness. The great nations of the world are not neglecting adequate preparations for defense and emergencies that may arise.

The preparedness I shall treat in this chapter is of immeasurably more importance than any of the things mentioned. We must all meet God. There are some things in life we can escape and evade, but here is one thing that is absolutely certain—we must meet God. We shall meet Him at death when our spirit "goes to God who gave it" (Eccl. 12:7). We shall all meet Him in judgment, for "we shall *all* appear" at that place and time. "I saw the dead, small and great, stand before God" (Rev. 20:12). "So then every one of us shall give an account of himself to God" (Rom. 14:12). The supreme question of life is—Am I prepared and ready to meet God?

Man in sin is unprepared to serve God acceptably here, to fulfil life's purpose, to meet God's demands, and he is not fit to die, to meet the Lord in peace, and to enter heaven. God is infinitely holy, and no unholy person can stand in His awful [unimaginable, awesome, holy, glorious] presence (Isa. 6:5). To have boldness in the day of judgment we must be "pure even as he is pure" (1 John 3:3), "righteous even as he is righteous" (1 John 3:7), and "be found of him in peace, without spot and blameless" (2 Pet. 3:14). Heaven is a holy place. The road that leads there is "the way of holiness" (Isa. 35:8). And to enter and enjoy its eternal felicities [great happiness, bliss] we must be holy, free from sin, for no sin can enter there. The holiness of God clothes the holy man with majestic glory, and this awful glory will drive the wicked from His presence forever (2 Thess. 2:7-9).

The preparation is ours. "Set thy house in order, for thou shalt die" (Isa. 38:1). "Prepare to meet thy God" (Amos 4:12). It is up to us; the responsibility is ours. Salvation is conditional. The principle of preparedness is right and reasonable. When people are about to take a long journey they always prepare in advance. In the fall of 1920 my wife, son, and I started on an eleven-thousand-mile trip, by an indirect route, from Akron, Indiana, U.S.A., to Beirut, Syria [Editor's note: Beirut now is the capital of Lebanon]. We first made extensive preparation. Our passport was secured from the United States government and endorsed and stamped by representatives from the various countries we expected to visit. Our baggage was already packed and properly checked, and our tickets secured. Not an item was overlooked. The result was we had a successful trip, and after nineteen weeks of travel on land and sea we safely reached our destination. We are all soon to take a journey "through the valley of the shadow of death" (Ps. 23:4) when "man goeth to his *long* home, and the mourners go about the streets" (Eccl. 12:5). Is it not strange that so few take time for preparation? Life and time is our only opportunity to get ready for this solemn event, our trip into *"long"* eternity. Every hour of our short life is laden with the great responsibility of getting ready for this solemn change.

In cold countries people in summer time prepare for the winter. Life is our summer time, and it is a tragedy to let it pass carelessly by without preparation. Soon the frosts of an eternal winter will settle upon you; the chill of death will be felt; and then in despair you will cry: "The harvest is past, the summer is ended, and we are not saved" (Jer. 8:20). It will then be too late forever. [Editor's bold]

In some of the Western States people have caves near their homes. On inquiry, I learned that these were prepared so that in case of tornado or cyclone [hurricane] the family could hastily flee to this place and be secure. Friend, the storms of judgment are approaching, the oncoming day of wrath, and what preparation have you made? "And the heaven departed as a scroll when it is rolled together; and every mountain and island were moved out of their places. And the kings of the earth, and the great men, and the rich men, and the chief captains, and the mighty men, and every bondman, and every freeman, hid themselves in the dens and in the rocks of the mountains; and said to the mountains and rocks, Fall on us, and hide us from the face of him that sitteth on the throne, and from the wrath of the Lamb: For the great day of his wrath is come; and who shall be able to stand?" (Rev. 6:14-17). Are you ready to stand amid scenes like this? Oh "prepare to meet thy God."

As to the preparation required the Bible speaks plainly. No one need go through this world in uncertainty. The future is not a lottery, not a guess. We can "make our calling and election *sure*" (2 Pet. 1:10), "Unto us which *are* saved" (1 Cor. 1:18), "He *hath saved* us" (2 Tim. 1:9), "*We know* we are of God" (1 John 5:19). "Hereby *we do know* that we know him" (1 John 2:3). "We know that we have passed from death unto life" (John 5:24; 1 John 3:14). "Knowing in yourselves that ye have in heaven a better and enduring substance [possession]" (Heb. 10:34).

What brings such knowledge? 1.—A deep, thorough repentance toward God. 2.—A living faith in Jesus Christ, resting upon the immutable promises of the Word. 3.—A sound conversion [one that perseveres to the end (2 Tim. 4:6-8; Matt. 24:13; Gal. 6:9; Heb. 12:1-2; Rev. 3:11)]. 4.— Holiness in heart and life. "Follow peace with all men, and holiness, without which no man shall see the Lord" (Heb. 12:14). "Blessed are the pure in heart: for they shall see God" (Matt. 5:8).

Now is the only time to prepare for the future. It will be too late at death; too late at the judgment. Oh, the blessedness of being ready. Listen to the testimony of a man who came to death fully ready: "I am now ready to be offered, and the time of my departure is at hand. I have fought a good fight, I have finished my course, I have kept the faith: Henceforth there is laid up for me a crown of righteousness, which the Lord, the righteous judge, shall give me at that day" (2 Tim. 4:6-8). Millions of saints have faced death with this same assurance. Among other things, this is why I am a Christian. I want to be ready for death and the judgment.

Oh, the terribleness of not being prepared. Hear the testimony of a man who faced death unprepared: "I am sore distressed; for the Philistines make war against me, and *God is departed from me,* and answereth me no more, neither by prophets, nor by dreams" (1 Sam. 28:15). The next day this poor man [King Saul] fell upon his own sword and committed suicide. While touring Palestine in the month of September, 1922, I visited the reputed place of Saul's death on the northern slopes of Mount Gilboa. I thought, "Here ended a life that began with a bright outlook and continued for a time with a successful career and then ended a miserable failure." We judge the success or failure of an enterprise, or a life, by its ending. I have known of many undertakings that had a good beginning, a sensational career, and then ended in failure. No matter what the accomplishments of life may be, if we come to death unprepared to meet God, our whole life is a failure.

In Cambridge Springs, Pa., a young woman was dying. She had neglected the one important thing in life—salvation. A good sister was with her the night of her death. Shortly after midnight the dying woman sat up in bed and remarked to the sister, "Do you know that there is a terrible storm coming? Why, I can see the lightning flash. Did you hear that thunder? The sky must be black." The other woman went outside and found it a beautiful moonlit night, without a cloud in the sky. She returned and assured the dying woman that there was no storm. But this did not console the woman who was in the agonies of death. She again said: "There is a storm, and it is coming nearer. Did you see that lightning? My, what a clap of thunder. I can hear the crash of an awful storm." About 1 A.M. she again sat up in the bed and said, "It is here," and fell over dead. My God, save me from such a death. This is what it means to come to the end of life unprepared.

YOUR SOUL ON THE AUCTION-BLOCK

"For what is a man profited, if he shall gain the whole world, and lose his own soul? or what shall a man give in exchange for his soul?" (Matt. 16:26). "But God said unto him, Thou fool, this night thy soul shall be required of thee" (Luke 12:20).

These texts express a number of facts: 1.—The value of the human soul. It is worth more than all this world. To gain the world and lose our soul is to suffer an irreparable loss. 2.—The value of salvation. The salvation of the soul is of more worth than "houses and barns," "goods and lands," for these will perish, but the soul will live on forever. 3.—Profit and loss. In a life of sin there is some gain—the "pleasures of sin for a season," the riches and honors of the world (Heb. 11:24-26). But all this is at the loss of the soul. To place this fleeting world in the gain column means to put your priceless soul in the loss column, and the loss is greater than the gain. In the life of a Christian we may lose the friendship, honors, and pleasures of the world, but we gain the eternal salvation of the soul.

I desire in this chapter to present the force of these scriptures as I believe Christ had in mind. Friend, your soul is on the auction-block. It is not houses and lands, horses and cattle, stocks and bonds, that are offered, but your SOUL. In this you are the auctioneer, and it lies in your power to deliver it to whom you will. This makes every man responsible for the destiny of his soul. Two bidders stand before you. On your right is the Lord with outstretched hand, pleading for your soul. He wants it for Himself. "All day long," He says, "have I waited" (Rom. 10:21; Isa. 65:2). On your left stands the devil [diábolos, Satan], bidding for your soul. He is a liar, murderer, thief, knave [dishonest], the biggest cheat that ever stalked this earth, and he wants your soul. He knows its value better than you do.

There are two things that every person should consider:

1.—Which of these two bidders has the best right to your soul? This is easily answered. The Lord has, for two reasons. By creative right it belongs to Him. He says, "All souls are mine" (Ezek. 18:4; Ps. 24:1) Here is the reason: "I have created him for my glory, I have formed him; yea, I have made him" (Isa. 43:7). By redemption right the soul belongs to God: "Ye are not your own, for ye are bought with a price: therefore glorify God in your body, and in your spirit, which are God's" (1 Cor. 6:19-20). Note this fact— "Ye ARE BOUGHT with a price." What is the price God paid for your soul's redemption? Here is the answer: "Forasmuch as ye know that ye were not redeemed with corruptible things, as silver and gold … but with the precious blood of Christ, as of a lamb without blemish and without spot" (1 Pet. 1:18-19). The agonies of the Savior in dark Gethsemane, His scourging at Pilate's whipping-post, bearing His cross to Calvary, being nailed upon it, and for six hours suspended between heaven and earth, and then His cruel death, friend—that is the price God paid for your soul. Has He not the best right to it? It rightfully belongs to Him by both creation and purchase. When you yield to Him you simply hand over His rightful property. However, when you hand over to Satan your soul, you deliver to him stolen goods, the property of Almighty God. What a sin "against heaven" (Luke 15:18).

2.—Which of these two bidders will give you the most for your soul? What does the Lord offer? "The Lord will give grace and glory; no good thing will he withhold from them that walk uprightly" (Ps. 84:11). "According as his divine power hath given unto us all things that pertain unto life and godliness" (2 Pet. 1:3). "The same Lord over all is rich unto all that call upon him" (Rom. 10:12). "The living God, who giveth us richly all things to enjoy" (1 Tim. 6:17). "Now unto him that is able to do exceeding abundantly above all that we ask or think, according to the power that worketh in us" (Eph. 3:20). "God is able to make all grace abound toward you; that ye, always having all sufficiency in all things, may abound to every good work" (2 Cor. 9:8). The Lord will give us honor, for He says: "If any man will serve me, him will my Father honor; and we will come and make our abode with him" (John 12:26; John 14:23). He will give us the "true riches": "All things are yours." And pleasures: "He maketh us to drink of the rivers of his pleasures" (Ps. 36:8), and He gives us "joy unspeakable, and full of glory" (1 Pet. 1:8). Best of all, He gives perfect soul rest and satisfaction: "I will give you rest unto your soul" (Matt. 11:28-29). "The Lord satisfieth the longing soul, and filleth the hungry soul with goodness" (Ps. 107:9). Of all these good things God promises Jesus said we "shall receive an hundred fold now in this time" (Mark 10:30). "And we know that all things work together for good to them that love God, to them who are the called according to his purpose" (Rom. 8:28).

There is one thing certain—the Lord will give just what He promises. There will be no disappointment. Millions have proved this to be true. But what is the Lord's promise for the future? A peaceful death, "for the end of that man is peace" (Ps. 37:37). Angels to carry the happy spirit to the paradise of God (Luke 16:22). Between death and the resurrection "they may rest from their labors; and their works do follow them" (Rev. 14:13). "There the wicked cease from troubling; and there the weary be at rest" (Job 3:17). "Depart and be with Christ, which is far better" (Phil. 1:23). Then at Christ's coming "the resurrection of life" to eternal rewards in heaven. Friend, this is the Lord's offer. It is up to us to accept or reject.

On the other hand, what has the devil to offer? "The pleasures of sin for a season," worldly friendship, carefree society, earthly fame, riches, and a general good time here. All this at the cost of your soul. But Satan is a liar and murderer. He never gives what he offers. If you are fool enough to deliver to him your soul, here is what you will get: disappointment, misery, remorse, heartaches, trouble, addictions, drunkenness, disease, ruined character, humiliation, debauchery, broken homes, ruined lives, jails, insane asylums, wars, hell on earth, and premature death. This is just a partial list of what the world in general is getting from Satan because they have delivered to him their souls. "To whom ye yield yourselves servants to obey, his servants ye are" (Rom 6:16).

But what about the future? What has Satan to offer you there? NOTHING. It is his trick to keep your mind on the present and away from the future. But it is the purpose of this book to help you to see the future, "BEYOND THE TOMB." Let us look at that. You deliver your soul to the devil here, serve sin all your life, reject the kind offers the Lord has made, and close your life in rebellion against God, and here is what you will get:

1.—A Christless death without hope: "This night is thy soul required of thee" (Luke 12:20).

"A rich man was he, and his acres were broad;
And his barns he tore down to build more:
'But thy soul is required, thou fool,' said his God,
'Then to whom shall thy goods be restored?'

"He looked all aghast at the sound of that voice,
Then gazed on his rich earthly store.
But it faded away, he had made a sad choice,
He was poverty's slave evermore.

"Out, out from his mansion he wandered away,
To the depths of eternity's night,
To beg for relief, and to long for a day
Which shall gladden, no never, his sight.

"Eternity's beggar. The call he had heard;
But the warning he turned it away.
O sinner, then list to the voice of thy God,
And turn to the Lord while you may."

If angels come to waft the happy spirits of the saints to paradise, it is reasonable to believe that Satan will send his demons to carry the lost souls of his servants to the pits of gloom where they are reserved and kept in "chains of darkness unto the judgment of the great day" (2 Pet. 2:4; Jude 6). Many saints have testified in their dying hours that they heard the angels sing and these heavenly messengers surrounded their bed; and a multitude of sinners have also declared that demons were present to receive their departing spirits.

A number of years ago in a town where I resided was a man who lived a hypocritical life. He made a very loud profession in church, but at home he abused his good wife and was anything but a Christian. When he came to die, he was very conscious that he was not ready. Just before he passed away he testified that his bed was surrounded with demons, and he was terribly frightened. In his fear and agony, he leaped out of bed, ran out into the yard, and died.

Another man with whom I was well acquainted, and who was converted in a meeting I held, finally grew careless and lost his experience of salvation. While in this condition his son, also unsaved, was accidentally killed. He grieved much over this. One Sunday afternoon he and his wife visited the boy's grave, and while there he lay upon the grave and asked God to send him to hell to keep company for his son. God is not mocked nor to be trifled with (Gal. 6:7). That same night he awoke his wife saying, "I am dying. My God, I am dying. Run quickly and get some of the brethren to pray for me." She ran up the street in her night clothes and got a brother and sister to accompany her home. When they arrived, the man was out of the bed on the floor dead. Dear reader, deliver your soul to God, and do it today.

2.—Torment after death. A certain man died, "and in hell he lift up his eyes, being in torments. ... And he cried and said ... I am tormented in this flame, ... this *place* of torment" (Luke 16:23-28). Jesus related this and it must be so.

3.—A resurrection "to shame and everlasting contempt" (Dan. 12:2).

4.—Hell forever beyond the judgment day: "Depart from me, ye cursed, into everlasting fire, prepared for the devil and his angels" (Matt. 25:41).

O friend, this is what you will receive if you deliver your soul to Satan. You cannot afford to do it. Heaven is so precious you cannot afford to miss it. And hell is so fearful you cannot afford to be lost eternally. It is bad when we lose health, but we may be able to regain it. A fortune lost, a ship lost at sea, a child kidnapped and lost, a friend lost by death, terrible as these appear and are, are nothing compared with the loss of your soul. Your priceless soul LOST, forever lost, hopelessly, ruinously, eternally lost. Lost in the blackness of an eternal night, amid the howling of demons and the piercing shrieks of the damned—lost, *lost,* LOST. And when once lost, what now would such "give in exchange" for their souls? What would they give to have their souls back again with the opportunities of life they once enjoyed? Reader, to whom will you deliver your soul?

RUSHING ON TO PERDITION

"I hearkened and heard, but they spake not aright [did not speak what is right]: no man repented him of his wickedness, saying, What have I done? every one turned to his course, as the horse rusheth into the battle. Yea, the stork in the heaven knoweth her appointed times; and the turtle and the crane and the swallow observe the time of their coming [migration]; but my people know not the judgment of the Lord" (Jer. 8:6-7).

The emigration [the act of leaving] of this old world is towards hell, and people are rushing on at a terrible speed. The figure here used is the horse dashing into battle. There are three things that the battle-horse does:

He rushes *desperately,* and will not be detracted from his course. So it is with the sinner. There is a spirit that gets hold of people, the spirit of the world, and under it they lose the fear of God out of their hearts, the fear of the future is stifled, and they speed onward in their course with such recklessness it is very difficult indeed to stop them in their mad rush long enough to interest them in eternal things.

Next, the battle-horse is *heedless of danger*. He speeds furiously upon the line of bayonets in the face of artillery and musketry. The world of the ungodly are like that. Crowding, pushing forward in the face of impending wrath and judgment, so engrossed amid the rattle of social, commercial, and political life, that they "know not the judgment of the Lord."

The battle-horse *overleaps hounds*. He breaks through at any cost. So it is with the sinner. God sets certain bounds and gives most positive warnings of the grave danger of overstepping them, but people heed not, and as a result land in hell.

On Brooklyn Bridge, New York, about 5 P.M., when the rush of traffic is on, if a person is caught in the press of the crowd, he is simply forced along with them. There is such a thing as getting so carried away in the whirl of sin that to break away from the multitude going the downward course takes a great effort, and very few can do it or will make the effort.

Another striking figure employed in our lesson is, "the stork in the heaven [sky] knoweth her appointed times" (Jer. 8:7). Instinct tells the stork to change its location, for preservation. The storks migrate to warmer climates and flee from the winter. Man is not as wise as the birds. When God's judgments loom, he will not alter his course nor change his place. The stork, turtle dove, crane, and swallow observe the seasons, but man heeds them not. Life and time is the season of grace and salvation, but man carelessly lets it pass. The birds know when to start but man neglects and delays until death overtakes him.

Listen, friend: what are you doing to save your soul? What are you doing for Jesus, for His church, and for the world's betterment? Your sins are destroying your soul; your conscience is drugged thereby. You have stifled conviction too long now, and your chances to be saved are lessening every hour. Act at once, or you are lost.

"Crowded is your heart with cares,
Have you no room for Jesus?
Captured by earth's gilded snares,
Have you no room for Jesus?
Lo, He's standing at your door,
Knocking, knocking, o'er and o'er,
Hear Him pleading evermore,
Have you no room for Jesus?

"Wasting all your precious hours,
Have you no work for Jesus?
Spending those God-given powers,
Have you no work for Jesus?
Striving not to conquer sin,
Seeking not a soul to win,
Bringing not a wanderer in,
Have you no work for Jesus?

"Chasing bubbles through the air,
Have you no time for Jesus?
None for gracious deeds to spare,
Have you no time for Jesus?
Earthly pleasures, wealth and ease,
Seeking, grasping toys like these,
Striving only self to please,
Have you no time for Jesus?

"Bearing only worthless leaves,
Have you no fruit for Jesus?
In your hands no precious sheaves,
Have you no fruit for Jesus?
Not a grain to store away,
Naught your labor to repay,
Not a joy for that great day,
When you shall meet with Jesus."

RED LIGHTS OF WARNING ON THE
BROAD WAY TO HELL

"So thou, O son of man, I have set thee a watchman unto the house of Israel; therefore, thou shalt hear the word at my mouth, and warn them from me. When I say unto the wicked, O wicked man, thou shalt surely die; if thou dost not speak to warn the wicked from his way, that wicked man shall die in his iniquity; but his blood will I require at thine hand. Nevertheless, if thou warn the wicked of his way to turn from it; if he do not turn from his way, he shall die in his iniquity; but thou hast delivered thy soul.... Say unto them, As I live, saith the Lord God, I have no pleasure in the death of the wicked; but that the wicked turn from his way and live: turn ye, turn ye from your evil ways; for why will ye die, O house of Israel" (Ezek. 33:7-11).

No one need go to perdition with his eyes closed. There is a hell of torment that awaits the guilty and there is a road that leads there. To keep men out, God has hung red lights of warning all along the way. As you know, red lights are usually danger signals. When there is an excavation on the road or street, a bridge has been washed out, or there has been a mountain slide, red lights are hung there as warning signals, and a person would be considered a fool to run past these and give no heed to them.

God has no pleasure in the death of the sinner (Ezek. 33:11), and He has done and is doing all that He can to keep the sinner from plunging into eternal ruin. This has been God's method in all ages. He faithfully warned the ungodly world in the days of Noah. The building of the ark was a warning; Noah's preaching was a warning, while the Spirit strove with men (2 Pet. 2:5; Gen. 6:3). "The longsuffering of God waited in the days of Noah" (1 Pet. 3:20). God warned the Ninevites, and they heeded the warning and were saved (Jonah 3). Jesus said they will rise in the day of judgment and condemn this generation of impenitents. Under both the Old and New Testaments, it will be seen that the Lord always faithfully warned individuals and nations of impending judgment. Note how Jesus time and again warned the Jews of the wrath that would be poured upon their nation and city unless they repented; and it came.

1.—God warns people through their *conscience*. Conscience is an original faculty in man's nature, and it operates in all, whether enlightened or heathen. Every man is endowed with this faculty; it is an essential part of his being. It is that which recognizes the fact of right and wrong, and demands compliance therewith, an intuitive moral impulse. It is an inward witness— "If our heart condemn us; if our heart condemn us not" (1 John 3:19-21). Conscience keeps a minute record and is an intelligent, true witness:

"Their conscience also bearing witness" (Rom. 2:14-15). Yes, it is a faithful witness and will not be bribed, but it is as true to the king as to the beggar, and it thunders in the soul of the rich as well as the poor. It is a loud witness. A deaf man can hear the voice of conscience. Its voice is terrible. It made Felix [a Roman procurator of Judea, whom Paul stood before while on trial] tremble, caused Joseph's brethren to quake and fear while they were before the governor of Egypt, and tormented Judas Iscariot until he threw down the pieces of silver and hanged himself.

When Cain fled from Abel's grave, conscience cried louder than his brother's blood cried from the ground (Gen. 4:10). The voice of conscience has wrung confessions out of many people guilty of heinous crimes. There is at Washington, D.C., a large fund accumulated, known as the "Conscience Fund." People who have either stolen or taken advantage of their fellowmen and cannot find the parties to make restitution send in the amount to the government to silence the voice of their conscience. In conscience, even the rudest person carries the voice of God within him. There is no refuting its testimony or setting aside its verdict. Some try to drown its voice in riot, pleasure, business, drink, drugs, and even suicide; but while other witnesses may die, conscience NEVER.

"Hope will end, but conscience never.
With thy spirit it will fly.
Yea, torment and chide thee ever,
Where the worm shall never die."

It will speak after death— "Son, remember." You may stab, wound, stifle, try to smother its voice, and even try to run away from it; but it will speak back to you— "I will meet you at the judgment." An accusing conscience is an inward trumpeter summoning your nobler powers to the great battle between the right and the wrong, and oh, how blessed to heed this trumpet call. The prickings of conscience are painful, but if rightly heeded in time, they will lead to repentance. You may speak of burying the past, but conscience will not let you. The blood of Christ is the only thing that will blot out the past, and during your life is the only time to have that blood applied.

2.—God warns through the *Spirit:* "My Spirit shall not always strive with man" (Gen. 6:3). "He will reprove the world of sin, and of righteousness, and of judgment" (John 16:8). The striving of the Spirit is the energy of God applied to the mind and heart of man, setting facts and truths before him, reasoning, convincing, and persuading him of the folly of sin, and of the danger of continuing such a life. Under the Spirits' striving, people's attention is arrested to the great concerns of their souls. The Spirit of God strives in many ways and all these have a meaning, a message, and a warning in them.

But the time of God's grace is limited. The Spirit "will *not* ALWAYS strive." "For rebellion is as the sin of witchcraft [mysticism, occult, sorcery], and stubbornness is as iniquity and idolatry. Because thou hast rejected the word of the Lord, *he hath also rejected thee*" (1 Sam. 15:23). "God is departed from me, and answereth me no more" (1 Sam. 28:15). "And the Lord God of their fathers sent to them by his messengers, rising up betimes, and sending; because he had compassion on his people, and on his dwelling place: but they mocked the messengers of God, and despised his words, and misused his prophets, until the wrath of the Lord arose against his people, *till there was no remedy*" (2 Chron. 36:15-16).

"Your iniquities have separated between you and your God, and your sins have hid his face from you, that *he will not hear*" (Isa. 59:2). "How often would I have gathered thy children together ... but ye would not. Behold, your house is left unto you desolate" (Luke 13:34-35). "There shall be great distress in the land, and wrath upon this people" (Luke 21:23). These are but a few of the many texts that could be cited to show that people have rejected the Spirit until they became incorrigible [set in their ways, hardened beyond cure], beyond hope.

After giving ample warning and invitation to be saved, God will, as a just judgment upon the unbelieving and impenitent, withdraw His Spirit and let them alone. On this point Charles G. Finney says: "Why will God's Spirit not strive always? (1)—Because longer striving will do the sinner no good; (2)—because sinners sin willfully when they resist the Holy Ghost; (3)—because there is a point beyond which forbearance is no virtue. Consequently, the Spirit ceases to strive with men. Result. (1)—A confirmed hardness of heart; (2)—a seared conscience; (3)—certain damnation."

How sad, when Almighty God, foiled by human obduracy [stubbornness] in all His manifestations of grace and mercy, at last after "his longsuffering has waited" for man's salvation, retires, exclaiming: "In returning and rest shall ye be saved; in quietness and confidence shall be your strength; and ye would not. But ye said, No" (Isa. 30:15-16). How long continued, constant, and persevering have been the Lord's efforts through the Spirit to save men, to stop them in their mad rush, and to turn them back to Him; but like a mighty torrent they sweep along, growing "worse and worse" until the stroke of judgment like a lightning flash hurls them to their doom.

3.—The Lord warns by His *gospel:* "For we must all appear before the judgment seat of Christ; that every one may receive the things done in his body, according to that he hath done, whether it be good or bad. *Knowing therefore the terror of the Lord, we persuade men"* (2 Cor. 5:10-11). The day of judgment will be a day of terror for the wicked and a fearful doom awaits them. Even in the Old Testament frequent reference is made to it, and in the gospel, people are repeatedly warned to "flee the wrath to come" (Matt. 3:7). Christ will come in the glory of His Father and "then he shall reward every man according to his works" (Matt. 16:27). There will be no more escape from sin, and the wicked will forever have lost their souls. The revelation of Jesus Christ from heaven will be a day of wrath, when the Lord will render "to every man according to his deeds," and this will eternally fix the fate of all men, whether pure or sinful. "Whosoever was not found written in the book of life was cast into the lake of fire" (Rev. 20:12-15). "When the Lord Jesus shall be revealed from heaven with his mighty angels, in flaming fire taking vengeance on them that know not God, and that obey not the gospel of our Lord Jesus Christ: who shall be punished with everlasting destruction [away] from the presence of the Lord, and from the glory of his power" (2 Thess. 1:7-9).

In different places we read that the Lord will come "with power and great glory" (Matt. 24:30; Mark 13:26; Luke 21:27). This awful glory is what will drive the wicked into everlasting destruction away from His presence to the flames of eternal hell. Oh, how many plain and solemn warnings God has given to all men of that day when all must either stand or fall in the presence of His majesty and glory!

"For if God spared not the angels that sinned, but cast them down to hell, and delivered them into chains of darkness, to be reserved unto judgment; and spared not the old world, but saved Noah the eighth person, a preacher of righteousness, bringing in the flood upon the world of the ungodly; and turning the cities of Sodom and Gomorrha [Gomorrah] into ashes condemned them with an overthrow, making them an ensample [example] unto those that after should live ungodly; the Lord knoweth how to deliver the godly out of temptations, and to reserve the unjust unto the day of judgment to be punished" (2 Pet. 2:4-9).

Peter refers to these past dealings of the Almighty as a solemn warning and example "unto those that after should live ungodly." Angels that sinned were cast down to hell. The antediluvian [pre-flood] "world of the ungodly" were destroyed by the flood. God rained fire and brimstone upon Sodom and Gomorrah in His wrath and vengeance. How forcible comes the language of the apostle to us: "Knowing therefore the *terror* of the Lord, we persuade men" (2 Cor. 5:11).

In all God's dealings, the impenitent and ungodly have always received the just measure of His wrath and vengeance, and in the foregoing text Peter clearly shows that God will deal with men in the same manner in the great day of judgment. Sinner, take warning. Instead of Christ's coming ushering in a day of mercy and salvation to the unsaved, He hath reserved "the unjust unto **the day of judgment** *TO BE PUNISHED*."

"Therefore be ye also ready: for in such an hour as ye think not the Son of man cometh. Who then is a faithful and wise servant, whom his lord hath made ruler over his household, to give them meat in due season? Blessed is that servant, whom his lord when he cometh shall find so doing. Verily I say unto you, That he shall make him ruler over all his goods. But and if that evil servant shall say in his heart, My lord delayeth his coming; and shall begin to smite [strike] his fellow servants, and to eat and drink with the drunken; the lord of that servant shall come in a day when he looketh not for him, and in an hour that he is not aware of, and shall cut him asunder [in pieces], and appoint him his portion with the hypocrites: there shall be weeping and gnashing of teeth" (Matt. 24:44-51).

Here a solemn charge is given to be ready. The "faithful and wise servant" represents those who in life obtain salvation and who diligently serve God, walking in all holy conversation and godliness, "blessed is that servant, whom his Lord when he cometh shall find so doing." Such will be rewarded in heaven. But how will the "evil servant" fare? God shall "cut him asunder, and appoint him his portion with the hypocrites; there shall be weeping and gnashing of teeth." (Matt 24:51) "And cast ye the unprofitable servant into outer darkness: there shall be weeping and gnashing of teeth" (Matt. 25:30). "But the heavens and the earth, which are now, by the same word are kept in store, reserved unto fire against the day of judgment and perdition of ungodly men. But, beloved, be not ignorant of this one thing, that one day is with the Lord as a thousand years, and a thousand years as one day. The Lord is not slack concerning his promise, as some men count slackness; but is longsuffering to us-ward [towards us], not willing that any should perish, but that all should come to repentance. But the day of the Lord will come as a thief in the night; in the which the heavens shall pass away with a great noise, and the elements shall melt with fervent heat, the earth also and the works that are therein shall be burned up. Seeing then that all these things shall be dissolved, what manner of persons ought ye to be in all holy conversation and godliness, looking for and hasting unto the coming of the day of God, wherein the heavens being on fire shall be dissolved, and the elements shall melt with fervent heat? ... Wherefore, beloved, seeing that ye look for such things, be diligent that ye may be found of him in peace, without spot, and blameless" (2 Pet. 3:7-14).

That awful day of fire will be "the day of judgment and perdition of ungodly men" (2 Pet. 3:7). Truth declares that now is the day of salvation, and that the present day of grace is drawn out by the mercy of God to enable more lost sinners to be saved. "The longsuffering of our God is salvation" (2 Pet. 3:9; 2 Pet. 3:15). When Christ comes salvation will forever cease, and the judgment and perdition of all the wicked will take place. We are solemnly charged in view of this coming crisis to live "in all holy conversation and godliness" (2 Pet. 3:11), and be found of Him "in peace, without spot and blameless" (2 Pet. 3:14). Oh, that all men would heed these loud warnings from the Almighty.

All through the gospel are found awful and solemn warnings to mankind of the doom that awaits the ungodly. Jesus emphatically declares that all who die in their sins cannot go where He is, "Then said Jesus again unto them, I go my way, and ye shall seek me, and shall die in your sins: whither I go, ye cannot come" (John 8:21). Since He is in heaven, the only conclusion we can draw from His language is that no man who lives and dies in sin will ever enter heaven. Again, Jesus said: "He that believeth not the Son shall not see life; but the wrath of God abideth on him" (John 3:36). Consider these words: "Shall not see life." No more hope of recovery; eternally cut off; the punishment of deprivation. And with this is coupled the awful punishment of sense: "The wrath of God abideth on him." What a destiny! Yet as sure as God has spoken it will come to pass. Oh, that the careless, indifferent, slumbering souls of men would heed these solemn warnings!

Life is a probationary state of mercy and salvation. Christ now sits upon a mediatorial throne at the right hand of the Father (Mark 16:19; Col. 3:1; 1 Tim. 2:5). The Holy Spirit, "with groanings which cannot be uttered" (Rom. 8:26), is pleading for lost sinners to be saved. But the Bible clearly teaches that the time is coming when this day of mercy will be forever past, when the tender pleadings of the Holy Spirit will cease, when Christ will leave the mediatorial throne and take the judgment seat. Then the world will be without an Advocate, without a Savior. Yes, the "ungodly are reserved unto the day of judgment to be punished" (2 Pet. 2:9), and that punishment will exceed any of the calamities that have befallen men in past ages.

4.—The Lord's *past dealings with men* are warnings. He has dealt severely with nations, as Israel and Babylon. He has dealt severely again and again with communities, as Sodom and Gomorrah; and with individuals, as Korah, Dathan and Abiram, King Saul, Ananias and Sapphira, and Elymas the Sorcerer. Paul informs us that "these things are written for our learning upon whom the ends of the world have come" (1 Cor. 10:11). Every sad death is a warning.

While holding a meeting at Stoneboro, Pa., a few years ago, my wife and I were called to visit a young man who was on his death-bed. He had lived a careless, wicked life, and when he found that there was no hope of recovery he professed to get saved. He prayed with us, sang hymns, and from all appearance gave evidence of conversion. A few days after closing the meeting I received a long-distance call to come and preach his funeral. I arrived at the church just as the procession drove in. At once I inquired of the father how the son died. With tears streaming down his face he related to me the following: "George gathered us all around his bed and bade us farewell, requesting us to meet him in heaven. Then from all appearance he died. We stood weeping around his bed for some time, when suddenly he opened his eyes with a look of horror, and said, 'I am lost. I have gone down into death, and found that hell is my doom. I came back to warn the family. I have put it off too long. When I was well, I didn't want to serve the Lord. When I found I must die, I was afraid and tried to get saved to escape hell; but I am lost, lost forever. My God, I am lost.' He then asked for a glass of beer, and some neighbors brought it, and he drank it saying, 'I am going to hell, lost.'" Great God, save us from such an end.

A number of years ago there was a drought in the State of Georgia. Crops were burning up. One Sunday, a number of neighbors gathered into a rich man's home. He had a large farm and his crops were practically destroyed as a result of the drought. That was the topic of conversation, and the man became enraged. He went to the cupboard and drew out a butcher knife, walked out into the yard and brandished it, saying, "If I had God Almighty here I would cut his heart out." Instantly he was struck with a flame of fire and burned up in his tracks, while his neighbors ran away from him in consternation. "God is not mocked" (Gal. 6:7).

While living at Cambridge Springs, Pa., an incident took place that was an awful warning to us all. Near my home a man was bringing in from the field a load of fine clover hay. A storm was approaching and he was endeavoring to reach the barn before the rain would spoil the hay. But before he reached his barn the rain began to fall in torrents. He became very angry and began to curse God. Suddenly a bolt of lightning struck him and burned the hay, wagon, and horses, and the man perished with them.

These are but a few incidents that have come under my observation, and every one of them is a solemn warning.

5.—The prevalence of death, and the uncertainty of life are a warning. Sudden deaths that have come under our notice, close calls that many of us have had, deaths in our own family circles, yes, every lightning flash, every thunder peal is a warning. One leading authority says that approximately 90 persons die every minute, 5,400 every hour, 129,600 every day, and 42,000,000 a year. It is really a wonder we are alive at all. As I look back to boyhood's days, I discover that the great majority of my early associates are dead.

God's warnings are expressions of His infinite love to us, the outflow of His great mercy and forbearance, and they are general and personal, loud and long. To land in perdition people must run the gauntlet past all of them, and the remembrance of this fact alone will make hell fearful. "He that being often reproved, and hardeneth his heart, shall suddenly be destroyed, and that without remedy" (Prov. 29:1).

THE LONGSUFFERING OF GOD,
ITS DESIGN, AND HOW ABUSED

"And thinkest thou this, O man ... that thou shalt escape the judgment of God? Or despisest thou the riches of his goodness and forbearance and longsuffering; not knowing that the goodness of God leadeth thee to repentance?" (Rom. 2:3-4).

We live under a moral government administered by a holy and righteous God, who is possessed with infinite knowledge and unlimited power. People in sin live in open disregard of all this. Paul in this passage appeals to such persons and shows the guilt and folly of disregarding the Divine law and authority and the danger of presuming too far upon the longsuffering and forbearance of the Almighty. "Account that the longsuffering of our Lord is salvation" (2 Pet. 3:15). That is, it is offered to men now, that more lost sinners may be saved. Here we see the world's need of a Savior. Whether Jew or Gentile, enlightened or heathen, all are under sin, all are lost, and all need to be saved on the same conditions of repentance and faith. The groundwork of this salvation is not merit but Divine goodness offered [by God's grace] to man in much forbearance and longsuffering, all the outflow of infinite love.

This is not a new thing, but as old as the seasons and sunshine. God is the personification of goodness, and His longsuffering "waited in the days of Noah" (1 Pet. 3:20). Out of His inexhaustible store of compassion, mercy, and patience, "he has not dealt with us after our sins, nor rewarded us according to our iniquities" (Ps. 103:10). The light of the gospel, and all the privileges and provisions of grace, are the tokens of His goodness, and this constitutes a wealth upon which we all may draw. "O taste and see that the Lord is good" (Ps. 34:8).

There are three things God manifests towards all the unsaved:

First.—The riches of His goodness. This finds expression in His great kindness to the unsaved, and this is manifest in innumerable ways and in profusion and bountifulness—in temporal blessings, physical blessings, and spiritual blessings. His wealth of goodness is an ocean unfathomable. Thus, people are under infinite obligations to the God they provoke, because His table has fed them, His wardrobe has clothed them, His sun has warmed them, and His kindness continued notwithstanding all their ingratitude. He still "waits to be gracious" (Isa. 30:18).

Second.—The riches of His forbearance. He withholds judgments that are due, and measures to man His mercy in His condescension to suffer such treatment from rebellious sinners.

Third.—The riches of His longsuffering. He now delays punishment beyond all expectation. He patiently *"waited"* in the days of Noah, hoping for the world to repent (Gen. 6:3; 1 Pet. 3:20). Had they done so, the hand of judgment would have been withheld. Sinners are now on praying grounds, on interceding terms with God.

The greatness of God elevates all this to a higher point of value. The dignity of the one against whom the offense is committed rates its terribleness. O sinner, God, before whom all the nations of the earth are as nothing, is the One insulted, and the offenders are as groveling worms. And yet He bears with us. His wisdom enters in. We cannot be affected with affronts of which we are ignorant; but how would we feel if we knew all that our friends and neighbors thought and said about us? God knows it all (2 Chron. 16:9; Heb. 4:13; Prov. 15:3). None of our offenses are hid from Him (Luke 8:17), but are open and naked, and yet He is good. Consider His holiness. If we do not *think* and *feel* a thing to be an affront, there is not much difficulty to endure it, but when it touches us to the quick, the trial comes. Now sin is "exceeding sinful" to God, and yet He is long suffering.

Think of His power. We often put up with many wrongs. We know and feel them, but are compelled reluctantly to submit, because we are powerless to resist. When Moses provoked the Egyptians, he saved himself by flight. But we cannot flee from God's Spirit and presence. He has power to destroy every offender. And yet He bears it all and extends goodness. Oh, "the *riches* of his goodness and forbearance and longsuffering" (Rom. 2:4).

Now we enquire—what is God's purpose in all this? None of God's gifts and dealings are without meaning: all are designed for our good and salvation. "Account that the longsuffering of our God *is salvation*" (2 Pet. 3:15). Reflection here should cause repentance. The Lord gives people time to alter their lives and employs agencies adapted to this end. His admonitions are intended to arouse the lethargy and carelessness in man and bring him to salvation. If this will not awaken and win hearts nothing will. Even nature is full of voices speaking to men (Ps. 19:1-4; Rom. 1:19-21). All this "leadeth" to repentance. Contrition [remorse, repentance] to which people are driven is false. Pharaoh was driven by fear and judgments. Judas was driven by the terror of his conscience. Some are driven by death and coming judgment; but to genuine repentance, people are *led.*

Now we come to man's treatment of all this. Men should use it rightfully, improve, benefit by it, for it is unmerited at best. But instead they "despise" it, treat God's kindness with contempt and utter disregard, and thus expose their ignorance and folly. They treat the longsuffering and mercy of God as unworthy of notice; with amazing indifference and coldness. The Lord calls and they close their ears and will not answer. He knocks and they refuse to open (Rev. 3:20). They turn all the Lord's mercy into instruments of deeper rebellion and sin. They are evil because He is good. How unreasonable this is!

There can be but one result. They cannot escape "the judgment of God." They despise and reject until further proffered [held out to someone for acceptance] mercies cease to be a virtue, until God says, "Ephraim is joined to his idols, let him alone" (Hos. 4:17). To treat the Lord's proffered mercies thus is wicked and heartless in the extreme. Imagine if a drowning man despised the rope that is thrown to him, a person in a burning building scorned the fire escape, or the one who has fallen into a deep pit cursed those who offer him escape. That is terrible, but not to compare with this. To sin against the goodness and forbearance of God, to fight against mercy, to accept the gifts of Christ and then reject *HIM,* what a hell of torment justly awaits those who thus despise the richness of His goodness and longsuffering!

Such aggravate their own punishment, and the pent-up storm of wrath will burst with greater fury. The more the advantages, the weightier the account demanded. The longer the time granted for amendment, the severer the stripes [punishment] for wasted opportunities. The smoothly gliding river of God's longsuffering, if barred out of the heart, will change and swell into a mighty torrent of wrath that will sweep into eternal ruin all those who continue in sin and die unsaved.

AMASSING OR ACCUMULATING WRATH
AGAINST THE DAY OF WRATH

"But after thy hardness and impenitent heart treasurest up unto thyself wrath against the day of wrath and revelation of the righteous judgment of God; who will render to every man according to his deeds: ... But unto them that are contentious, and do not obey the truth, but obey unrighteousness, indignation and wrath, tribulation and anguish, upon every soul of man that doeth evil" (Rom. 2:5-9).

That the present day of mercy and salvation (Rom. 2:4), confined to our natural life here on earth, will be followed by a day of wrath, indignation, tribulation and anguish, the apostle in graphic language most clearly teaches. This time will be ushered in by the "revelation of Jesus Christ from heaven," which is also called the "righteous judgment of God." The wrath and judgment of a king is terrible, the wrath of an angel would be tremendous, but the wrath of God is more terrible than human imagination can compass [imagine or understand].

In the present life, God blends mercy with judgment, but in that day, mercy will retire and wrath will be unmitigated. It will be "judgment without mercy" (James 2:13). Now wrath is *warned:* then it will be *felt.* "He that believeth not the Son shall not see life; but the wrath of God abideth on him" (John 3: 36). On this last passage Dr. Adam Clarke remarks: "It evidently means punishment, which is the effect of irritated justice. Taken in this sense, we may consider the phrase as a Hebraism: punishment of God—the most heavy and awful of all punishments; such as sin deserves, and such as it becomes Divine justice to inflict. And this *abideth on him*—endures as long as his unbelief and disobedience remain. And how shall these be removed in a hell of fire. Reader, pray God that thou may never know what this *continuing punishment* means."

No pen can describe this. No imagination can conceive it. It is sure to fall upon every impenitent sinner, as certain as God Almighty's throne; for eternal and omnipotent Justice has decreed it, Revelation has declared it on almost every page, and God's providences confirm it.

"But when he saw many of the Pharisees and Sadducees come to his baptism, he said unto them, O generation of vipers, who hath warned you to flee from the wrath to come?" (Matt. 3:7).

"Endured with much longsuffering the vessels of wrath fitted to destruction" (Rom. 9:22).

"Let no man deceive you with vain words: for because of these things cometh the wrath of God upon the children of disobedience" (Eph. 5:6).

"For which things' sake the wrath of God cometh on the children of disobedience" (Col. 3:6).

"And to wait for his Son from heaven, whom he raised from the dead, *even* Jesus, which delivered us from the wrath to come" (1 Thess. 1:10).

"And said to the mountains and rocks, Fall on us, and hide us from the face of him that sitteth on the throne, and from the wrath of the Lamb: For the great day of his wrath is come; and who shall be able to stand?" (Rev. 6:16-17).

"And the nations were angry, and thy wrath is come, and the time of the dead, that they should be judged, and that thou shouldest give reward unto thy servants the prophets, and to the saints and them that fear thy name, small and great; and shouldest destroy them which destroy the earth" (Rev. 11:18).

"And he treadeth the winepress of the fierceness and wrath of Almighty God" (Rev. 19:15).

"Behold, the Lord cometh with ten thousands of his saints, To execute judgment upon all, and to convince [convict] all that are ungodly among them of all their ungodly deeds which they have ungodly committed, and of all their hard *speeches* which ungodly sinners have spoken against him" (Jude 14-15).

In the face of such solemn truth how dare men presume upon God's mercy and close their probationary state in rebellion against His throne?

The Apostle clearly shows that such during life are *treasuring up* unto themselves wrath against this awful day of wrath, amassing and accumulating wrath. The sinner is represented as the author of much of his own punishment, heaping and piling up wrath continually as he goes on in sin throughout his life. As a person amasses a fortune by depositing his wage and income regularly, and this accumulates at compound interest, so wrath accumulates daily, adding and multiplying at an enormous rate to our stock of wrath. It is "unto thyself." Just think—one dollar a day at 6 per cent interest in forty years amounts to $49,200. Similarly our daily life is continually adding to some kind of stock that is laid up for us. "Laying up for yourselves against the time to come" (1 Tim. 6:19). The righteous are accumulating blessings, and the sinners wrath.

Just as a mountain slide closes the valley and dams up the stream until a lake is formed, and then bursts in fury, sweeping everything before it, so sin dams up the stream of life until a "lake of fire" (Rev. 20:15) and wrath accumulates, and before long it will burst with fierceness, when Mercy's door is forever closed.

"The treasure of wrath in this verse is opposed to the riches of goodness in the preceding. As surely as thou despises, or neglects to improve the riches of God's goodness, so surely thou shalt share in the treasures of his wrath. The punishment shall be proportioned to the mercy thou has abused" (Dr. Clarke on Rom. 2:5).

A LIFE OF SIN HARD AND ITS WAGES SURE

"For the wages of sin is death; but the gift of God is eternal life through Jesus Christ our Lord" (Rom. 6:23).

Sin is here an employer, and whoever "commiteth sin is the servant of sin" (John 8:34), and is doing his employer's work. This work is hard, for "the way of transgressors is hard" (Prov. 13:15). This is a voluntary service: "To whom ye yield yourselves servants to obey, his servants ye are to whom ye obey; whether of sin unto death, or of obedience unto righteousness" (Rom. 6:16). We choose our own master and are wholly responsible for the results.

Sin is like a big factory. Satan owns and controls the plant. Every man is assigned his work. What a motley crowd of servants! Here are found young and old, rich and poor, kings, statesmen, paupers, beggars, moral reformers, criminals, whoremongers [one who involves himself with prostitutes, sexually immoral, fornicators], all grades of society working side by side. They all work without pause or rest. "There is no rest to the wicked" (Isa. 48:22). No vacations or holidays, none superannuated [retired], nor any pensioners. To one the hard master says, "Get rich" and he bends all his efforts in that direction. To another, "Indulge in lust and be a sensualist," and that one ruins his character forever. To still another, "Act the hypocrite," and that person obeys, but his is tremendous work and it commands the highest wage, a "greater damnation." The greater the light these slaves have received, the darker their sin and the stronger grows their earning power.

Every sinner is working under the wage system, for every sin has its wage. This is a proportionate wage. Certain kinds of work command the largest pay. And the more work done, the greater the pay. Payday is coming. However, sin pays out in part as work is being done. We see this in present disappointments, misery, woe, trouble, broken homes, ruined lives, jails, insane asylums, disease, alcoholism, all forms of addictions, etc., etc. These present installments of hell on earth are but a prelude of the final recompense. In the end, the great wage that has accumulated through life will be paid in full. People are sure to get all they earned, and eternity will be one long pay-day.

Every lost being will *"depart"* from the pay station (the judgment) with his package (mind and soul) full of "shame and everlasting contempt," and in hell subsist on the wage of "everlasting punishment."

What a disappointment that will be! Pay-day is usually a happy day, a time when people line up, eager to receive their wage. But not so here. All will be lined up, and "every man will receive." Satan deceived them in life to believe they are working for riches, fame, and pleasure, but when they open their package on pay-day it will be *DEATH!* "The wages of sin is *death*" (Rom. 6:23). This means separation from God forever, a final, eternal separation, with no hope of a reunion. A separation from loved ones, and from all that is good, lovely, and pure.

"There shall be weeping and gnashing of teeth, when ye shall see Abraham, and Isaac, and Jacob, and all the prophets, in the kingdom of God, and you *yourselves* thrust out" (Luke 13:28).

It will be death to peace of mind, to all noble feelings, to a pure character, to joy and happiness, and to all hope eternally. It will mean "tribulation and anguish" (Rom. 2:9). These terms signify extreme suffering, despair, and ruin. It will be confinement to the society of demons and the lowest of ages, the absence of all that can afford [provide or supply] comfort and pleasure, and the presence of all that can create misery. An eternal consciousness of abiding wrath, of moral loathsomeness, growing worse as ages roll on, the working of uncontrolled passions and ungratified desires. There will be a constant sense of its all being self-caused and justly merited, and an utter inability to escape, or obtain mitigation, ever conscious that it is *"everlasting."* This is *death,* the true and sure wages of sin.

LIFE'S RECORD SUMMED UP

"Who will render to every man according to his deeds" (Rom. 2:6). We are daily making a record which is registered in God's book of remembrance in heaven, and also upon the tables of our own conscience. We also are making a record upon the lives of those about us, as each person casts an influence upon others, either for good or bad. "No man liveth to himself, no man dieth to himself" (Rom. 14:7). Our "deeds" are what counts. Our thoughts, words, and actions count [and our motives]. This is the sum-total of life which forms character, and character fixes our destiny. The Lord keeps a full, accurate, and true record of each life, and not a single item is lost. "God will bring every work into judgment, with every secret thing, whether it be good or evil" (Eccl. 12:14). So then every one of us must give an account of himself to God.

"Every idle word that men shall speak, they shall give an account thereof in the day of judgment" (Matt. 12:36) "In the day that God shall judge the secrets of men by Jesus Christ according to the gospel" (Rom. 2:16).

"And must I be to judgment brought,
And answer in that day,
For every vain and idle thought,
And every word I say?
* * * * * *
"How careful then ought I to live,
With what religious fear,
Who such a strict account must give,
Of my behavior here."

—*Wesley*

Many on earth escape the just reward of their evil deeds, and in our earthly courts, justice is often retarded and defeated because shrewd lawyers plead the case, and many times favor is shown to the rich and influential; but there will be no trickery in that final reckoning, no tricky barrister [lawyer] to plead our case when God "will render to every man *according to his deeds*" (Rom. 2:6).

Out of all classes, races, and grades of men, the Lord recognizes but two groups—namely "every soul of man that doeth evil" (Rom. 2:9) and "every man that worketh good" (Rom. 2:10). The deeds declare the man. The good have a noble aim in life. The object aimed at counts. Those who have lofty endeavors place before themselves a great objective and then strive for the goal with a great spirit. They are conscious of something worth striving and enduring for. The evil are without settled aims. The riches, fame, and pleasures of the world they seek are uncertain and fleeting. They never seek to rise above the leadings of their animal natures and are sure to come to a sad end. The structure of life they laboriously erect will fall with a fearful crash.

Life's actions will determine our destiny. To a Christian faith saves, but good works follow. Our deeds will be recompensed according to their nature, quality, frequency, and their circumstances, and will be rated according to the light received. The effect of our deeds upon others will count, and thus the reward in heaven will be immeasurably greater than the mere act in itself deserves; and in hell, on the same principle some will receive "few stripes" (Luke 12:48) and others "many." It will be "more tolerable" (Luke 10:12) for some than others, and there will be those who receive a "greater damnation" (Matt 23:14) and "much sorer punishment" (Heb. 10:29). The judgment will take account of men's aims in life, and our motives will be carefully examined. God will take us for what we really are, and not what we seem or pretend to be.

While visiting the United States mint in Philadelphia, Pa., we were told that there is a scale there so accurate that two pieces of tissue paper of exactly equal size placed one on each side, would balance. But if you would remove one and with a pencil write your name and address on it, and then place it back on the scales, it would overbalance the other. The lead that adheres to the paper is thus weighed. That is getting near to perfection. But the judgment balances will weigh not only our deeds—the acts of life, but also the motives that prompted those deeds. This, inspiration calls "the secrets of men," the hidden incentive that lies back of all we think, say, and do. How much then it means to live so that "when he shall appear, we may have confidence, and not be ashamed before him at his coming" (1 John 2:28).

THE CERTAINTY OF DIVINE RETRIBUTION, AND TERRIBLE CONSEQUENCES OF DIVINE ABANDONMENT

In Rom. 9:22 we read of the "vessels of wrath fitted to destruction." This does not mean that they are unconditionally foreordained to wrath, and by an unchangeable Sovereign decree from all eternity fitted for destruction and eternal misery. These two great truths stand out prominently in the gospel: 1.—The misery and ruin of the sinner are of himself; and, 2.—The salvation and happiness of the Christian are of God. People become vessels of wrath and fit themselves for eternal misery by their own unbelief, rebellion, and sins. Satan tempts, allures, and deceives, but they themselves yield and sin against God. Wicked men and evil influences have their effect, but every man is what he is by choice. Sinners will not apply the only remedy [which is Christ]. They close their hearts against Christ, heed not the warnings, choose the broad way, and refuse to repent and be saved.

"For the wrath of God is revealed from heaven against all ungodliness and unrighteousness of men, who hold the truth in unrighteousness" (Rom. 1:18). The Lord reveals to all men His righteousness, and also His wrath. Both are conditional, and it is in our power to choose either. The history of the humanity is a living record of both, and they really exhibit to us the Divine character. This is not a hidden mystery but an awful, visible revelation. History is replete with concrete examples. In the bosom [heart] of every awakened sinner is a terrible apprehension of impending judgment at the commission of wrong. "The wicked trembleth at the shaking of a leaf" (Lev. 26:36). "He fleeth when no man pursueth" (Pro. 28:1). "Tho hand join in hand, the wicked shall not be unpunished" (Pro. 11:21).

This is an eternal, established law. Do good and reward is certain. Violate Nature's law, physical law, or moral law, and you must suffer for it. If you sow you must reap; and "*whatsoever* a man soweth, that shall he also reap" (Gal. 6:7). The punishment for sin is not a mere corrective measure, a restraining force, but the retribution of a holy God, whose hatred of sin is infinite, and the commission of which is disagreeable and repugnant to His righteous nature. He *must* punish sin according to its true desert [what it deserves]. In God, wrath is a righteous principle. The principle runs through the entire universe, and wrong never fails to receive punishment. It cannot but result from the perfection of the Divine nature.

The legislator is not angry in passion when he promulgates [enacts] his law, nor the judge when he pronounces sentence. Society cannot be maintained without laws with severe penalties. How could we love and respect God if He treated equally truth and lies, honesty and dishonesty, benevolence and cruelty, morality and criminality, obedience and disobedience, and holiness and sin? God must be just and cannot but punish the rebels in His kingdom. Retribution is certain.

"Wherefore God also gave them up to uncleanness through the lusts of their own hearts" (Rom. 1:24), "For this cause God gave them up unto vile affections" (Rom. 1:26). "And even as they did not like to retain God in their knowledge, God gave them over to a reprobate mind" (Rom. 1:28). To be utterly forsaken and cast out from society, or from home and its endearments and from loved ones, must be terrible in the extreme. Life imprisonment is terrible of contemplation. To be despised and hated by everybody, without a friend in the world, is almost unthinkable; but all this is no approach [comparison, coming near to what it feels like] to being forsaken and abandoned by God. To be without friends and home is dreadful, but to be "without Christ and hope" is horrible in the extreme.

In the texts just quoted, Paul tells us what befell the pagan world and why, but the same principle is true among all nations of men. Israel were debarred [excluded, prohibited] from entering Canaan because they hardened their hearts through unbelief (Heb. 3:7-19). God swore in His wrath, "they shall not enter into my rest" (Heb. 3:11). We have striking examples all through the Bible of individuals and nations that rendered themselves unworthy of God's favor and were utterly abandoned by God, so that "there was no remedy" (2 Chron. 36:16). They reached a place of confirmed hardness of heart, and were numbered among those "whose damnation slumbereth not" (2 Pet. 2:3). They lived to ruin others with their influence and just waited to be finally damned and eternally ruined themselves. God simply let loose of them, "gave them up," "gave them over," and said, "your house is left unto you desolate" (Matt. 23:38), and "it is a fearful thing to fall into the hands of the living God" (Heb. 10:31). Beyond the judgment of the great day such will *"depart"* from God into "everlasting destruction [away] from the presence of the Lord, and from the glory of his power" (2 Thess. 1:9). This means to be abandoned by God to all eternity.

On the Rocky Mountains in Colorado is a certain point termed the Great Continental Divide. Here stands a building, the eaves of which slope east and west. The apex of the roof is exactly on the Divide. Two friendly raindrops falling from a cloud strike this point and separate never to meet again. One starts on a long journey toward the Gulf of Mexico and the Great Atlantic Ocean and the other flows toward the Pacific. Just so with the readers of this book. One decides for Christ; the other rejects Him. That moment they separate in spirit and start in opposite directions, the one toward hell and eternal misery, the other toward heaven and eternal bliss. Finally, they reach the end of life's journey and pass through the portals of death. The one is carried by the angels to the paradise of God, and there rests from his labors and is comforted. The other lifts his eyes in torments and is reserved in chains of darkness unto the judgment-day to be punished. Between them is a great gulf fixed, so there is no passage from one world to the other. Beyond this state is the final resurrection. The one takes part in the resurrection of life (Rev. 20:6), and the other comes forth in the resurrection to shame and everlasting contempt (Dan. 12:2; Rev. 20:5). This is followed by judgment. The one is gathered to the right hand of the judgment throne, and the other the left (Matt. 25:31-46). The one hears the gladsome word "come," and the other the awful sentence, "depart." The one enters the kingdom of glory and life eternal, and the other "everlasting punishment" in "everlasting fire."

O reader, your eternal destiny hinges upon a single choice, and it is in your power to make it.

THE REWARD OF INIQUITY

"Now this man purchased a field with the *reward of iniquity* [using money obtained by fraud, deception, treachery or theft]; and falling headlong, he burst asunder in the midst, and all his bowels gushed out" (Acts 1:18).

The physical laws by which the material world is governed are no more fixed and certain than the moral law of God. Every act of life has its sure and just reward. The deed determines the reward; so man secures his own recompense. In this chapter, I desire to consider five states in the life and character of Judas Iscariot.

First.—An apostle. "He was numbered with the twelve" (Acts 1:17) We assume that he was saved, for he enjoyed the fellowship and companionship of Jesus and was chosen and ordained by Him to be one of His twelve disciples. Along with the others, he was given power to heal the sick and to cast out demons, and "obtained part of this ministry" (Acts 1:17) in that he was a preacher of the gospel. Being a shrewd business man, the Lord selected him to be the treasurer of the company. What great privileges were his! He spent three years with Christ, heard His gracious teaching, and beheld His notable miracles. He was present when the Master stilled the midnight storm on Galilee (Mark 4:35-41), when five thousand were fed with a few loaves and fishes (Mark 6:30-44), and when Lazarus was raised to life (John 11:1-44). He had the grandest of opportunities before him. He could daily eliminate the weaknesses and failings in his life, and by humbleness of heart and much seeking God by prayer become more like his Savior and thus develop the better qualities of his nature and be an overcomer. In short, he was on probation. His present and future success or failure was placed within his own power. What was true of Judas is true of all.

Second.—His spiritual decline. "Why was not this ointment sold for three hundred pence, and given to the poor? This he said, not that he cared for the poor; but because he was a thief, and had the bag [purse]; and bare [stole] what was put therein" (John 12:5-6). The three years of Christ's personal ministry were a testing time for all the disciples. Eleven of them stood the test and emerged victorious in the end. Judas failed. **Everyone of us must pass through the testing.** [Editor's bold] It is up to us to make good. Judas had an equal chance with the rest, but he ended in failure. His was a gradual descent. He went down by degrees. So with all who fail in life. Some fall more rapidly than others, but all more or less by degrees. No one leaps in one jump from the summit of a mountain to its base. There are a number of definite steps in a good man's fall, and no doubt every one was taken by Judas, if all the facts were known. Harboring evil thoughts until there is a decided dearth of spiritual grace and devotion, is one step. Carelessness and looseness of action is another. This weakens the sense of moral obligation and results in a relaxation of holy habits and occasional violations of the law of conscience. Soon such a one becomes lost in temporal anxieties. Lust conceives in the heart, and now there are occasional acts that require repentance. All this brings the poor soul to the brink of an awful precipice.

Third.—His fall. "Judas by transgression *fell*" (Acts 1:25). He gradually drew near to the cliff, and then suddenly took a tremendous leap and plunged into the abyss below. It is similar with every backslider. Suddenly all his light turned to darkness, and how great was that darkness. "He went out, and it was dark" (John 13:30). The higher the elevation attained the deeper the fall. In the case of Judas he fell from "this ministry and apostleship." He opened his heart to sin, and the devil put it in there to betray Jesus. Judas bargained for thirty pieces of silver, the price of a field, and "Satan entered into him" (John 13:27). Judas became the leader of a mob that carried lanterns, torches, and weapons, and Judas "was guide to them who took Jesus" (Acts 1:16). He openly betrayed and sold Christ. He proved himself to be a traitor. He rendered himself unworthy of eternal life.

He sold out his soul for a feather,
No hope in the whirlwind's fierce blast.
He's undone forever and ever,
He missed heaven, yes missed it at last.

Fourth.—His miserable end— "Hanged himself." "Falling headlong burst asunder" (Acts 1:18). Now the storm was gathering and bursting with fury. Remorse begins its terrible work. Vain regret, agonizing fear, terrible self-reproach, and unbearable shame all rush in upon his poor soul. Conscience stricken, with a thousand phantoms starting from their habitations, filled with maddened thoughts of despair, he flings away the thirty pieces of silver. But the guilt of his crime remains with him. He rushes away in the darkness of the night and becomes his own swift executioner. He dies in ignominy and shame, and it is supposed this occurred in the very field bought with the reward of his iniquity (Acts 1:18). His sin has gained its recompense. The "son of perdition" dies in awful despair.

Fifth.—His future. "That he might go to his own place" (Acts 1:25). A place suited to one who by transgression fell and thus became a "child of hell," one of the "sons of perdition."

Let us just a moment count up Judas' gains and losses. He hoped to gain thirty pieces of silver with which to buy a small rocky field he coveted. What did he lose? His apostleship, the highest office on earth. His peace of mind, his self-respect, and all the enjoyments of life. He lost the esteem of all good men in all ages, and instead there were heaped upon him ignominy, disgrace, and everlasting abhorrence. He lost his life and all the pleasures of time. He lost his soul and all the joys of eternity. He missed heaven and gained hell. What a warning!

THE GOODNESS AND SEVERITY OF GOD

"Behold therefore the goodness and severity of God" (Rom. 11:22). In this text, we have introduced two sides of God's character. God is love, the fountain of goodness, the spring of infinite mercy. He says, "I love them that love me" (Pro. 8:17), and not only so, but "while we were yet sinners, Christ died for the ungodly" (Rom. 5:8), thus demonstrating His love for the whole world. But man can limit the field of God's operations by stubbornly rejecting His goodness, love, and mercy. Therefore, the Lord gives warning such as this: "Towards thee, goodness, if thou continue in his goodness" (Rom. 11:22), and "showing mercy unto thousands of them that love me and keep my commandments" (Exod. 20:6). This clearly shows who will reap the benefits of His goodness and mercy eternally.

But what of those who rebel and refuse to love and serve God? "Indignation and wrath, tribulation and anguish, upon every soul of man that doeth evil" (Rom. 2:8-9). "Vengeance is mine; I will repay, saith the Lord" (Rom. 12:19). "I will execute vengeance in anger and fury" (Mic. 5:15); "in flaming fire taking vengeance on them that know not God" (2 Thess. 1:8). "Our God is a consuming fire" (Heb. 12:29). "A certain fearful looking for of judgment and fiery indignation, which shall devour the adversaries. ... Of how much sorer punishment, suppose ye, shall he be thought worthy, who hath trodden under foot the Son of God ... and hath done despite unto the Spirit of grace? For we know him that hath said, Vengeance belongeth unto me, I will recompense, saith the Lord. And again, The Lord shall judge his people. It is a fearful thing to fall into the hands of the living God" (Heb. 10:27-31).

What a striking picture! God is severe as well as good; and the Word of God cannot be broken. To those who continue in doing good and faithfully serve God upon earth, He will pour out His goodness. "At his right hand are pleasures evermore" (Ps. 16:11). But the positive testimony is that a "sore punishment" awaits the guilty who dare to trample beneath their feet the mercy of God and reject that love which gave Christ's blood that we might live. Such can expect a "fearful looking for of judgment and fiery indignation" (Heb. 10:27), "wrath" in "anger" and awful "fury." O friend, "behold the goodness and the severity of God" (Rom. 11:22).

The dealings of Jehovah with mankind in past ages are given as an example of what the future will be. We can judge the future by the past. [For God never changes (Heb. 13:8; Num. 23:19; James 1:17).] God has been severe as well as merciful. When God "saw that the wickedness of man was great in the earth" (Gen. 6:5), He said, "I will destroy man whom I have created" (Gen. 6:7), "But Noah found grace in the eyes of the Lord" (Gen. 6:8). The Almighty had faithfully warned the people that His Spirit would not always strive with them (Gen. 6:3). They failed, however, to heed the warnings. No doubt they said, as scoffers also say today: "God is too good, too merciful, ever to destroy us. We would not drown our worst enemy in a flood of water, and God is more gracious than we." But the decrees of Jehovah stood fast; His word was fulfilled. A day of wrath came upon the degenerate world. Mercy's door was closed; the Spirit of God ceased to strive; and the teeming millions were in the hands of the living God. When it was too late to pray, they awakened to the awful fact that God meant what He said. God warned them, but they would not heed. Hence, they paid the penalty. They were engulfed in one common grave. Noah, however, found grace in the eyes of the Lord in that awful day of wrath. Why? Because his works were righteous. He lived in the fear of God. "Behold the goodness and the severity of God." (Rom. 11:22) "And as it was in the days of Noe [Noah], so shall it be also in the days of the Son of man" (Matt. 24:37). Again, we have in the destruction of Sodom and Gomorrah another example of the goodness and the severity of God. The sin of those people was very grievous. God decided to take vengeance upon them. Lot, who was righteous, warned some of them. His words, however, were as an idle tale [not believed or heeded]. The people thought that a merciful God would not do such a thing. They were, I presume, like modern folks.

They said, "We would not burn our worst enemy, and God is kinder than we." Ah! God is not man. God is not mocked. Who art thou that repliest against God? Lot was delivered because he was righteous (2 Pet. 2:7-8). He found mercy in that awful day. But what of the disobedient, wicked Sodomites? They were in the hands of the living God. With them mercy's day was forever past. The day of wrath had come. "Then the Lord rained upon Sodom and upon Gomorrah brimstone and fire from the Lord out of heaven ... and lo, the smoke of the country went up as the smoke of a furnace" (Gen. 19:24, 28). O reader, take warning. "Even thus shall it be in the day when the Son of man is revealed" (Luke 17:30).

In all the past, God has been severe with the transgressor as well as merciful to the righteous. At times His mercy was extended to all. When, however, individuals or nations rejected His mercy, mocked and killed His servants, and refused to obey Him, He visited upon them wrath; His anger was kindled, and He punished severely. On account of the rebellion of Pharaoh, God visited Egypt with awful plagues. He smote with death all the first-born of all the land. He led Israel through the Red Sea, and then destroyed Pharaoh's host [army].

When the Israelites made a golden calf to worship, God said to Moses, "Let me alone, that my wrath may wax hot against them, and that I may consume them" (Exod. 32:10). Had it not been that Moses acted as a mediator and interceded for the people, God would have consumed them in His anger.

Time and again He sent plagues among the Israelites and destroyed them by the thousands because of their disobedience. He opened the earth and destroyed Korah, Dathan and Abiram, and their hosts [households], all on account of the Jews' corrupting themselves in idolatry. He sent Nebuchadnezzar to Jerusalem, who destroyed it and the sanctuary, slaughtering the Jews and leaving their city a heap of ruins.

Finally, His own chosen people rejected the Messiah and condemned Him to be crucified. They cried, "His blood be upon us" (Matt. 27:25). For this cause came "days of vengeance," "great distress in the land, and wrath upon the people" (Luke 21:23). They fell into the hands of the living God. Such a time of trouble had never been known, nor so long as the world stands ever will be (Matt. 24:15-21; Luke 21:20-24). God wreaked vengeance until over 1 million perished in the siege and destruction of Jerusalem, according to the Jewish historian Josephus. The remainder were scattered among all nations of the earth. Blindness came upon them. Even their land was cursed.

Thus, we could review all God's dealings with man in the past and prove beyond question the awful severity as well as the mercy of God. All these things are for examples to the ungodly, warnings of the severe impending doom that will fall on the transgressor in the great day of God's wrath, which day will far exceed any that this world has ever seen.

THE GENERAL RESURRECTION

The doctrine of the resurrection is well grounded in scripture. Both in the Old and New Testaments it is clearly taught. Yes, the dead shall rise again. Martha said to Jesus concerning her dead brother, Lazarus, "I know that he shall rise again in the resurrection at the last day" (John 11:24). Four times Jesus declared of the righteous, "I will raise him up at the last day" (John 6:39-40, 44, 54). Daniel declared that the bodies "that sleep in the dust of the earth shall awake, some to everlasting life, and some to shame and everlasting contempt" (Dan. 12:2).

Beloved reader, the last great day is coming. Jesus is going to return again. The same Christ that once trod [walked] the shores of Galilee, that bore His cross to Golgotha's rugged hill, and there was suspended between heaven and earth for the redemption of mankind, the Man of sorrows, the humble Nazarene, is coming back again; coming "with power and great glory" (Matt. 24:30). One object of His coming is stated by Paul in these words:

"But I would not have you to be ignorant, brethren, concerning them which are asleep, that ye sorrow not, even as others which have no hope. For if we believe that Jesus died and rose again, even so them also which sleep in Jesus will God bring with Him. For this we say unto you by the word of the Lord, that we which are alive and remain unto the coming of the Lord shall not prevent [precede] them which are asleep. For the Lord himself shall descend from heaven with a shout, with the voice of the archangel, and with the trump [trumpet] of God: and the dead in Christ shall rise first: then we which are alive and remain shall be caught up together with them in the clouds, to meet the Lord in the air: and so shall we ever be with the Lord" (1 Thess. 4:13-17).

Here the order of the resurrection is clearly given. Those who are alive upon earth at the time of His coming will not *prevent* those asleep. The word *"prevent"* is more correctly rendered by other translations "precede" "*go* before," "enter into his presence sooner than the dead," etc. This is the correct idea of the text. Those upon earth at the time of Christ's return will not be changed into immortality and rewarded before the dead are raised but the dead in Christ shall rise first, i.e., before we, the living, are changed. The instant that the Lord will descend from heaven with a shout, with the voice of the archangel, and with the trumpet of God, the slumbering dead will arise, after which we, the living, "shall all be changed, in a moment, in the twinkling of an eye, at the last trump [trumpet]: for the trumpet shall sound, and the dead shall be raised incorruptible, and we shall be changed" (1 Cor. 15:51-52). The judgment will occur and eternal rewards and punishments will be meted out to all men. "Then we which are alive and remain shall be caught up together with them [the righteous dead just raised] in the clouds, to meet the Lord in the air: and so shall we ever be with the Lord" (1 Thess. 4:17).

In the resurrection morning, the dead will appear from two directions. "They also which sleep in Jesus will God bring with him" (1 Thess. 4:14). The Lord will come "with ten thousands of his saints" (Jude 14). "At the coming of our Lord Jesus Christ with all his saints" (1 Thess. 3:13). He has the keys of that spirit world (Rev. 1:18). These texts prove that all the saints—all who sleep in Jesus, that is, all the righteous who have died—He will bring with Him. They will accompany Him on His return. Only the spirit goes to God at death (Eccl. 12:7; 2 Cor. 5:8), hence that is the part that will return with Him.

Only our bodies will be raised at the trumpet sound. Only our bodies sleep in the dust of the ground (Eccl. 12:7; Matt. 27:52-53); and those who sleep "in the dust of the earth shall awake" (Dan. 12:2). "We look for the Savior, the Lord Jesus Christ: who shall change our vile body, that it may be fashioned like unto his glorious body" (Phil. 3:20-21). It is not our soul, but our body that will be changed in the resurrection day. "So also is the resurrection of the dead ... It is sown a natural body; it is raised a spiritual body" (1 Cor. 15:42-44). Only our bodies are mortal (proof, Rom. 6:12), "and this mortal must put on immortality" (1 Cor. 15:53). This is clear.

Those who sleep in Jesus, the spirits, the souls of all the departed, God will bring with Him; namely, all His saints. In that moment, the bodies will be raised from the graves immortal and incorruptible. The soul will then reanimate these immortal bodies and dwell therein forever.

This will be the order of the final resurrection of the dead, according to the united testimony of all Scripture. Thus far, we have only considered the righteous. But the wicked will also be raised. The Lord shall descend with a shout, with the trump [trumpet] of God, the last trump [trumpet], and not only will the righteous hear His voice but in that very *hour* "all that are in the graves shall hear his voice, and shall come forth; they that have done good, unto the resurrection of life; and they that have done evil, unto the resurrection of damnation" (John 5:28-29). A universal resurrection. Being universal it includes both classes of the human family. Daniel saw this and thus described it: "And many [the many] of them that sleep in the dust of the earth shall awake, some to everlasting life, and some to shame and everlasting contempt" (Dan. 12:2).

"There shall be a resurrection of the dead, both of the just and unjust" (Acts 24:15). There is but one resurrection future—*a resurrection* of the dead. Who are included in it? Both the just and unjust. This accounts for the fact that when "he cometh with clouds; *every eye* shall see him, and they also which pierced him" (Rev. 1:7). Yes, in that day "the dead, small and great," shall "stand before God" (Rev. 20:12). Both the righteous and wicked will be raised, the former in glorified bodies, fashioned like unto His glorious body; a resurrection unto eternal life and rewards. But the latter unto damnation, shame, and everlasting contempt.

AFTER DEATH, THE JUDGMENT

"And as it is appointed unto men once to die, but after this the judgment" (Heb. 9:27). "Because he hath appointed a day, in the which he will judge the world" (Acts 17:31).

That a day of final judgment awaits us the Scriptures clearly teach. It is an event we cannot escape. "For we must all appear before the judgment seat of Christ; that everyone may receive the things done in his body, according to that he hath done, whether it be good or bad" (2 Cor. 5:10). In view of this solemn fact, and "knowing therefore the terror of the Lord, we persuade men" (2 Cor. 5:11).

The day of judgment will be the day of final retribution, when eternal rewards and punishments will be meted out to all men. This will be the greatest of all days. There have been days of awful visitations of God's wrath during the history of the world: the flood, the destruction of Sodom and Gomorrah, the slaying of the first-born in Egypt, the awful destruction of Jerusalem, etc.; but no day exceeds this one. It will be the day when God will come down to take vengeance on the wicked of all ages, and pent-up fires will envelop this globe in a general conflagration (2 Peter 3:1-12). Nor is this day of judgment to be deferred till after a thousand years' millennial reign, but Christ "shall judge the quick and the dead at his *appearing* and his kingdom" (2 Tim. 4:1) [see also editor's note at chapter end]. First in order, the resurrection of the dead will take place, and immediately following this will be the general judgment.

"For the Son of man shall come in the glory of his Father with his angels; and *then* he shall reward every man according to his works" (Matt. 16:27).

"And to you who are troubled rest with us, when the Lord Jesus shall be revealed from heaven with his mighty angels, in flaming fire taking vengeance on them that know not God, and that obey not the gospel of our Lord Jesus Christ: who shall be punished with everlasting destruction from the presence of the Lord, and from the glory of his power; when he shall

come to be glorified in [the persons of] his saints, and to be admired in all
them that believe (because our testimony among you was believed) in that
day" (2 Thess. 1:7-10).

These texts declare in the clearest language that the reward of the
righteous and the punishment of the wicked will be given "*when* the Lord
Jesus shall be revealed from heaven" (2 Thess. 1:7-8), when the Son of
man shall come. In Matthew 25, a clear description of the final judgment
is given:

"When the Son of man shall come in his glory, and all the holy angels
with him, then shall he sit upon the throne of his glory: and before him
shall be gathered all nations: and he shall separate them one from another,
as a shepherd divideth his sheep from the goats: and he shall set the sheep
[the saved in Christ] on his right hand, but the goats [the unsaved, the lost]
on the left. Then shall the King say unto them on his right hand, Come, ye
blessed of my Father, inherit the kingdom prepared for you from the
foundation of the world. ... Then shall he say also unto them on the left
hand, Depart from me, ye cursed, into everlasting fire, prepared for the
devil and his angels" (Matt. 25:31-34, 41).

Here again it is declared that the final separation between the righteous
and wicked, their reward and punishment, will take place and be given
"when the Son of man shall come in his glory, and all the holy angels with
him." Yes, dear reader, "God shall bring every work into judgment, with
every secret thing, whether it be good or whether it be evil" (Eccl. 12:14).

Nothing will escape that searching hour. "Every one of us shall give
an account of himself to God" (Rom. 14:12). Oh, how solemnly the
injunction of Peter should fall upon every heart, in view of that day, when
all must stand or fall eternally in the presence of His majesty and awful
glory:

"Seeing then that all these things shall be dissolved, what manner of
persons ought ye to be in all holy conversation and godliness, looking for
and hasting unto the coming of the day of God, wherein the heavens being

on fire shall be dissolved, and the elements shall melt with fervent heat? Nevertheless, we, according to his promise, look for new heavens and a new earth, wherein dwelleth righteousness. Wherefore, beloved, seeing that ye look for such things, be diligent that ye may be found of him in peace, without spot, and blameless" (2 Pet. 3:11-14).

This will be "the day of judgment and perdition of ungodly men" (2 Pet. 3:7). Note the solemn language. That great day will usher in the final *"perdition* of ungodly men."

[Editor's note: The widely taught, promoted, publicized and preached "pre-tribulation rapture" theory, where the "rapture" of the church occurs while the lost are left behind here on earth, to be followed by a "7-year great tribulation period" and then followed by a "millennial 1000-year kingdom here on earth" is false and not in accord with Scripture. Christ is right now ruling and reigning, seated at the right hand of the Father in heaven; we are right now at this very moment IN the "1000 year" period mentioned in the book of Revelation (Rev 20)! There will be no "7 year" period after a "rapture of believers" during which those who are left behind can change their mind and still choose to accept Christ and be saved; there will be no second chances! The next event will be Christ returning in power and glory to judge the world on the great day of judgement (2 Pet. 3:10; 2 Thess. 1:7-8; Matt. 24:30; Matt. 25:31-46; Rev. 1:7). Be not deceived! Please do not take my word for this either, but search the Scriptures for yourself to determine the truth (Acts 17:11).]

THE NATURE OF GOD'S LAW UNDER THE OLD COVENANT; UNDER THE LAW

Everything in God's vast creation is placed under law. The galaxies, infinities, and immensities of the universe with which we are surrounded, the mechanism of the planetary system, the earth and all its works, convince us of the existence of certain fixed laws, and these, God has ordained. Man, the crowning work of creation, was also placed under law, the moral government of heaven. The principles of this moral code were originally written in man's conscience. Adam and Eve were under it and on probation before sin ever entered into the world. This moral, eternal law is "holy, just, and good" (Rom. 7:12).

God's eternal law of righteousness existed before the law of Moses was given. This is self-evident. Surely God had a law by which He governed His creatures, both angels and men, long before Sinai. The law, the first written code ever given to man, as worded in the Decalogue [the Ten Commandments] and in the book of the law [the Pentateuch, the first five books of the Bible], was given through Moses about twenty-five hundred years after the creation of Adam. Hence moral obligations did not begin with that law, nor did they cease when that [Mosaic] law was abolished [nailed to the cross (Col. 2:14)]. "All unrighteousness is sin" (1 John 5:17); and "sin is lawlessness" (1 John 3:4, *Revised Version*).

The "angels sinned" (2 Pet. 2:4). But they did not violate the law of Moses; for it was not given until thousands of years after they fell, and they were not under it anyway. Adam sinned (Rom. 5:12-14). Cain sinned (Gen. 4:7). The Sodomites were "sinners" (Gen. 13:13) and vexed Lot with their "unlawful deeds" (2 Pet. 2:8). All this was many centuries before the Mosaic law of Sinai was delivered. Abraham kept God's laws (Gen. 26:5). All this shows clearly that God's eternal law existed as a moral principle of righteousness, no doubt from all eternity. After the creation of the world, in whatever form or manner the Lord chose to communicate His will to man, this was His commandments, His statutes, and His laws (Gen. 26:5) to them.

This original law is superior to the law of Moses:

"Master, which *is* the great commandment in the law? Jesus said unto him, Thou shalt love the Lord thy God with all thy heart, and with all thy soul, and with all thy mind. This is the first great commandment. And the second is like unto it, Thou shalt love thy neighbor as thyself. On these two commandments hang all the law and the prophets" (Matt. 22:36-40).

The national [Mosaic] law to Israel was hung onto this higher law, and of course was inferior to it. These principles, clad in the armor of eternal immutability, lay back of the Mosaic law and existed before and throughout that dispensation as they had existed before and exist now since that national code is abolished. In its very nature this great law of supreme love to God and equal love to fellow creatures must be as eternal and everlasting as God Himself. This law governs angels, governed Adam, the patriarchs, the pious Jews while under the law of Moses, and governs all Christians now. The gospel of Christ is a clear expression of this eternal law. It is applicable to all God's creatures in all ages.

The code from Sinai, the whole book of the law given by Moses, was only a national law. It was given to one people—Israel: "Who are Israelites; to whom pertaineth the adoption, and the glory, and the covenants, and the giving of the law" (Rom. 9:4). Of course, this national law contained moral, civic, and ceremonial precepts, and like all State and National laws, was founded upon the principles of God's great moral and eternal law. Even while it was in force from Moses to Christ, it did not supersede that higher law; and when it ended at the cross, it in no way affected the moral law, for that continued right on unchanged and unchangeable.

The rewards and penalties of Moses' law were all temporal. A careful reading of that particular code reveals no promises of future rewards nor any warnings of future punishment. If they kept the law they should be blessed in children, in health, in goods, in cattle, and in lands. If they disobeyed they should be cursed in all these. The highest penalty for disobedience was death: "He that despised Moses' law *died* without mercy under two or three witnesses" (Heb. 10:28). But are we to understand by this that this temporal punishment, and these temporal rewards were all the punishment of which Israelites were conscious? No indeed. When they violated the law of Moses and paid the penalty for their crime, they were conscious also of violating the higher and moral principles, and these they will meet at the judgment. That higher and moral law will face them in the last day.

We have somewhat of a parallel in our own State and National laws. A man commits murder and in some cases pays the extreme penalty of the law by being sentenced to death. Is that all? No, indeed. When he broke the law of the State and Nation he also violated the moral principles of God's eternal law, and these he must face in the final judgment.

Being under this higher moral and eternal law, the people of Old Testament times must have had a concept of the future life beyond the grave. It could not be otherwise. While "life and immortality are brought to light in the gospel" (2 Tim. 1:10) much clearer than in the Old Testament, yet the people back then did have a conception of what awaits us in the great future. Yes, the patriarchs and saints of old "confessed that they were strangers and pilgrims on the earth" (Heb. 11:13). David, the king of Israel, said, "I am a stranger with thee, and a sojourner, as all my fathers were" (Ps. 39:12). These Old Testament worthies [saints] were seeking another country, "a *better country,* that is, an heavenly" (Heb. 11:16). They understood that heaven would be their eternal reward. The Psalms and other literature of the Old Testament are sprinkled with sparkling expressions relative to future eternal rewards.

If they anticipated this on condition of faithfulness till death is it not reasonable to believe that they had some comprehension of future punishment as a result of disobedience? To my mind there is plenty of proof that they did have that. Jesus informs us that the Sodomites will be at the final judgment, and that punishment awaits them there; but it will be "more tolerable" for them than for those who rejected Him (Matt. 10:15; 11:24; Luke 10:12). Not only were those ancient cities destroyed and turned into ashes, but the inhabitants are destined to suffer "the vengeance of eternal fire" (Jude 7). The fact that men feared God shows that they were aware of future judgment; and we are not left to guess at this either for "Enoch also, the seventh from Adam, prophesied of these, saying, Behold the Lord cometh with ten thousands of his saints, to execute judgment upon all" (Jude 14-15).

Such expressions as the following would indicate that they had some knowledge of a fearful punishment to fall upon the wicked: "Upon the wicked he shall rain snares [burning coals], fire and brimstone, and an horrible tempest: this shall be the portion of their cup" (Ps. 11:6). "The wicked shall be turned into hell, and all the nations that forget God" (Ps. 9:17). In Dan. 7:9-11 appears a description of the final judgment, and the beast—the false religion and its devotees—was "given to the burning flame." The description is almost identical with Rev. 20:11-15, which ends with the wicked cast into the lake of fire. In Dan. 12:2 the final resurrection is mentioned, and the lost shall awake "to shame and everlasting contempt."

The gospel is a clear expression of God's eternal moral law by which all men must either stand or fall in final judgment. Therefore, the gospel will be the standard of judgment, for God shall judge the secrets of men by Jesus Christ, according to the gospel (Rom. 2:16). Jesus said, "The word I speak unto you, the same shall judge you in that day" (John 12:48).

THE ENORMITY OF SIN

"But sin, that it might appear sin, working death in me by that which is good; that sin by the commandment might become exceeding sinful" (Rom. 7:13). The greater the light the more *"exceeding sinful"* volitional transgression becomes. "For I know your manifold transgressions and your mighty sins" (Amos 5:12). "How mighty are your sins" (*American Standard Version*). In the language of Eliphaz, "Are not thine iniquities *infinite?*" (Job 22:5).

The law of God cannot, from the nature of its author, allow the commission of a single sin; and to transgress this holy, just, and good law, is sin. The tendency of this age is to minimize sin. One of the arguments used against eternal punishment is the supposition that it is out of proportion to the offense committed; and then sin is pictured as a trivial trespass. This is entirely wrong. The sinfulness of sin against God, that which makes volitional transgression *"mighty"* and *"infinite,"* is its nature. We readily grant that our finite minds cannot fully grasp its enormity, and we can only gather this in part as we endeavor to comprehend God's view of it.

Sin and holiness are opposite principles. The more holy a being is, the more detestable and abhorrent sin becomes. Holiness is one of the Lord's attributes. "Holy, holy, Lord God Almighty" (Rev. 4:8). He is infinitely holy, hence infinitely opposed to sin. The very holiness of His nature demands that all of His creatures be holy— "Be ye holy, for I am holy" (1 Pet. 1:16). The holiness of His nature clothes Him with majestic glory. This glory of His power will drive every sinner away from His presence forever (2 Thess. 1:7-9). Sin is open rebellion against this holy, infinite God, hence in its nature it is an infinite transgression. Even committing only one sin incurs an infinite debt to Divine justice.

The enormity of a crime is not measured by the standing of the one who commits it, but by the dignity of the one against whom it is committed, as well as by the thought and intent of the criminal. The lowest serf in the community commits the crime of assassinating the rulers of his country, and must pay the same penalty as would a senator if he committed the deed. The standing and dignity of the one against whom the offense is committed has much to do in rating the enormity of the crime.

Man lifts his hand against God, and in open rebellion sins against his Creator, transgresses His law and government, resists the overtures of His mercies, and dies in opposition to God's throne. This is a crime against the Sovereign of earth and sky, the King of heaven and earth, the Ruler of the universe, the one before whom angels fall and the redeemed hosts of heaven worship. This is vastly, immeasurably greater than a mere trespass against a fellow creature. It is sin against the infinite God to whom we are obligated and who has a just claim upon us all. It is sin against Christ, our only hope and Savior, a trampling under foot of the blood of His cross, a rejection of Him who suffered and died for us, the one before whom we all must appear in the judgment, and who will then dispose of us [render to each as deserved and send to their eternal place, heaven or hell]. It is "doing despite to the Spirit of grace" (Heb. 10:29), grieving, insulting, resisting, rejecting, and locking the heart against the sensitive Holy Ghost and His tender strivings and pleadings. It is against heaven— "I have sinned *against heaven* and in thy sight," said the returning Prodigal (Luke 15:21). Sin is against light, your own judgment, and your soul's present and eternal interests. In the light of these facts, "how mighty are your sins." "Are not thine iniquities *infinite?*" (Job 22:5)

"Our sins are infinite not only in number, but also in criminality. Every sin is, in fact, infinitely evil, and deserving of infinite punishment:

"1) Because it is committed against an infinite being, against God, a being infinitely powerful, wise, holy, just, and good.

"2) Because it is a violation of an infinite, perfect law.

"3) Because it tends to produce infinite mischief.

"4) Because committed in defiance of motives and obligations infinitely strong.

"If our sins are thus infinite in number and criminality, then, of course, they deserve an infinite or everlasting punishment. God is perfectly right in inflicting an infinite punishment upon sinners. If it is just to inflict infinite punishment upon impenitent sinners, God is bound by the strongest obligations to inflict it."—*E. Payson, D.D.*

The following quotations give us an idea of the enormity of sin:

"The science of chemistry teaches us that a single grain of iodine will impart color to seven thousand times its weight of water. So one sin affects the whole life."—*Moody*

"No sin against God can be little, because it is a sin against the great God of heaven and earth. If a sinner can find out a little God, it may be easy to find out a little sin."—*Bunyan*

"One small leak will in time sink the ship. One worm will, in a few years, destroy the largest tree. One sin will taint a whole life."

"O sin! how has thou cursed us! Thou has thrown up a barrier between ourselves and God. With thy chilling breath, thou has extinguished the light of our household joys; thou has unstrung our harp, and filled the air with discordant cries; thou has unsheathed the sword, and bathed it in human blood; thou has dug every grave in the bosom of fair earth; but for thee, we should not have known the name of widow or orphan, tear and sigh, sorrow and death; but for thee, our hearts had been untorn by a pang, and our joy pure as the ecstasies of heaven."—*Joseph Parker*

THE PENALTY FOR SIN

A law without penalty attached for its violation would be a nullity [have no effect, be void]. We have State and National laws, and in order for these to be effective, penalties are affixed for their violation. This makes law impressive and of force. Temporal laws have temporal penalties. The nature of the law governs the punishment. The law of God under which man is placed is unlike all other laws in that it is infinite and eternal. Being infinite, the transgression of His law is an infinite sin and cannot but incur an infinite debt on the part of the guilty violator to the justice and judgment of the Divine Lawgiver.

An infinite God has placed us under His infinite and holy law. Sin is a willful, knowing transgression of this law. Man has the promise of eternal felicity and a blessed union with his Maker in heaven forever provided he lives in obedience to the law of the Creator and fully submits to the Divine government. It is in the power of every individual to obey or disobey; to remain forever happy or to be eternally separated; to choose life or death. Man willfully and knowingly transgresses. The justice and immutability of God demands the payment of the penalty for the crime, and each transgressor must suffer the punishment of a broken law. God cannot be a just God and waive the exaction of the penalty.

Now, I ask in all candor and reason, does this reflect upon the Lawgiver and His law? Who is to blame—the Lawgiver, or the guilty violator? Reason answers, "The violator." It reflects *only* on him. When someone openly violates the laws of our land, and as a result is punished, who is responsible? When a condemned criminal is sentenced and pays the penalty for his misdemeanor who would think of reflecting upon the State and National lawmakers and the laws they have enacted when those laws are just and good? Censure falls upon the guilty every time. [Editor's note: at the time this book was first published, society and statutes were much simpler than today. Nonetheless, the author's point still stands.] Just so with God and His law. Eternal damnation does not reflect upon the Divine character but upon the guilty sinner.

And this is doubly true when we consider the fact that God has made provision whereby man can escape the awful penalty of a broken law. Mercy rejoiced against judgment, and the love of God provided an atonement in the person of Jesus Christ. "God was in Christ, reconciling the world unto himself" (2 Cor. 5:19). "Jesus Christ the righteous" (1 John 2:1) became the atoning sacrifice for our sins. The stroke of justice fell on Him. He suffered in our stead, "the just for the unjust, that he might bring us to God" (1 Pet. 3:18). "He by the grace of God tasted death for every man" (Heb. 2:9). Thus, He satisfied Divine justice. What infinite love; What wondrous mercy!

Through the transgression of God's eternal law man had contracted an infinite, or external debt to Divine justice. He had nothing to pay. Thus, he was hopelessly, ruinously, and eternally lost. There was but one way this infinite debt could be removed. That was, by pardon, or forgiveness— "Forgive us our debts" (Matt. 6:12). But forgiveness was made possible only through someone's satisfying the demands of justice by paying the debt. This is the great atonement. In the language of the poet—

"Jesus paid it all,
All to him I owe."

This puts man infinitely in debt to Divine mercy. God offers pardon to all who plead guilty and confess their lost condition.

But what of those who reject the benefits of the atonement of Christ, trample upon His mercy, refuse to be saved, and close their probationary state [their life] in rebellion against His throne? There can be but one answer. They must suffer the penalty of a broken law. To draw any other conclusion is to cast reflection upon God. A universal salvation has been provided. A universal invitation is given. But when the majority of mankind reject these proffered mercies, refuse to accept Christ, trample the benefits of His atonement beneath their feet, and lift their arms in rebellion against the government of heaven, and refuse to be saved, who is responsible? Every man is responsible for his eternal future. And this is no reflection on the just God of heaven.

The sentence of eternal death is hanging over all. But Christ in mercy came from heaven to earth "to proclaim liberty to the captives, and the opening of the prison to them that are bound" (Isa. 61:1). Some accept, but the majority reject and choose to remain in a life of sin. They alone can be responsible.

Christ has provided salvation at a great sacrifice. He freely offers it to man. If man refuses to accept the offer, then who is responsible? To illustrate: Let us suppose the people of a certain city are afflicted with a dreaded disease. As a result, they are dying by the thousands. But a certain individual provides a remedy that will counteract all the effects of the disease and grant a perfect cure. He sends out a broad invitation to all the afflicted ones to come and apply His remedy. He offers it free to all. A limited few accept the invitation, apply the remedy, and are cured. Of the remainder, some curse and revile the man who offers them the cure; others scoff, jeer, and make light of the proposed remedy. Still others believe the remedy to be all right, but simply neglect to apply it. When these individuals are in the throes of death, upon whom can they reflect? Would any intelligent man think for a moment of reflecting upon [blaming] the kind friend who provided the remedy and offered it to them freely? Not one. The individuals themselves are wholly responsible because they would not accept the invitation and apply the only cure at hand.

This illustration clearly shows the responsibility on the unsaved. Sinners are morally diseased and corrupted by sin. They must, as a result, suffer the "second death" (Rev. 20:14), or final separation from God in the lake which burns with fire and brimstone. But a remedy has been provided, which is a "double cure" for sin. It is the precious blood of Christ. All are invited to come to this fountain of cleansing, and those who will accept the invitation and plunge into the crimson flood will be saved. All who refuse it will be lost. And who is responsible? Jesus said, "Ye will not come unto me, that ye might have life" (John 5:40).

As an illustration, suppose a train is bound for a certain city where a plague is raging and people are dying by the thousands. We warn the people who have boarded the train of what is before them. We exhort them to get off the train or certain destruction will befall them. But they close their ears to our warnings and merrily ride on to certain death. When the people arrive in the city and the plague takes hold upon them who is responsible? Can they for a moment reflect upon [blame] those who gave them warning? No indeed. They themselves are responsible.

Sinners are headed for the city of destruction. They are traveling on the broad road that leads there. God has given the most solemn warnings to all men that if they travel this road certain destruction awaits them. Through the preaching of the gospel we sound out the warnings of the Almighty. But, the majority of people close their ears and harden their hearts, and as a result plunge their souls down to certain ruin. Are they not responsible? Does this reflect upon the character of God? Not in the least.

A farmer prepares his field. Two bushels of seed stand before him. One contains tares [weeds], the other wheat. He has the privilege of sowing either one, but he chooses to sow the tares. When harvest-time comes can he expect to reap golden grain? No, indeed. "Whatsoever a man soweth, that shall he also reap" (Gal. 6:7-9). And is he not responsible? You are sowing in time; you will reap in eternity. The harvest will be in proportion to the seed sown. "They have sown the wind, and they shall reap the whirlwind" (Hos. 8:7). Does this reflect upon God? No.

The regard God has for His law is shown by His opposition to the transgression of that law. And this is understood by the penalty He inflicts upon the guilty sinner. The awful penalty God inflicts upon the sinner measures His opposition to sin and His view of its enormity. I quote the following forceful argument on this point from *Philosophy of the Plan of*

Salvation: "Holiness signifies the purity of the divine nature from moral defilement, while justice signifies the relation which holiness causes God to sustain to men as the subjects of the divine government. ...

"A lawgiver can manifest his views of the demerit of transgression in no other way than by the *penalty* which he inflicts upon the transgressor. ... And the measure of punishment which conscience dictates is just in proportion to the opposition which the lawgiver feels to the transgression of his law, i.e., the amount of regard which he has for his own law will graduate the amount of opposition which he will feel to its transgression. The amount of opposition which any being feels to sin is in proportion to the holiness of that being, and conscience will sanction penalty up to the amount of opposition which he feels to crime. ...

"The principle, then, is manifest, that the more holy and just any being is, the more he is opposed to sin, and the higher penalty will his conscience sanction as the desert [due consequences] of transgressing the divine law. ... This is the foundation of penalty in the divine mind. .... Penalty, therefore inflicted upon the transgressor, is the only way by which the standard of justice as it exists in the mind of God could be revealed to men.

"The truth of this principle may be made apparent by illustration. Suppose a father were to express his will in relation to the government of his family, and the regulations were no sooner made than some of his children should resist his authority and disobey his commands. Now, suppose the father should not punish the offenders, but treat them as he did his obedient children. By so doing he would encourage the disobedient, discourage the obedient, destroy his own authority, and make the impression upon the minds of all his children that he had no regard for the regulations which he had himself made. And, further, if these regulations were for the general good of the family, by not maintaining them he would convince the obedient that he did not regard their best interests, but was the friend of the rebellious. And if he were to punish for the transgression but lightly, they would suppose that he estimated but lightly a breach of his commands; and they could not, from the constitution of their minds, suppose otherwise. But if the father, when one of the children transgressed, should punish him and exclude him from favor until he submitted to his authority and acknowledged with a penitent spirit his offense, then the household would be convinced that the father's will was imperative, and that the only alternative presented to them was affectionate submission or exclusion from the society of their father and his obedient children. Thus, the amount of the father's regard for his law, his interest in the wellbeing of his obedient children, and the opposition of his nature to disobedience, would be graduated in every child's mind by the penalty which he inflicted for the transgression of his commands.

"So in the case of an absolute Lawgiver: his hostility to crime could be known only by the penalty which he inflicted upon the criminal. If for the crime of theft he were to punish the offender only by the imposition of a trifling fine, the impression would be made upon every mind that he did not at heart feel much hostility to the crime of larceny. If he had the power and did not punish crime at all, he would thus reveal to the whole nation that he was in league with criminals, and himself a criminal at heart.

"So in relation to murder: if he were to let the culprit go free or inflict upon him but a slight penalty, he would thus show that his heart was tainted with guilt, and that there was no safety for good men under his government. But should he fix a penalty to transgression, declare it to all his subjects, and visit every criminal with punishment in proportion to his guilt, he would show to the world that he regarded the law, and was opposed directly and forever to its transgression.

"In like manner and in no other way could God manifest to men his infinite justice and his regard for the laws of his kingdom. Did he punish for sin with but a slight penalty, the whole universe of mind would have good reason to believe that the God of heaven was but little opposed to sin. Did he punish it with the highest degree of penalty, it would be evident to the universe that his nature was in the highest degree opposed to sin and attached to holiness. ... The mind of man would receive an idea of the

amount of God's opposition to sin only by the amount of penalty which he
inflicted upon the sinner."

THE BIBLE MEANING OF HELL

The word *hell* occurs in our standard English Bible fifty-three times. In the Old Testament, it appears thirty-one times, always translated from the Hebrew *sheol* and in the New Testament twenty-two times, in ten texts taken from the Greek *hades,* in eleven texts from the Greek *gehenna,* and once from *tartaroo,* or *tartarus. Sheol* occurs sixty-five times in the Old Testament Scriptures. It is rendered *grave* thirty-one times, *hell* thirty-one times, and *pit* three times. In the New Testament *hades* is generally held to be a corresponding term to the Old Testament *sheol,* and it occurs ten times. Robert Young, Ll.D., in his *Analytical Concordance,* defines *sheol*— "the unseen state," and *hades*— "the unseen world."

Scholars differ as to the signification of these terms. Some, as the Adventists, Russellites, and the various branches who hold the soul-sleeping doctrine, apply them exclusively to the grave. Then a large number hold that these terms never apply to the grave, but exclusively to the world and state of departed spirits between death and the judgment. From a footnote in Smith's Bible Dictionary, I quote: "The word *sheol* is never used of the grave proper, or place of burial of the body. It is always the abode of departed spirits, like the Greek *hades.*" Others apply these terms to the future state beyond death, to include the eternal world. Then still others, and probably the large majority, hold that they are generic terms with more than one meaning, sometimes applying to the grave, sometimes to the world of departed spirits, and again to the state of the lost eternally.

I am strongly inclined to this last view. The signification in any text must be determined by the sense in which the word is used and by the context. Russell R. Byrum in his splendid work, *Christian Theology,* has well said: "The Scriptures represent the future punishment of the wicked as being in a place called *'hell'* in the common English Bible. In the Revised Version, the original Hebrew word *sheol* and the Greek terms *hades* and *gehenna* are usually retained either in the text or margin. The theory that these terms refer merely to the grave or to the valley of the Son of Hinnom outside Jerusalem is too unscholarly to deserve any extended notice or serious refutation. A casual reading of the Scriptures affords abundant disproof of it. The inspired writers employed these figures and such words as their language afforded to designate the place of the eternal abode of the wicked" (p. 656).

In such texts as the following *sheol* and *hades* evidently mean the grave: "Ye shall bring down my gray hairs with sorrow to the grave [*sheol*]" (Gen. 44:38). "He bringeth down to the grave, and bringeth up [*sheol*]" (1 Sam. 2:6). "Let not his hoar head [gray head, growing old] go down to the grave [*sheol*] in peace" (1 Kings 2:6). "If I wait, the grave [*sheol*] is my house" (Job 17:13). "They shall go down to the bars of the pit [*sheol*], when our rest together is in the dust" (Job 17:16). "O grave [*hades*], where is thy victory?" (1 Cor. 15:55).

The following texts, with many others, do not and cannot apply to the grave: "Shall burn unto the lowest hell [*sheol*]" (Deut. 32:22). "The wicked shall be turned into hell [*sheol*], and all the nations that forget God" (Ps. 9:17). "Delivered my soul from the lowest hell [*sheol*]" (Ps. 86:13). "Hell [*sheol*] from beneath is moved for thee" (Isa. 14:9). "With hell [*sheol*] are we at agreement" (Isa. 28:15); "Your agreement with hell [*sheol*] shall not stand" (Isa. 28:15, 18). "Shall speak to him out of the midst of hell [*sheol*]" (Ezek. 32:21). "Out of the belly of hell [*sheol*] cried I" (Jonah 2:2). "Thou ... shalt be thrust down to hell [*hades*]" (Luke 10:15). "The gates of hell [*hades*] shall not prevail against it" (Matt. 16:18). "Thou ... shalt be brought down to hell [*hades*]" (Matt. 11:23). "In hell [*hades*] he lift up his eyes, being in torments" (Luke 16:23). "Thou wilt not leave my soul in hell [*hades*]" (Acts 2:27). "His soul was not left in hell [*hades*]" (Acts 2:31). "I...have the keys of hell [*hades*] and of death" (Rev. 1:18). "Death and hell [*hades*] were cast into the lake of fire" (Rev. 20:14).

In Ps. 9:17 the ultimate state and place of the finally lost are evidently intended. As *sheol* means "the unseen state," the "unseen world," or that which lies beyond the present life, the Psalmist here uses it to denote the eternal place of punishment, whatever his conception of that may have been. Of the rich man after death we read, "And in hell he lift up his eyes, being in torments." "And he cried and said ... I am tormented in this flame"; "This *place* of torment" (Luke 16:23-24, 28). Of course, this was not the grave. Torment awaits the unsaved beyond death. They go into a "*place* of torment." So whether *hades* is used to denote the place and state of the lost after death, or *gehenna* beyond the resurrection and judgment, it will be hell in tormenting flames.

In 2 Pet. 2:9 we read that God has reserved "the unjust unto the day of judgment to be punished." There is a place then where these lost spirits are thus reserved or kept: "And the angels which kept not their first estate, but left their own habitation, he hath reserved in everlasting chains under darkness unto the judgment of the great day" (Jude 6). "God spared not the angels that sinned, but cast them down to hell [Greek, Tartarus], and delivered them into chains of darkness, to be reserved unto judgment" (2 Pet. 2:4). "For if God spared not messengers when they sinned, but to pits of gloom consigning them *the lowest hades* delivered them up to be kept unto judgment" (*Rotherham's Translation*). "Plunging them into Tartarus, delivering them up in chains to be kept in darkness until the judgment" (*Sawyer's Translation*). "With chains of thick gloom, having cast them down to Tartarus" (*Young's Translation*). "Confined them in Tartarus in chains of thick darkness" (*Emphatic Diaglott*).

From all this we learn that fallen angels are reserved in "the *lowest hades,*" called by Peter *"Tartarus,"* and here in "chains of darkness" and "pits of gloom" they are kept "until the judgment of the great day," when they will receive their full punishment. The demons said to Jesus, "Art thou come hither to torment us *before the time?*" (Matt. 8:29). A time of awful torment awaits them beyond the judgment (Matt. 25:41; Rev. 20:10). They "believe and tremble" in view of this. Until that time, their place is the lowest of hades, or Tartarus. They are *reserved* there. But God has also reserved the ungodly unto the day of judgment to be punished. Since the final place of punishment of demons and wicked men will be the same (Matt. 25:41), we may rightly conclude that after death they all occupy the same place. Dying men have testified, "I am taking an awful leap into the dark"; "the demons are here to take me"; "I am going to hell, I am lost"; and "I am in torment; my God, what torment!"

It was into this place that the rich man passed at death. Here fallen angels, demons, and the lost and wretched of all ages are gathered and kept in chains of darkness until the judgment, when they will be cast "into everlasting fire." With fearful anticipation of that eternal future of woe, and reflection upon past life closed out in rebellion against God, stung and tormented by a guilty conscience, aware that all hope and mercy are forever gone, and conscious of being lost forever, what must be the state of a lost soul beyond death in that "unseen world"?

We shall now consider *gehenna,* the word generally employed in the New Testament to designate the place of eternal punishment beyond the resurrection and judgment:

"Shall be in danger of hell fire [*gehenna*]" (Matt. 5:22).

"Thy whole body should be cast into hell [*gehenna*]" (Matt. 5:29-30).

"Fear him which is able to destroy both soul and body in hell [*gehenna*]" (Matt. 10:28).

"To be cast into hell fire [*gehenna*]" (Matt. 18:9).

"Twofold more the child of hell [*gehenna*] than yourself" (Matt. 23:15).

"How can ye escape the damnation of hell [*gehenna*]?" (Matt. 23:33).

"To go into hell [*gehenna*]" (Mark 9:43).

"To be cast into hell fire [*gehenna*]" (Mark 9:47).

"To cast into hell [*gehenna*]" (Luke 12:5).

"The tongue...is set on fire of hell [*gehenna*]" (James 3:6).

Gehenna is from the Valley of Hinnom. This deep, narrow valley lies immediately south of Mount Zion, Jerusalem. The following passages of scripture will give the reader a history of the place: Josh. 15:8; 2 Chron.

28:3; 33:6; 2 Kings 23:7-14; Jer. 7:31; 19:1-5. Dr. Adam Clarke, in his comments on Matt. 5:22, remarks: "This place was near Jerusalem, and had been formerly used for those abominable sacrifices in which the idolatrous Jews had caused their children to pass through the fire to Molech. A particular place in this valley was called Tophet, the fire-stove, in which some supposed they burnt their children alive to the above idol. ... From the circumstance of this valley having been the scene of those infernal sacrifices, the Jews, in our Savior's time, used the word for hell, the place of the damned."

It was the fire of this idolatrous worship in the offering of human sacrifices which gave this valley—*Gehenna*—its bad notoriety. This caused it to be associated in the minds of the Jews with heinous sin and terrible suffering, and this led to the employment of the term to the place of final and everlasting punishment. There was no word in Jewish language more appropriate than the name of this hideous valley. So Jesus used it as *figurative* of the future punishment of the wicked. Spirit is from *ruach* (Hebrew) and *pneuma* (Greek), which literally means *wind*. But to apply *wind* for *spirit* in the Bible would destroy the true sense and meaning of the term. So with "hell"—from *gehenna*. It never was intended by our Lord to mean *literally* the Valley of Hinnom south of Jerusalem. This place was but a figure of future punishment.

Pastor Russell used to lecture in many cities on a favorite topic: "To hell and back." The rich man in Luke 16, however, never got back. If, as some materialistic writers affirm, hell means no more than the literal Valley of Hinnom south of Jerusalem, then I have twice been there and returned. In April, 1921, and again in April, 1923, I traveled the entire length of this deep valley and found it to be quite a comfortable and scenic place of rocky ledges and olive groves. To substitute "Valley of Hinnom" for "hell" will show the absurdity of this teaching, e.g. Matt. 10:28: "Fear not them which kill the body, but are not able to kill the soul; but rather fear him which is able to destroy both soul and body in the Valley of

Hinnom south of Jerusalem." James 3:6: "The tongue is a fire ... and it is set on fire of the Valley of Hinnom south of Jerusalem." Rev 20:15: "And whosoever was not found written in the book of life was cast into the Valley of Hinnom south of Jerusalem." Anyone can see that hell does not mean this literal valley. The scholarship of the world is against such a position.

As certain as the Bible teaches a place and state of eternal rewards called "heaven," the abode of the righteous, it also teaches a place and state of punishment after death and beyond the judgment called "hell," the abode of the wicked. One clear text on this point is as good as a thousand, for truth never contradicts: "How can ye escape the damnation of hell?" (Matt. 23:33). One denies that there is a God and a heaven in which He dwells, if one is to deny what is plainly set forth in this text.

HELL, A PLACE AS WELL AS A STATE

Of the Rich Man after death, we read that his was not only a state of "being in torments," but he spoke of being in "this *place of torment.*" (Luke 16:23, 28). Hell, then is a place. If this is true between death and the judgment, it will also be true beyond that great day of judgment in the eternal state. "The wicked shall be turned into hell, and all the nations that forget God" (Ps. 9:17). Dr. Clarke on "turned into" remarks: "The original is very emphatic. Headlong into hell, down into hell." Note the fact that hell in this text is peculiar to the wicked and the nations that forget God. The grave is common to all, both good and bad. It certainly signifies the *place* and state of the lost, the end of the wicked. I here insert a few brief comments on the text. "It is hell. This is inevitable and certain. There the wicked are abandoned by God, without excuse, without recourse, without hope forever" (*W. Forsyth, M.A.*). "Hell here is the opposite of heaven" (*George Bamton*). "They shall be turned into hell. There will be tormenting pains, a sleepless conscience, mutual reproaches, unrestrained and full grown passions, and the certainty of eternal despair" (*J. Jowett, M.A.*). "It means hell. ... The loss of all worldly good, the society the lost will find there—vile men and devils, and the lake of fire. If this be figurative, then how awful must be the punishment which requires such a figure" (*W. Barns*).

"Thy whole body should be *cast into hell*" (Matt. 5:29-30).

"Both soul and body *in hell*" (Matt. 10:28).

"Cast *into hell fire*" (Matt. 18:9).

"To *go into hell,* into the fire that never shall be quenched" (Mark 9:43).

"To be *cast into hell fire;* where their worm dieth not, and the fire is not quenched" (Mark 9:47-48).

All these scriptures teach in so many words that there is a place called hell into which the wicked will "go" and be "cast," and both soul and body will suffer in that unquenchable fire.

"And whosoever was not found written in the book of life was *cast into the lake of fire*" (Rev. 20:15). "These both were *cast alive into a lake of fire burning with brimstone*" (Rev. 19:20). "But the fearful, and unbelieving, and the abominable, and murderers, and whoremongers, and sorcerers, and idolaters, and all liars, shall have their part *in the lake* which burneth with fire and brimstone" (Rev. 21:8). "And shall *cast them into a furnace of fire:* there shall be wailing and gnashing of teeth" (Matt. 13:42). "And the devil that deceived them *was cast into the lake of fire* and brimstone" (Rev. 20:10). Such language would be meaningless if there be not a place of future and eternal punishment. But it seems to me the Scriptural statements on this point are decisive. They clearly establish the fact that hell is a real place, the final destiny of demons and the wicked, not simply a condition, a state of being, but an actual place into which all the ungodly will be cast.

Of the righteous we read that they shall "*enter in* through the gates *into the city*" (Rev. 22:14). Heaven is a place. The same is true of hell, the eternal abode of the lost. If one is true, the other is true. The soul is the volitional part of our being, that which sins against God. The members of the physical body are the instruments of the soul in its transgressions. Nearly all of the sins that men commit are performed through or with the body. Hence beyond the resurrection *"both soul and body"* will be cast into hell (Matt. 10:28). Both will suffer there. Such will be the ultimate abode of the incorrigible sinner.

"Then shall he say also unto them on the left hand, Depart from me, ye cursed, into everlasting fire, prepared for the devil and his angels" (Matt. 1 25:41). Hell is a prepared place, originally prepared for Satan and his demons, but no less for man who rejects Christ, his only hope of salvation, and chooses to serve sin and the devil. In the day of judgment, the lost will depart into this awful place of everlasting punishment.

THE NATURE OF FUTURE PUNISHMENT

All we know of this is what is revealed in the Scriptures. Punishment is promised upon the finally incorrigible wicked and pertains to immutable and eternal justice and conveys the idea of retribution. In its true idea, it is suffering judicially inflicted as a satisfaction to justice. There is an infinite, immutable, eternal mind, the intelligent first cause and source of all things—God—and the principles of His administration are based on eternal rectitude [morally correct behavior or thinking]. His holy and Divine nature furnishes the foundation for an immutable distinction between the right and wrong, the just and the unjust, and measures reward and punishment accordingly. Punishment for sin then is suffering inflicted for ill-desert, and its essential element is retribution. The Bible testimony on this point is unmistakably clear.

"Avenge not yourselves. ... Vengeance is mine; I will repay, saith the Lord" (Rom. 12:19). "In flaming fire taking vengeance on them that know not God" (2 Thess. 1:8). "Suffering the vengeance of eternal fire" (Jude 7). "A certain fearful looking for of judgment and fiery indignation, which shall devour the adversaries" (Heb. 10:27). "The same shall drink of the wine of the wrath of God, which is poured out without mixture into the cup of his indignation" (Rev. 14:10). The right then to punish sin because it deserves to be punished and to render vengeance upon criminals because they are wicked, is God's. God in His eternal and infinite wisdom has annexed [attached] penalties to His law that are in perfect harmony with the nature of the law, and He will inflict such penalty. His moral law is eternal and is based upon the nature of God Himself, and He intends all rational beings to obey it and conform to His moral character. How infinite then must be God's abhorrence of all moral evil and sin. Thus we get an idea of the true nature of sin and the punishment that must follow. That punishment is consistent with justice, wisdom, and goodness, whether we finite creatures are able to perceive and understand it or not.

Our position is that sin is such an infinite evil that it will be justly followed by an endless punishment. Our annihilationist friends insist that they believe in eternal punishment but that this punishment is an eternal blotting out of existence, a cessation of being. They deny eternal suffering. Here the issue is drawn. Now, if the wicked can suffer punishment without being conscious of it, why cannot the righteous enjoy eternal happiness unconsciously? The one looks as consistent as the other.

We might ask: Will a person who is annihilated *forever* feel it more than one who is annihilated *for a few thousand years?* Our materialist friends hold that all at death are unconscious, go into utter nonexistence. That is all they claim will happen to the wicked at the resurrection. Why take them out of a non-existent state, and then again suddenly blot them out of existence again? What is the difference? If the righteous at death go into non-existence, what is the difference between them and the wicked who will go into the same state beyond the judgment? If mere physical death, passing into a state of non-existence, is eternal punishment, then will not the death of the brutes also be everlasting punishment? Where is the difference?

Can that which does not exist suffer punishment? If the wicked cease to exist, have no consciousness whatever, do they not therefore cease to be punished, and is not this the very opposite of what Jesus taught when He said— "And these shall go away into everlasting punishment?" (Matt. 25:46) Referring to future retribution, our Savior declared that it shall be more tolerable for Sodom, and Tyre and Sidon at the judgment than for Chorazin and Capernaum (Matt. 11:21-24). Now, as there cannot be different degrees of annihilation, this cannot be the punishment of the damned.

We shall come then to the direct question: What will the eternal punishment of the lost consist in and of, or what will be its nature? We believe the Bible clearly teaches that it is a state of endless, irrecoverable misery and conscious suffering.

First, *torment.*

"And when he was come to the other side into the country of the Gergesenes, there met him two possessed with devils, coming out of the tombs, exceeding fierce, so that no man might pass by that way. And, behold, they cried out, saying, What have we to do with thee, Jesus, thou Son of God? art thou come hither to torment us before the time?" (Matt. 8:28-29).

In Thayer's Greek-English Lexicon *basanizo,* the verb form for the Greek noun translated "torment" is: "To vex with grievous pains of body or mind, to torment." *Torment*— "That which gives pain, vexation, or misery. Extreme pain, anguish, the utmost degree of misery, either of body or mind. To torture, hence to put to extreme pain or anguish, to inflict excruciating pain and misery."—*Webster.* The text describes a man possessed with a legion of demons. At the approach of Christ, the devils cried out, "Jesus, thou Son of God: art thou come hither to *torment* us *before the time?*" On this Dr. Adam Clarke remarks: "They knew there was a time determined by the divine Judge, when they should be sent into greater torment." Torment awaits these devils beyond the judgment, and this text proves that they are fully cognizant of the fact. That is why they "tremble" (James 2:19). They did not say to Jesus, "Do not annihilate us," but "I adjure thee by God, that thou *torment* me not" (Mark 5:7). Further proof that this will be their awful punishment is found in Rev. 20:10: "And the devil that deceived them was cast into the lake of fire and brimstone, and shall be *tormented* day and night forever and ever."

This hell of torment was "prepared for the devil and his angels," and the wicked will be cast into the same place and state (Matt. 25:41). So, *torment,* and not obliteration, awaits the guilty. After death, the Rich Man "lift up his eyes, *being in torments*" (Luke 16:23). He cried for mercy, begged for water, and said, "I am *tormented* in this flame" (Luke 16:24). He called his abode "this *place of torment.*" Hell, then, is not a state of non-existence, but a place of torment, suffering. This was not said of the moldering corpse that had been buried on earth, but it was the state and condition of a man whose spirit was alive in the eternal world.

"If any man worship the beast and his image, and receive his mark in his forehead, or in his hand, the same shall drink of the wine of the wrath of God, which is poured out without mixture into the cup of his indignation; and he shall be tormented with fire and brimstone in the presence of the holy angels, and in the presence of the Lamb: and the smoke of their torment ascendeth up for ever and ever: and they have no rest day nor night" (Rev. 14:9-11).

This is the opposite of annihilation. An unconscious being reduced to nonentity could not be tormented, and these scriptures teach that the wicked, with demons, will be tormented in hell forever.

A faint idea of the future state of the lost may be gathered by considering the condition of those who were demon possessed: "And, behold, a man of the company cried out, saying, Master, I beseech thee, look upon my son: for he is mine only child. And, lo, a spirit taketh him, and he suddenly crieth out; and it teareth him that he foameth again, and bruising him hardly departeth from him. … And as he was yet a coming, the devil threw him down, and tare him [threw him into convulsions]. And Jesus rebuked the unclean spirit, and healed the child, and delivered him again to his father" (Luke 9:38-39, 42).

We read of another demoniac that the devil threw into the water and fire, and it could not be controlled (Matt. 17:15; Mark 9:22). Of the man in the tombs we read, "He ware no clothes, neither abode in any house, but in the tombs" (Luke 8:27). "He was kept bound with chains, and with fetters; and he brake [broke] the bands, and was driven of the devil into the wilderness" (Luke 8:29). "No man could bind him, no not with chains. Because that he had been often bound with fetters and chains, and the chains had been plucked asunder by him, and the fetters broken in pieces: neither could any man tame him. And always night and day, he was in the mountains, and in the tombs, crying, and cutting himself with stones" (Mark 5:3-5). "Exceeding fierce, so that no man might pass that way"

(Matt. 8:28). What a terrible state! Here was a poor man, a human being, under the direct control of demons. What then must be the state of the finally lost who will be utterly abandoned by God and under the absolute control and in the same abode eternally of these demons, "delivered to the tormentors" (Matt. 18:34)? Great God, save us from such a destiny.

Second, *tribulation and anguish.*

"But unto them that are contentious, and do not obey the truth, but obey unrighteousness, indignation and wrath, tribulation and anguish, upon every soul of man that doeth evil" (Rom. 2:8-9).

Paul's theme here is the "righteous judgment of God" that all men must face in the final "day of wrath." Read the context. The Divine penalty upon the ungodly is "indignation and wrath," and its effect upon them is not annihilation but "tribulation and anguish." Tribulation here means pressure—extreme anguish and excruciating pain. The anguish simply intensifies the other. The idea conveyed is that of extreme suffering.

Third, *damnation.* —Judgment, condemnation.

"He that believeth not shall be damned" (Mark 16:15-16).

"That they all might be damned who believed not the truth" (2 Thess. 2:12).

"Their damnation slumbereth not" (2 Pet. 2:3).

"They that have done evil, unto the resurrection of damnation" (John 5:29).

"How can ye escape the damnation of hell" (Matt. 23:33).

This cannot mean annihilation, for it is "eternal damnation" that they shall suffer, and some will receive "greater damnation" than others (Mark 3:29; Matt. 23:14).

Fourth, *shame and contempt.*

"Some to shame and everlasting contempt" (Dan. 12:2).

To evade the force of this text, Elder Uriah Smith in *Here and Hereafter* (pp. 276, 277) argues that it is not the *shame—their* emotion—that will be everlasting, but the *contempt,* the emotion felt by others toward them. But Smith's deductions are not sound. In the Septuagint, this is rendered, "Some to reproach and everlasting shame." "Some to shame and infamy everlasting," is another rendering; and again— "To ignominy, to shame eternal." Eternal shame shall be the portion of the ungodly, a consciousness of their own loathsomeness, and this shall cover them with eternal confusion.

Fifth, *suffering vengeance of the Almighty, who is a consuming fire.*

"Suffering the vengeance of eternal fire" (Jude 7). This is the opposite of blotting out of existence. When God rained fire and brimstone upon Sodom and Gomorrah, the buildings, etc., were reduced to ashes; but the wicked inhabitants of those cities who committed fornication, "going after strange flesh" (Jude 7), are "suffering the vengeance of eternal fire." The fire of Divine wrath is upon them and will be forever. This is not annihilation, but a perpetual suffering.

Sixth, *the punishment of loss, or deprivation.*

"Depart from me, ye that work iniquity" (Matt. 7:23). "What a terrible word! What a dreadful separation! Depart from me! From the very Jesus whom you have proclaimed, in union with whom alone is eternal life to be found. For, united with Christ, all is heaven; separated from him, all is hell."—Dr. Adam Clarke. "Depart from me, ye cursed" (Matt. 25:41). "And these shall go away" (Matt. 25:46). "Bind him hand and foot, and take him away, and cast him into outer darkness; there shall be weeping and gnashing of teeth" (Matt. 22:13).

In life salvation was within their reach; they could have secured it and have become qualified for the enjoyment and companionship of God, and of the good and pure of all ages: but they disdained it, refused it, and disqualified themselves for the holy society of heaven. Now, since by their action such chose to be separated from the holy and redeemed hosts of heaven, they must be associated with the impure and unholy in both character and doom. An utter severance and banishment from the presence of the Lord, and an abode and association with demons and the refuse of all ages is the necessary consequence of all the workers of iniquity, and this is the eternal misery of the damned.

There is for them no other alternative. This doom is deprivation of eternal life, endurance of God's displeasure, and an utter rejection and banishment from the society of Jesus and the blessed in heaven. This state is final. He shall "sever the wicked from among the just" (Matt. 13:40-43, 48, 50). Eternal separation from God. "This is the second death" (Rev. 20:14). "When once the master of the house is risen up, and hath shut to the door, and ye begin to stand without, and to knock at the door, saying, Lord, Lord, open unto us; and he shall answer and say unto you, I know you not whence ye are: then shall ye begin to say, We have eaten and drunk in thy presence, and thou has taught in our streets. But he shall say, I tell you, I know you not whence ye are; depart from me, all ye workers of iniquity. There shall be weeping and gnashing of teeth, when ye shall see Abraham, and Isaac, and Jacob, and all the prophets, in the kingdom of God, and you yourselves thrust out" (Luke 13:25-28). "And while they went to buy, the bridegroom came; and they that were ready went in with him to the marriage: and *the door was shut*. Afterward came also the other virgins, saying, Lord, Lord, open to us. But he answered and said, Verily I say unto you, I know you not" (Matt. 25:10-12). Barred from heaven forever. Here we have a glimpse of the soul's eternal loss.

"Blessed are they that do his commandments, that they may have right to the tree of life, and may enter in through the gates into the city. For *without* [outside] are dogs [the morally impure], and sorcerers [those who practice occult crafts, use altering drugs, etc.], and whoremongers [sexually immoral, fornicators, molesters, adulterers], and murderers, and idolaters, and whosoever loveth and maketh a lie" (Rev. 22:14-15).

Here are some of the saddest statements to be found in the Bible. The place is where time and eternity meet and eternal destinies are apportioned to all men. "They that were ready went in," "through the gates into the city"—heaven. Then "the door was shut," and the whoremongers, idolaters, liars, and all characters of the lost were "thrust out," left "without," lost, ruined, cursed, damned, and in torment. "There shall be weeping and gnashing of teeth." What a disappointment and sense of misery when heaven's door, the door of mercy and opportunity, is forever closed, and the lost hear the awful sentence, "depart," and find themselves in "outer darkness."

Uriah Smith, in *Here and Hereafter* (p. 280), argues against eternal, conscious suffering from the word *"punishment"* in Matt. 25:46. It is from *kolasis,* which he defines "cutting off," and then identifies "cutting off," with the idea of blotting out of existence, or annihilation. Everlasting punishment is defined to be everlasting non-existence. The followers of Pastor Russell use the same argument. But truth squarely contradicts their doctrine. There is a vast difference between cutting off and annihilation. In fact, it does not mean that at all. Were we to grant that punishment in Matt. 25:46 means an everlasting cutting off, the nature of this cutting off is clearly defined by Christ Himself in the same connection—namely— "depart from me into everlasting fire." This is not annihilation, but an eternal cutting off from association with Christ in heaven, the loss of all the felicities [great happiness, joy, bliss] of eternal glory, just what the many scriptures cited in this chapter so clearly teach. "He that is unjust, let him be unjust still: and he which is filthy, let him be filthy still: and he that is righteous, let him be righteous still: and he that is holy, let him be holy still" (Rev. 22:11).

Here we have the eternal state. The great judgment is past (Rev. 20:11-12). Satan and the wicked are in the lake of fire (Rev. 20:10, 15; 21:8; 22:15). The righteous are now in the new heaven and earth—their eternal home (Rev. 21:26; 22:1-5). What is now their condition? The righteous are "righteous and holy still." The wicked—how about them? Are they no more, blotted out of existence, utterly extinct? No, indeed. They are there in that eternal world, "unjust, and filthy still." Character formed in life has fixed their destiny.

"Here we have the misery of the unjust and impure, and the happiness of the righteous and holy. It connects time with eternity. The character wherewith we sink into the grave at death is the very character with which we shall reappear on the day of resurrection. The moral lineaments [distinctive features or characteristics] which are graven on [deeply imprinted or carved into] the tablet of the inner man, and which every day of an unconverted life marks deeper and more indelible [cannot be removed] than before, will retain the impress they have received unaltered by the transition to the future state of our existence. Propensity is strengthened by every new act of indulgence; any virtuous principle is more firmly established than before by every new act of resolute obedience to its dictates. Then the hell of the wicked may be said to be already begun, and the heaven of the virtuous. The one has a foretaste of the wretchedness before him, the other of the happiness before him. The inward sense of dishonor which haunts and humbles the sinner here is but the commencement of that shame and everlasting contempt to which he shall awake hereafter. In stepping from time to eternity he carries in his own distempered bosom [sinful or sick heart] the materials of his coming vengeance along with him. He will carry his unsanctified habits and unhallowed passions thitherward. When probation is over, character is unalterably fixed, and there is but one probation."—*T. Chalmers, D.D.*

Eternal torment, tribulation, anguish, damnation, shame and contempt, suffering the vengeance of Almighty God, cast into outer darkness, barred from God's presence and heaven forever, weeping, wailing, gnashing of teeth, "where *their* worm dieth not, and the fire is not quenched"—such is the Bible description of the nature of future punishment. What the realities will be, only fallen angels and the wicked shall ever know.

"Pray always, that ye may be accounted worthy to escape all these things that shall come to pass, and to stand before the Son of man" (Luke 21:36).

FIGURES EMPLOYED TO DENOTE THE PUNISHMENT OF THE FINALLY IMPENITENT

Referring to the eternal abode of the redeemed in heaven we have such expressions as "many mansions," "city," "better country," "new heaven and new earth," "walls of jasper," "streets of gold," "precious stones," "sapphire," "pearls," "tree of life," "living fountains of waters," "fruit every month," healing "leaves," "crowns," "harps," "palms," etc., etc. In the Scriptures, such language is employed as could best convey to finite minds the glories of that heavenly realm. No one would think of taking all these expressions strictly literally. To regard them as figures of the real does not detract from the anticipated beauties and glories of heaven, for a figure cannot be as great and wonderful as the reality. This too is true of the eternal state and abode of the ungodly [hell]. The inspired writers employed such language and figures as could vividly portray to the human mind the awful doom of the unsaved. This does not deny nor lessen the reality of future punishment.

First—*Fire.*

"Unquenchable fire" (Matt. 3:12). "Hell fire" (Matt. 5:22). "Furnace of fire" (Matt. 13:42, 50). "Into hell fire," "Everlasting fire" (Matt. 18:8-9; 25:41). "Into hell fire, the fire that shall never be quenched" (Mark 9:43-47). "In flaming fire taking vengeance" (2 Thess. 1:8). "Suffering the vengeance of eternal fire" (Jude 7). "Tormented with fire and brimstone" (Rev. 14:10). "A lake of fire burning with brimstone" (Rev. 19:20; 21:8). "Cast into the lake of fire" (Rev. 20:15). In James 3:6, we read that "the tongue is a fire; ... and it is set on fire of hell." This, of course, is not literal fire, and yet the fires of hell burn in men's uncontrolled tongues. The disembodied spirit of the Rich Man in Luke 16 found himself in a "flame of torment." The "devil and his angels," who are immortal spirits, will be punished in this "everlasting fire."

Second—*Darkness.*

"Shall be cast into outer darkness: there shall be weeping and gnashing of teeth" (Matt. 8:11-12). "Cast ye the unprofitable servant into outer darkness; there shall be weeping and gnashing of teeth" (Matt. 25:30). "Bind him hand and foot, and take him away, and cast him into outer darkness; there shall be weeping and gnashing of teeth" (Matt. 22:13). "There shall be wailing and gnashing of teeth" (Matt. 13:50).

This is directly opposite to annihilation. None of these texts refer to turning human beings into ashes.

"They shall never see light" (Ps. 49:19). On this text Dr. Adam Clarke remarks: "Rise again they shall; but they shall never see the light of glory, for there is prepared for them the blackness of darkness forever." What awful truth! Yet, as sure as God's Word declares it, this will come to pass. This will be the fearful doom of the ungodly. They go into a place of punishment and remain there. They suffer there. No ray of light will ever penetrate that awful darkness; no sunbeam of hope will ever gladden their hearts. "Outer darkness. There shall be weeping, wailing, and gnashing of teeth" (Matt. 8:12; Matt. 25:30).

"These are wells without water, clouds that are carried with a tempest; to whom the mist of darkness is reserved for ever" (2 Pet. 2:17). "Raging waves of the sea, foaming out their own shame; wandering stars, to whom is reserved the blackness of darkness for ever" (Jude 13).

Here is pictured in graphic figure the eternity of lost souls. Eternity's night, dark, deep, unfathomable, impenetrable, the "blackness of darkness forever." Amid howling devils and the piercing shrieks of the damned, rocking upon the billows of eternal despair, hopelessly and forever lost. "To whom the mist of darkness is reserved," that is, an eternal separation away from the presence of God and the glory of His power. "They shall be thrust into outer darkness; into the utmost degree of misery and despair. False and corrupt teachers will be sent into the lowest hell; and be the most downcast underfoot vassals of perdition."—*Dr. Clarke*

Third—*Perdition.*

A figure of loss, ruin, destruction. "The day of judgment and perdition of ungodly men" (2 Pet. 3:7). "Shall ascend out of the bottomless pit, and go into perdition" (Rev. 17:8). "Which drown men in destruction and perdition" (1 Tim. 6:9). Judas Iscariot was called "the son of perdition"— "a child of hell" (John 17:12). The man of sin is also termed the "son of perdition" (2 Thess. 2:3-4).

THERE WILL BE DEGREES OF PUNISHMENT
RATED BY THE LIGHT RECEIVED

While hell will be the place and state of future punishment for all the lost, the Scriptures clearly teach that some in perdition will have a "sorer punishment" than others, that is, their sense of torment will be greater: "The Lord of that servant will come in a day when he looketh not for him, and at an hour when he is not aware, and will cut him in sunder [in pieces], and will appoint him his portion with the unbelievers. And that servant, which knew his lord's will, and prepared not himself, neither did according to his will, shall be beaten with many stripes. But he that knew not, and did commit things worthy of stripes, shall be beaten with few stripes. For unto whomsoever much is given, of him shall be much required: and to whom men have committed much, of him they will ask the more" (Luke 12:46, 48).

Reference is here made to the Jews' mode of punishment: "For petty offenses they in some cases inflicted as few as four, five, and six stripes. For a criminal offense forty stripes were administered. For a double offense, eighty stripes were given" (*Lightfoot*). Paul says, "Of the Jews five times received I forty stripes save one" (2 Cor. 11:24). Here he alludes to this very thing.

Jesus is here speaking of the day of final rewards, the day of Christ's coming and judgment. He applies in principle the Jews' mode of punishment to that which will be meted out to the unfaithful. It will be a proportionate punishment, and the light and knowledge people have received will rate this. He "which knew his Lord's will"—had a clear revelation—and then "prepared not himself," will receive the "many stripes," and justly so. While he that "knew not"—was limited in his knowledge of God and His will—and yet "did commit things worthy of stripes," shall receive "few stripes," or a lighter punishment. This will be rated on the principle that "unto whomsoever much is given, of him shall be much required" (Luke 12:48). In this is revealed the justice of God. While the duration of this punishment will be to all eternal in its nature, some will have greater anguish and torment than others.

On this point I quote Dr. Adam Clarke: "From this and the preceding verse we find that it is a crime to be ignorant of God's will; because to every one God has given less or more of the means of instruction. Those who have had much light, or the opportunity of receiving much, and have not improved it to their own salvation, and the good of others, shall have punishment proportioned to the light they have abused. On the other hand, those who have had little light, and few means of improvement, shall have few stripes—shall be punished only for the abuse of the knowledge they possessed."

"Woe unto you, scribes and Pharisees, hypocrites! For ye devour widows' houses, and for a pretense make long prayer: therefore ye shall receive the greater damnation" (Matt. 23:14). "These shall receive greater damnation" (Mark 12:40). "The same shall receive greater damnation" (Luke 20:47). This language of Christ is emphatic and clear. He Himself will be the future judge, and He will sentence to everlasting misery the hosts of lost sinners assembled on the left hand of His judgment throne. What He said on this point is authentic. The damnation of some will be "greater" than others. In this immediate connection, Christ denominates this future state of the wicked "the damnation of hell" (Matt. 23:33). Then in hell there will be those who suffer a *greater* sense of condemnation than others, a "more abundant" torment, for that is the meaning of "greater" in these texts, which is from *perissoteros* in the Greek.

"But after thy hardness and impenitent heart treasurest up unto thyself wrath against the day of wrath and revelation of the righteous judgment of God; who will render to every man according to his deeds" (Rom. 2:5-6). "For the Son of man shall come in the glory of his Father with his angels; and then he shall reward every man according to his works" (Matt. 16:27). "And the dead were judged out of those things which were written in the books, according to their works" (Rev. 20:12). "I the Lord search the heart, I try the reins [examine the mind], even to give every man according to his ways, and according to the fruit of his doings" (Jer. 17:10). These texts apply directly to the future state and plainly say that every man's punishment will be "according to his deeds," "his ways," and "the fruit of his doings." That is, it will be rated proportionately and justly, and the intents and deeds determine the amount.

As there are many grades of character among the unbelieving here upon earth, so there will be many degrees of woe among the lost hereafter. "Whatsoever a man soweth, that shall he also reap" (Gal. 6:7). "He that soweth bountifully, shall reap also bountifully" (2 Cor. 9:6). Here is a principle that will enter into future rewards and punishment. The more seed sown the greater the harvest. It cannot be otherwise. Every act of life, every word and thought, is a seed sown, and the more seeds of sin and wickedness cast, the greater will be the final harvest of punishment. "They have sown the wind, and they reap the whirlwind" (Hos. 8:7).

To the righteous Jesus said, "Lay up for yourselves treasures in heaven" (Matt. 6:19-21). In 1 Tim. 6:17-19, Paul speaks of people "laying up in store for themselves against the time to come." Such language certainly implies the thought of adding to our stock of future bliss and happiness. The more treasures laid up in store, the more shall be possessed when the reward is given. And the same is true of the unsaved. They daily treasure up, accumulate, and amass wrath unto themselves. "Treasurest up unto thyself wrath against the day of wrath" (Rom. 2:5). The sinner through life is simply adding to his stock of wrath and judgment. The more he accumulates, the greater will be his punishment.

Light rates the sinfulness of sin. According to the degree of light a man has, is sin sinful to him. Paul says that sin by the commandment became exceeding sinful. The knowledge of the commandment is what made sin "*exceeding* sinful." Jesus said to Pilate, "He that delivered me unto thee hath the *greater sin*" (John 19:11). By consenting to the wish of the Jews and condemning Christ to be crucified, Pilate committed an awful sin. Yet Christ said that the one who delivered Him into Pilate's hands had the "greater sin." That was Judas Iscariot. He had more light than Pilate. Judas had once a blessed part in that sacred ministry. Because he had more light, his sin was greater. The greater the light, the deeper the sin.

"And Jesus said, For judgment I am come into this world, that they which see not might see; and that they which see might be made blind. And some of the Pharisees which were with him heard these words, and said unto him, Are we blind also? Jesus said unto them, If ye were blind, ye should have no sin: but now ye say, We see; therefore your sin remaineth" (John 9:39-41). "If I had not come and spoken unto them, they had not had sin: but now they have no cloak for their sin. If I had not done among them the works which none other man did, they had not had sin: but now have they both seen and hated both me and my Father" (John 15:22, 24). Light, I repeat, rates the sinfulness of sin. That being true we can easily see how men will be punished "according to their deeds," and how they must reap what they sow. Those whose sins are "exceeding sinful" because they reject greater light will receive a "greater damnation." Although all will be cast into hell, conscience will doubtless be a principal part of eternal torment, and the punishment of *sense* and *separation* will be much greater to some than to others. Thus, we see not only that light rates the sinfulness of crime here, but that it will rate the punishment of the damned in hell forever. Whatever the damnation of the ungodly will be, it must and will be just (Rom. 3:8; 2 Thess. 1:7-9; Isa. 30:18; Job 34:12; Deut. 32:4; Ps. 9:7-8; Ps. 140:12; Eph. 6:9; Pro. 11:1; Rev. 20:12-13).

"And whosoever shall not receive you, nor hear your words, when ye depart out of that house or city, shake off the dust of your feet. Verily I say unto you, it shall be more tolerable for the land of Sodom and Gomorrah in the day of judgment, than for that city" (Matt. 10:14-15). "Then began he to upbraid [denounce] the cities wherein most of his mighty works were done, because they repented not: Woe unto thee, Chorazin! woe unto thee, Bethsaida! for if the mighty works, which were done in you, had been done in Tyre and Sidon, they would have repented long ago in sackcloth and ashes. But I say unto you, It shall be more tolerable for Tyre and Sidon at the day of judgment, than for you. And thou, Capernaum, which art exalted unto heaven, shalt be brought down to hell: for if the mighty works, which have been done in thee, had been done in Sodom, it would have remained until this day. But I say unto you, That it shall be more tolerable for the land of Sodom in the day of judgment, than for thee" (Matt. 11:20-24).

Jesus reproached these cities and declared that if He had done in Sodom the same works that He did in them, those ancient people of Sodom would have repented and would not have been destroyed. He also said that in the day of judgment the punishment of Sodom will not be so great. If that punishment were simply annihilation such language would be meaningless. Of one man Jesus said, "It had been good for that man if he had never been born" (Matt. 26:24).

Backsliders will receive a greater punishment than those who were never saved: "For it had been better for them not to have known the way of righteousness" (2 Pet. 2:21). "For if we sin willfully after that we have received the knowledge of the truth, there remaineth no more sacrifice for sins, but a certain fearful looking for of judgment and fiery indignation, which shall devour the adversaries. He that despised Moses' law died without mercy under two or three witnesses: of how much sorer punishment, suppose ye, shall he be thought worthy, who hath trodden under foot the Son of God, and hath counted the blood of the covenant, wherewith he was sanctified, an unholy thing and hath done despite unto the Spirit of grace? For we know him that hath said, Vengeance belongeth unto me, I will recompense, saith the Lord. And again, The Lord shall judge his people. It is a fearful thing to fall into the hands of the living God" (Heb. 10:26-31).

How solemn these truths! Of all the millions in the dark regions of despair, the men and the women that were once saved and then fell away from that state will have the greatest punishment. Their punishment will be a "much sorer punishment" than that of those who were never saved. To all eternity they will remember a time when they were saved and the sweet peace of heaven filled their souls. They will remember those seasons of grace and glory, the sweet hymns of Zion, the fellowship of their Creator. They will look back to a time when their hearts were pure and when they were ready to enter heaven and immortal glory. Oh, what a remembrance for lost souls! But they sold their souls for a feather. They bartered away the priceless treasure of salvation for some trifle, some of earth's vanities. Now they are lost—eternally lost; forever cut off from Christ and all that is pure and lovely; sinking away farther and farther from home, heaven, and loved ones—eternally separated. Oh, what a punishment!

From all the foregoing texts, we clearly see that men's punishment will be "according to their deeds"; that some will have "greater damnation," a "much sorer punishment," than others; that some will have "few stripes," others "many," according to the degree of light they have received; that it will be "more tolerable" for some than for others. This stands in direct contradiction to the doctrine of annihilation. If the ungodly will simply be burned into ashes, such scriptures have no meaning. An unconscious man, lifeless, and reduced to a bit of ashes, cannot suffer.

ETERNITY

In Isa. 57:15, it is said that God "inhabiteth *eternity*." This is the only text in the Bible where the word "eternity" occurs. It is one of the greatest and most comprehensive words in any language. In life, we are the subjects of Time. We are told, however, that the day is approaching when an angel shall swear "by him that liveth for ever and ever that there shall be time no longer" (Rev. 10:6). This means eternity.

Time has a beginning and ending. It is a fragment of eternity. It might be likened to a small island in the midst of the ocean. Gradually its sands are washed away by the mighty billows [waves] which sweep against its shores. By degrees it is being washed away until at length—God only knows how soon—the billows of eternity will sweep over and wash away the last sands of time, and nothing will remain but eternity.

Time is a measured portion of duration. Moments, hours, days, weeks, months, years, centuries, and ages, measure time. But eternity! No cycle of years can measure it. It is a boundless ocean, a shoreless sea, or as Paul expresses it, a "world without end." It is without beginning or ending. It takes ten hundred thousand years to make a million; a thousand million to make a billion; a thousand billion to make a trillion; a thousand trillion to make a quadrillion; a thousand quadrillion to make a quintillion; a thousand quintillion to make a sextillion; a thousand sextillion to make a septillion, a thousand septillion to make an octillion; a thousand octillion to make a nonillion; a thousand nonillion to make a decillion (which when expressed in numerical form looks like this very very large number: 1,000,000,000,000,000,000,000,000,000,000,000). But even this vast number does not express eternity.

Let us suppose that a bird comes from a far distant planet, making one trip in each decillion years. It carries away as much water in its tiny beak as it can contain. The length of time required by that bird thus to transfer to the distant planet all the waters contained in the springs, rivers, lakes, and oceans, would not measure eternity. After carrying away all the waters, suppose the bird still continues its journeys to earth, coming but once in a decillion of years, and carries away in its tiny beak a grain of sand from the seashore, or a bit of dust. That bird could carry away the entire globe on which we live, and yet eternity would not be measured.

Dear reader, you are going to eternity. We shall all soon be there. Death is the gateway each of us must pass through, and death fixes our destiny either in heaven or in hell. You are now forming a character for eternity. You are sowing seed, the harvest of which you must there reap. Now is the only time to prepare.

God inhabits eternity; it is His palace. When we attempt to span the marvels and glories of this divine dwelling-place, with its illimitable [without limits] corridors of space, we are lost in amazement. In the "high and holy place"—heaven—beyond galaxies, and stretching into immensities and infinities, God "inhabiteth eternity." As already expressed, the only way we finite creatures can form an idea of eternity is by going step by step up to the largest measures of time we know of, and then on and on, till we are lost in wonder. Eternity is vaster than the vastest.

"A perpetual duration which has neither beginning nor end."—*Charnock*

"Beyond is all abyss, eternity, whose end no eye can reach."—*Milton*

"Oh, if we could tear aside the veil, and see but for one hour what it signifies, to be a soul in the power of an endless life, what a revelation would it be."—*Horace Bushnell*

"Eternity has no gray hairs. The flowers fade, the heart withers, man grows old and dies, the world lies down in the sepulcher of ages, but time writes no wrinkles on the brow of eternity."—*Bishop Heber*

"Sow the seeds of life; and in the long eternity which lies before the soul, every minutest grain will come up again with an increase of thirty, sixty, or a hundredfold."—*F. W. Robertson*

THE PUNISHMENT OF THE WICKED
WILL BE TO ALL ETERNITY

Eternity is well expressed in the following text: "*From* everlasting *to* everlasting, thou art God" (Ps. 90:2). There are three words which in our English Bible in their true sense signify eternity and are so used in the Scriptures. They are *everlasting, eternal,* and *forever,* from the Greek *aionios.* Forever is also translated from *aiona.* I shall here submit the definition of *aionios* by some of the standard Greek lexicons:

"Everlasting; perpetual; eternal."—*Pickering*

"Without end, never to cease, everlasting."—*Dr. Thayer*

"Everlasting, eternal."—*Liddell and Scott.* Also *Donnegan*

"Everlasting, perpetual."—*Youge*

"Without end; perpetual and interminable."—*Schleusner*

"To eternity."—*Cremer*

"Indeterminate as to duration; eternal; everlasting."—*Baxter*

"Unlimited as to duration; eternal, everlasting."—*Greenfield*

"Ever enduring; perpetual; everlasting; implying eternity; without end."—*Robinson*

Aiona— "forever," is defined by Robert Young in his Analytical Concordance— "To the ages of the ages." From this we learn that when our translators rendered aionios as "everlasting" and "eternal," and aiona as "forever," and they had solid grounds for doing so.

Everlasting— "Lasting or enduring forever, eternal, endless."— *Webster*

Eternal— "Everlasting, endless, immortal."—*Webster*

Forever— "Throughout eternity, endless."—*Webster*

I shall now give a number of texts where the Greek word is aionios and the English rendering is everlasting:

The righteous "shall inherit everlasting life" (Matt. 19:29).

"In the world to come, life everlasting" (Luke 18:30).

"The end everlasting life" (Rom. 6:22).

"The everlasting kingdom" (2 Pet. 1:11).

"The everlasting God" (Rom. 16:26).

Now, we read— "Some to shame and *everlasting* (Greek Septuagint— *aionion*) contempt" (Dan. 12:2).

"Cast into *everlasting* fire" (Matt. 18:8).

"Depart from me ye cursed, into *everlasting* fire, prepared for the devil and his angels" (Matt. 25:41).

"And these shall go away into *everlasting* punishment; but the righteous unto life eternal" (Matt. 25:46).

As long as God Himself shall exist, and as long as He shall have dominion and a kingdom, the wicked will suffer "contempt and shame everlasting"; "everlasting punishment" in "everlasting fire." The same word that measures the endless existence of God Himself, of His kingdom, dominion, gospel, and the life and felicities of the righteous in heaven, measures the duration of the punishment of the wicked in hell. There is no appeal from this fact.

On Matt. 25:46 Robert W. Landis, in his splendid work, *The Immortality of the Soul,* says: "The passage before us, moreover, clearly supposes the future and interminable existence of both the righteous and the wicked. The one enters into reward, the other into punishment, and that reward and that punishment are both eternal. The idea of cessation of existence is in no way intimated, either directly or by implication, in either case. ... It is simply silly to say that non-existence is the antithesis of happiness, as a child can see with a moment's reflection. ... And they are said to go away *into* this everlasting punishment, as the righteous are said to go *into* their eternal reward. The reward, therefore, eternally finds the righteous in possession of it, and the punishment eternally finds the guilty and condemned in possession of it. Such is the obvious and unforced import [meaning] of the passage" (pp. 479-480).

I shall now quote Dr. Clarke: *"Depart*—This includes what some have termed the punishment of loss or privation [deprived of essential things like food and warmth]. Ye cannot, ye shall not be united to me. *Into everlasting fire.* This is the punishment of sense. Ye shall not only be separated from me, but ye shall be tormented, awfully, everlastingly tormented in that place of separation. *Prepared for the devil and his angels.* The devil and angels sinned before the creation of the world, and the place of torment was prepared for them: it never was designed for human souls; but as the wicked are partakers with the devil and his angels in their iniquities, in their rebellion against God, so it is right that they should be sharers with them in their punishment. ... They are cursed because they refused to be blessed; and they are damned, because they refused to be saved. *And these shall go away into everlasting punishment,* no appeal, no remedy, to all eternity. No end of the punishment of those whose final impenitence manifests in them an eternal will and desire to sin. By dying in a settled opposition to God, they cast themselves into a necessity of continuing in an eternal aversion from Him. But some are of the opinion that this punishment shall have an end: this is as likely as that the glory of the righteous shall have an end: for the same word is used to express the duration of the punishment, as it used to express the duration of the state of glory. ... The original word—*aionios* is certainly to be taken here in its proper grammatical sense, continued being, never ending. Some have gone a middle way, and think that the wicked shall be annihilated. This, I think, is contrary to the text; for if they go into punishment, they continue to exist; for that which ceases to be, ceases to suffer" (comments on Matt. 25:41, 46).

The next term is *"eternal,"* also derived from *aionios.*

"But the righteous unto life eternal" (Matt. 25:46).

"Eternal salvation" (Heb. 5:9).

"Eternal redemption" (Heb. 9:12).

"Eternal Spirit" (Heb. 9:14).

"Eternal inheritance" (Heb. 9:15).

"Eternal glory" (2 Tim. 2:10).

"King eternal" (1 Tim. 1:17).

"In danger of eternal damnation" (Mark 3:29).

"Suffering the vengeance of eternal fire" (Jude 7).

No earthly wisdom can overthrow these solid truths. The same word that measures the life, salvation, redemption, and inheritance of the righteous in heaven, the existence of the Spirit, and the eternal existence of God Himself, measures the damnation of the lost in hell, where they will suffer the "vengeance of eternal fire." As long as the heavens shall stand, as long as the righteous will enjoy their life with Christ, so long shall the damnation of the wicked last. There is no way to evade the plain testimony of the Bible on this point. Eternal truth teaches eternal damnation in eternal fire.

We shall now come to the word *"forever,"* from *aiona.*

"And he shall reign over the house of Jacob forever; and of his kingdom there shall be no end" (Luke 1:33).

"The Son abideth forever" (John 8:35).

"Jesus Christ, the same yesterday, and today, and forever" (Heb. 13:8).

"Thine is the kingdom, and the power, and the glory forever" (Matt. 6:13).

"To whom be glory forever" (Rom. 11:36).

"The word of God, which liveth and abideth forever" (1 Pet. 1:23-25).

"Him that sat on the throne, who liveth forever and ever" (Rev. 4:9).

"Thy throne, O God, is forever and ever" (Heb. 1:8).

"They shall reign forever and ever" (Rev. 22:5).

Now, concerning the future of the wicked we read:

"To whom the mist of darkness is reserved forever" (2 Pet. 2:17).

"To whom is reserved the blackness of darkness forever" (Jude 13).

"Shall be tormented day and night forever and ever" (Rev. 20:10).

"And he shall be tormented with fire and brimstone; ... and the smoke of their torment ascendeth up forever and ever" (Rev. 14:10-11).

As long as God shall reign and His throne shall endure, the torments of Satan and wicked men shall last.

On the strength of all the facts presented in this chapter I affirm in the name of the God of the Bible, that the Scriptures nowhere employ any stronger words to express the endless existence of God Himself and of all that pertains to His eternal life, kingdom, and glory, than it uses to set forth both the never-ending felicities of the righteous in heaven, and the never-ending torments of the wicked in hell, "where their worm dieth not, and the fire is not quenched" (Mark 9:44).

ANNIHILATIONISTS' ARGUMENTS CONSIDERED

Those who hold and teach against the doctrine of eternal, conscious suffering, "everlasting punishment" in "everlasting fire," lay great stress upon certain texts that to them support the idea of utter extinction of being, or annihilation. I desire to be fair in this treatment and take up the main points of argument and carefully consider them. **All truth runs parallel and never contradicts. To build a doctrine upon peculiar interpretations of certain portions of scripture that are contradicted by other clear texts is unsound and unsafe.** [Editor's bold] I do not question the sincerity of our friends who hold opposite views. There are many able and good men in that group. But I am fully confident their position is wrong, and a fair and candid investigation will prove this.

First.—The main and strongest argument presented is this: "Death is the wages of sin (Rom. 6:23). 'The soul that sinneth, it shall die' (Ezek. 18:4). 'Sin, when it is finished, bringeth forth death' (James 1:15). Death is a state which can be reached only on a complete extinction of life. As long as there is any *life* about a man, he is not dead" (*Here and Hereafter,* p. 266, by Uriah Smith). This is a fair sample of all the arguments I have examined. It is assumed: 1.—That the term *death* in these texts signifies a cessation of the souls conscious being, and 2.—That the death of the sinner blots him out of existence. I firmly believe that materialists cannot sustain either of these propositions and with their failure to do so their position fails and their doctrine falls.

They also argue like this: "Christ paid the sinner's penalty. If that penalty was eternal torment, then Christ must have suffered eternal torment. But the penalty is death, and Christ paid it by dying." They assert that "this is unanswerable." But let us apply this logic to their position. Death means extinction of life, eternal obliteration, annihilation, and this is accomplished by the wicked being burned up root and branch. Now, we ask—Was Christ annihilated, burned up, eternally obliterated? If so, there is no more Christ. The fact is, such talk presents no real argument, for

Christ, an infinite being, could pay the penalty for finite creatures in a moment of time. Atonement does not require the *exact amount* and *kind* of suffering to satisfy justice. Thus, the fallacy of such argument is clearly seen. Some of the arguments here presented on this point of "death" have been given in the chapter on "Conditional Immortality."

The death of the sinner is not applied exclusively to his future state, but it is his present condition and realization. God told Adam, *"In the day that thou eatest thereof thou shalt surely die"* (Gen. 2:17). The penalty of death was to fall on them not beyond the judgment, nor thousands of years in the future, but in the very day of their sin. *"In the day* that thou eatest thereof, thou shalt surely die."* The Divine testimony stands unbroken. On the very day that Adam transgressed the law of God he died—not a physical death, for he lived many years after he was driven from Eden. Physical death, it is true, came upon Adam as a result of the fall (Gen. 3:17-19; 1 Cor. 15:21-22); but the sense in which he died on the day of his sin was that his soul was cut off from union with God. He died a spiritual death, became dead in sin. Sin separates the soul from God (Isa. 59:1-2); it cuts man off from the grace of divine life. His soul is alienated from God and brought under the dominion of sin. That state of man in sin is called "death"; and this death of the soul begins the very day sin is committed.

The soul is the volitional part of man's being. "The fruit of my body for the sin of my soul" (Mic. 6:7). It is the soul which is responsible to God. It sins, and it must be converted—saved. "Converting the soul" (Ps. 19:7). "The salvation of your souls" (1 Pet. 1:9). It is the soul of man which receives spiritual life from God in regeneration. "Hear, and your soul shall live" (Isa. 55:3).

Adam's sin not only brought him under the dominion of sin and into a state of spiritual death, but it affected the whole human race. "Wherefore, as by one man [Adam] sin entered into the world, and death by sin; and so death passed upon all men, for that all have sinned" (Rom. 5:12). "Death by sin came upon all men." "Death reigned from Adam to Moses" (Rom.

5:14). Since the law could not give life (Gal. 3:21), death reigned from Adam until Christ. He came "that they might have life" (John 10:10). Christ came so that people would get saved and such have "passed from death unto life" (1 John 3:14).

So death—the state of the sinner, the wages of sin—is, in part, a present condition and state of the soul. This fact overthrows all the arguments in favor of annihilation based on the word "death."

"But every man is tempted, when he is drawn away of his own lust, and enticed. Then when lust hath conceived, it bringeth forth sin: and sin, when it is finished, bringeth forth death" (James 1:14-15). When an individual allows lust to conceive in his heart it (lust) will bring forth death. Just as soon as a man yields to the evils of lust he commits sin. Death is the immediate result. Hear Paul's testimony: "I was alive without the law once: but when the commandment came, sin revived, and I died" (Rom. 7:9). The time when he was alive was during his infancy [as a young child] before he had knowledge of good and evil. When he arrived at the years [age] of accountability and obtained a knowledge of the law, or commandment, sin revived and he died— "I died." The very first sin that Paul committed produced death to his soul; hence he was dead.

All sinners are "dead in trespasses and sins" (Eph. 2:1-5). "Even when we were dead in sins" (Eph. 2:5). "And you, being dead in your sins" (Col. 2:13). "He that loveth not his brother abideth in death" (1 John 3:14). "To be carnally minded is death" (Rom. 8:6). "Awake thou that sleepest, and arise from the dead" (Eph. 5:14). "She that liveth in pleasure is dead while she liveth" (1 Tim. 5:6). "Thou hast a name that thou livest, and art dead" (Rev. 3:1). Jude speaks of some people "twice dead, plucked up by the roots" (Jude 12).

All these scriptures, with many more, clearly prove that death is a present condition of every sinner.

"The soul that sinneth, it shall die" (Ezek. 18:20). When? In the day that it sins. Lo! [Pay Attention!] The sinner is now dead, the Bible declares. The whole unregenerated world is in this life abiding in death.

The present dead state of sinners is the result of sin, a part of its wages. If they fail to repent and obtain spiritual life through Jesus Christ in this world, they will continue in the same state of death in the eternal world.

Death does not mean annihilation—utter extinction of being. In the very day Adam sinned he died (Gen. 2:17). Was he annihilated that day? No; he lived a natural life for nine hundred and thirty years (Gen. 5:5). When Paul came to a knowledge of God's commandment he died— "I died." Was he then blotted out of existence? No; he lived to persecute the church of God and finally to preach the gospel of Christ. Multiplied scriptures teach that, all sinners are now dead, abiding in death, some of them "twice dead." Are all these annihilated? No; the world is full of them; they live all around us. Yet the Bible declares they are dead. So, the death of the sinner does not mean that the sinner is blotted out of existence. This fact utterly refutes and overthrows the Russellite and Adventist idea based upon the word "death"—that utter extinction of being will be the eternal portion of the impenitent.

But these teachers ask, "Can a person be dead and still living?" Yes; "she that liveth in pleasure is dead while she liveth" (1 Tim. 5:6). Dead, yet living. The prodigal son in a far country was dead, yet was still living (Luke 15:32). Not only is this true of the sinner here, but it will be true hereafter. If annihilation is what is meant by the second death in the lake of fire and brimstone, then all will receive the same punishment, all will be blotted out. The Bible, however, teaches that some will have "greater damnation" in hell than others. All this proves the contrary [opposite] of blotting-out. In the case of annihilation all would receive the same doom.

Annihilation is not lasting punishment. To blot the wicked out of existence would be the opposite of "everlasting punishment," "eternal damnation," "torment forever and ever," which the Scriptures so plainly teach will be the eternal future of the ungodly. When the wicked are brought before the judgment seat of Christ in "shame and everlasting contempt" and their guilty consciences lash them as they writhe beneath

His piercing gaze, then to be suddenly blotted out of existence would be a speedy end to their awful punishment and would be a glorious relief; because if they were to become unconscious they would cease to suffer. If the wicked are to be eternally unconscious, to be no more, they would not suffer everlasting punishment, or torment, which the Bible so plainly declares they will suffer.

While some people view annihilation as punishment, the Buddhists, who number many millions, regard annihilation as the highest good. Certainly these millions do not regard nirvana as punishment.

Some say that the punishment of the wicked will consist in the awful thought of missing the enjoyment of heaven and in going into utter extinction of life. If this argument be true, and the torments that they will suffer consist in such thoughts while they stand in judgment, then that torment and sense of punishment will last only until they are blotted out— just the brief moment that they stand before God. When once blotted out they cannot suffer or be tormented. Could a bit of ashes, with no consciousness, no feeling, no life, suffer? Incredible! Preposterous! But the Bible declares that the lost will be "tormented forever and ever," suffer "everlasting punishment" "in everlasting fire."

Again I say, to blot the wicked out of existence would bring a speedy relief instead of an everlasting punishment. Thousands in this life, suffering the pangs of a guilty conscience, have committed suicide, expecting thus to get out of misery. But such an act brings one from misery to everlasting agony and endless despair, for there is no end for the soul, a fact which we have proved by the Bible.

The death of the soul incurred by sin is not a cessation of the soul's conscious existence or being. That this death is the opposite of conscious suffering I shall prove to be utterly false. In giving the Scriptural meaning of the term "death" as applied to the sinner both in this world and in that which is to come, Webster defines it thus: (1) "Separation or alienation of the soul from God; a being under the dominion of sin, and destitute of grace and divine life; called spiritual death." (2) "Perpetual separation from God; and eternal torments; called the second death." These definitions exactly express the Scriptural application of the term "death" to the sinner, both here and hereafter. The death of the soul is an alienation from God, from His approving smile and favor—the normal sphere of the soul's happiness—a state where the soul no longer partakes of His divine life. This is the wages of sin.

Every sinner, the Bible declares, is dead. Not less than one hundred clear texts prove this fact (e.g. Eph. 2:1-5; Col. 2:13; Rom. 6:11; Rom. 6:23; Matt. 8:22; Luke 15:32; John 6:53). The same state of death that the sinner is now in, will be his eternal state. But is the dead sinner unconscious? Is he blotted out of existence? Is he annihilated? No; he lives among us; he has an existence. His soul is also conscious. It sins and condemnation rests upon it. It is sensitive toward God.

Though the sinner is now dead, yet he passes through conscious suffering—suffers remorse of conscience, suffers the guilt of his crime. This is the present experience of tens of thousands [indeed, today it is in the millions and hundreds of millions!]. Just so it is in the eternal world. As long as the soul continues in sin, it "abideth in death" (1 John 3:14). If such persons refuse to come to Christ that they "might have life" they will go into the eternal world dead in sin. In this world, they have a chance of life; but once they pass into eternity, all chance is forever cut off and they are doomed to suffer an eternal separation from God in that unquenchable fire where "their worm dieth not" (Mark 9:43-46).

With the resurrection of all the dead from their graves, physical death, "the last enemy," will be destroyed (1 Cor. 15:21-26). The state of both the righteous and the wicked beyond that day will be eternal. With physical death destroyed the righteous will enter life eternal; and the wicked, eternal damnation, where "they have no rest day nor night" (Rev. 14:11), in the "mist of darkness ... forever" (2 Peter 2:17).

Second.—It is claimed that everlasting fire will not burn forever; for eternal fire converted the cities of Sodom and Gomorrah into ashes, and now the saline waters of the Dead Sea cover the very spot.

Jude 7 and 2 Pet. 2:6 are cited as proof. The latter part of this statement that the Dead Sea covers the very spot is not recognized as a fact by standard authorities; but the argument, however, is one of the strongest used by materialists against an everlasting hell. But their deductions are wrong.

To sustain the foregoing proposition, they must prove that the terms "Sodom" and "Gomorrah" always refer to the houses or buildings that made up those cities. When we speak of New York and London as wicked cities, we mean the people, not the houses and buildings. Sometimes in referring to a city or cities we speak with exclusive reference to the streets, buildings, manufacturing plants, etc.; at other times in referring to the same cities we speak exclusively of the inhabitants. When the prophet said, "Behold, this was the iniquity of thy sister Sodom, pride," etc. (Ezek. 16:49-50), he spoke of the people. When the Lord said that it would be more tolerable for Sodom in the day of judgment than for Capernaum, He did not mean the buildings, for they had long passed out of existence, but He meant the people of that city. Yes, Sodom and Gomorrah will be at the judgment. When God rained fire and brimstone from heaven upon those ancient cities their buildings, vegetation, and the mortal bodies of the people were turned into ashes (2 Pet. 2:6). But the souls of those people of Sodom and Gomorrah who committed fornication in "going after strange flesh" are, the sacred writer says, "Set forth for an example, suffering the vengeance of *eternal fire*" (Jude 7), not that the fire which literally consumed them was eternal, but that the fire of God's vengeance which began with their literal destruction is an eternal fire and will continue to constitute their torment.

Third.—Annihilationists lay no small stress on those texts which say that the wicked will be destroyed. Such scriptures as "the transgressors shall be *destroyed* together" (Ps. 37:38), "whose end is *destruction*" (Phil.

3:18-19), "punished with everlasting *destruction*" (2 Thess. 1:9), etc., are freely quoted and are considered absolute proof that the impenitent will be annihilated. That these texts, using the term "destruction," express the ultimate state and condition of the ungodly, I readily admit. But before they can be wrested [forcefully turned/twisted] in favor of the annihilation theory, it must be proved that "destroy" always means to obliterate, or blot out of existence. This I emphatically deny.

Adventists and Russellites assume the thing that they cannot prove. They say "destroy" means to blot out of existence. Sometimes it means that, but by no means does it always signify "to annihilate." For example, "Egypt is *destroyed*" (Exod. 10:7). Pharaoh's servants declared that Egypt was destroyed. The awful plagues that the Almighty sent into that land destroyed it. Yet Egypt was not blotted out of existence, annihilated; it was ruined. "The prosperity of fools shall destroy them" (Prov. 1:32). Surely the prosperity of fools does not blot them out of existence. "An hypocrite with his mouth destroyeth his neighbor" (Prov. 11:9). No one believes that a hypocrite with his mouth can annihilate his neighbor. A hypocrite can, however, ruin his neighbor's reputation; say things that will cast reflection on him, and thus destroy him.

"A fool's mouth is his *destruction*" (Prov. 18:7). "Be not righteous over much; neither make thyself over wise: why shouldst thou destroy thyself?" (Eccl. 7:16). Here are two texts in which "destroy" and "destruction" cannot mean annihilation. Again, "My people are destroyed for lack of knowledge" (Hos. 4:6). They ruined themselves and rendered themselves unfit for service. Not one of them, however, was annihilated. "O Israel, thou hast destroyed thyself; but in me is thine help" (Hos. 13:9). I ask in all candor and reason, Did Israel blot herself out of existence? Was Israel as a nation annihilated? Not so. After she had destroyed herself God said, "In me is thine help." Paul preached the very faith that he once had destroyed (Gal. 1:23). How could Paul preach a thing that was no more? Ah, the very faith that Paul once destroyed was still a living faith, and he preached it to others. Thus, we could multiply scripture texts to prove the falsity of the doctrine that teaches that "destroy" only means to annihilate.

A storm may "destroy" your crops, but not "annihilate" them; a cyclone may overturn your buildings and "destroy" them, yes, leave a path of "destruction" for hundreds of miles, and yet not "annihilate" a single thing [for there is rubble left there, which while messy, was not "annihilated"—without a trace of existence remaining]. So also will sin destroy your soul, and in the day of judgment you will be sentenced to be punished with everlasting destruction in the flames of a fire that "never shall be quenched." Man was created to enjoy God and to live on the plane of God's nature; but when man is by sin eternally destroyed—ruined—he will never meet the object for which he was created. He is eternally separated from communion with God—the normal sphere of the soul's happiness. Thus, he is ruined forever. Sin in this life separates between man and his God. A great chasm, or gulf, divides them. This will be still more awfully true after souls pass into eternity; then that great gulf will be impassable (Luke 16:19-26). Lost souls can never pass over it; they are ruined, eternally ruined.

But let us pass beyond the judgment, beyond the awful day of the Lord's coming, and what is the testimony of Divine truth? "And to you who are troubled rest with us, when the Lord Jesus shall be revealed from heaven with his mighty angels, in flaming fire taking vengeance on them that know not God, and that obey not the gospel of our Lord Jesus Christ: who shall be punished with everlasting destruction [away] from the presence of the Lord, and from the glory of his power; when he shall come to be glorified in his saints, and to be admired in all them that believe (because our testimony among you was believed) in that day" (2 Thess. 1:7-10).

This eternal separation from God is not annihilation but banishment away "from the presence of the Lord, and from the glory of his power"; exclusion from His approbation [approval or praise] forever, so that the light of His countenance can be no more enjoyed, as there will be an eternal impossibility of ever being reconciled to Him: and as the destruction is everlasting, it is an eternal continuance and presence of evil and absence of all good. Thus, the wicked will be eternally ruined, destroyed from the lofty end for which they were created.

There will be degrees of remorse and conscience torment, but all the lost will be equally excluded from the Divine presence. They forsook God in life, and now He shall forsake them forever. Such will be deprived of the infinite good and feel the might of God's justice. In the language of T. DeWitt Talmage, "It is the awful, stupendous, consuming, incontrovertible fact of the universe."

Fourth.—The following texts are quoted to prove utter extinction of being: "Shall utterly perish in their own corruption" (2 Pet. 2:12); "Except ye repent, ye shall all likewise perish" (Luke 13:3). That the word "perish" is here used to teach the hopeless and lost condition of the guilty I admit; but that it teaches the doctrine of annihilation I deny. While Webster defines the word, "To be destroyed; to become nothing," he also defines it, "To incur spiritual death; to suffer spiritual or moral ruin." The latter definition conveys the Scriptural use of the word when applied to the future of the wicked. If "perish" means only to come to nothing and be no more forever then the righteous will also be blotted out of existence eternally: "The righteous perisheth, and no man layeth it to heart" (Isa. 57:1). With reference to the ungodly, the word is used to signify their hopeless and lost state in hell, where there is no hope of ever being recovered from their awful state of torment. Their hope and opportunities are forever cut off. In this sense, they perish.

Fifth.—Consume. There are a few texts that speak of the wicked being consumed. But does this mean annihilation? Listen: "We are consumed by thine anger" (Ps. 90:7). Thou "hast consumed us, because of our iniquities" (Isa. 64:7). "My zeal hath consumed me" (Ps. 119:139). And yet all these were still living. Thus, it will be seen that such terms as "consume," "perish," "destroy," etc., in their Scriptural application to the lost, do not mean to annihilate. They express the hopeless, lost, ruined state of the wicked in their "everlasting punishment."

"Fret not thyself because of evildoers, neither be thou envious against the workers of iniquity. For they shall soon be cut down like the grass, and wither as the green herb. ... For yet a little while, and the wicked shall not be: yea, thou shalt diligently consider his place, and it shall not be. ... I have seen the wicked in great power, and spreading himself like a green bay-tree. Yet he passed away, and, lo, he was not: yea, I sought him, but he could not be found" (Ps. 37:1-2, 10, 35-36). "For as ye have drunk upon my holy mountain, so shall all the heathen drink continually, yea, they shall drink, and they shall swallow down, and they shall be as tho they had not been" (Obad. 16).

These texts are regarded as decisive in proving that the wicked will be blotted out of existence. They are quoted over and over again, and so positively that the uninformed are led to believe that the texts clearly teach the opposite of everlasting punishment. Such teachers find little comfort in the teachings of Christ in the New Testament. Their proof-texts are largely drawn from the Old Testament, and they are wrested [twisted] from their true meaning and application to build up these theories. That the aforementioned texts prove the annihilation of the wicked beyond the great day of judgment is wrong. Materialists cannot prove that the texts have any reference to the state of man beyond the resurrection. There is not even a hint of such a thing. Let us briefly consider each one.

In the first we are commanded not to fret because of evil-doers, nor be envious at them; "For," the Psalmist assures us, "they shall soon be cut down like the grass." Does he refer to their state beyond the resurrection at the last day? No; he is speaking of natural death. "For he knoweth our frame; he remembereth that we are dust. As for man, his days are as grass: as a flower of the field, so he flourisheth. For the wind passeth over it, and it is gone; and the place thereof shall know it no more" (Ps. 103:14-16). "Man that is born of a woman is of few days, and full of trouble. He cometh forth like a flower, and is cut down: he fleeth also as a shadow, and continueth not" (Job 14:1-2). "Man that is born of a woman" "is dust," he is "of few days"; his days are "like grass"—soon cut down. This speaks of the shortness of life. Evildoers and workers of iniquity may prosper, but their prosperity lasts only a few short years. They are soon cut down by death and go hence. Does that overthrow the doctrine of eternal punishment? It has no bearing on the subject.

"Yet a little while and the wicked shall not be." "I have seen the wicked in great power, and spreading himself like a green bay-tree," says the Psalmist, "yet he passed away, and lo, he was not." And the prophet adds that the wicked is "as tho he had not been." After the wicked man had passed away, David said, "I sought him, but he could not be found." When he diligently considered his place, it was not.

What weight have these poetical sayings of the Psalmist's against the everlasting torment of the wicked in hell? None whatever. They have no reference to the subject. David was speaking of the folly of wickedness. He testified that he had seen wicked men making a great display in the earth and spreading themselves like a green bay-tree, but that they soon passed away and were not. Death cut them down in the midst of their great honor and prosperity, and they were no more seen on the earth. They soon passed out of people's memory and were "as tho they had not been." Their place in earth's circles and societies, in the hearts and minds of the people, could not be found.

We all have seen the same thing—men who for a time were swept to the height of worldly honor and drank to the full of worldly applause, who were very popular in the people's minds and had a place in their hearts and affections. Thus like a green bay-tree they spread themselves, but in a few years death cut them off. They passed away; they were no more. Soon the memory of them was almost forgotten. They lost their place in the affections of the people. They are "as tho [though] they had not been." This is precisely what the Psalmist and the prophet teach in the texts before mentioned. To apply them to eternity beyond the judgment as expressing the state of the ungodly is to wrest Scripture out of its true meaning.

Similar texts to the aforementioned refer directly to death and the grave. For example, Job 7:9-10: "As the cloud is consumed and vanisheth away: so he that, goeth down to the grave shall come up no more. He shall return no more to his house, neither shall his place know him any more." To take this text and build a theory upon it, a person might say that there will be no resurrection of the dead. The writer, however, has exclusive reference to this life and to natural death. So, with all similar texts; they have no bearing on the future state of the ungodly beyond the judgment day.

Sixth.—The wicked will be burned up. "For, behold, the day cometh, that shall burn as an oven; and all the proud, yea, and all that do wickedly, shall be stubble: and the day that cometh shall burn them up, saith the Lord of hosts, that it shall leave them neither root nor branch" (Mal. 4:1).

Before this text can be made to prove the future annihilation of the wicked two positions will have to be sustained: first, that this text applies to the state of the ungodly beyond the judgment; second, that it is not metaphorical language. Neither of these positions can be sustained. This I shall clearly prove.

Mal. 4:1 does not apply to the state of the wicked in the eternal world. This great day that was to burn up the proud and those who do wickedly was to be ushered in by the coming of Elijah the prophet: "Behold, I will send you Elijah the prophet before the coming of the great and dreadful day of the Lord: and he shall turn the heart of the fathers to the children, and the heart of the children to their fathers, lest I come and smite the earth with a curse" (Mal. 4:5-6).

When did this reach a fulfilment? "But the angel said unto him, Fear not, Zacharias: for thy prayer is heard; and thy wife Elizabeth shall bear thee a son, and thou shalt call his name John. And thou shalt have joy and gladness; and many shall rejoice at his birth. For he shall be great in the sight of the Lord, and shall drink neither wine nor strong drink; and he shall be filled with the Holy Ghost, even from his mother's womb. And many of the children of Israel shall be turned to the Lord their God. And he shall go before him in the spirit and power of Elias [Elijah], to turn the hearts of the fathers to the children, and the disobedient to the wisdom of the just; to make ready a people prepared for the Lord" (Luke 1:13-17). "For all the prophets and the law prophesied until John. And if ye will receive it, this is Elias, which was for to come" (Matt. 11:13-14). "And his disciples asked him, saying, Why then say the scribes that Elias must first come? And Jesus answered and said unto them, Elias truly shall first come, and restore all things. But I say unto you, That Elias is come already, and they knew him not, but have done unto him whatsoever they listed [liked]. Likewise shall also the Son of man suffer of them. Then the disciples understood that he spake unto them of John the Baptist" (Matt. 17:10-13).

John the Baptist was the Elias [Elijah] that was the harbinger of that "great and dreadful day of the Lord," that day of fire. But what day did John usher in? The gospel day, the present day of fire and grace. John's twilight gave way to the "Sun of righteousness" who arose "with healing in his wings" (Mal. 4:2). The whole fourth chapter of Malachi is a clear prediction of the coming of Christ in His first advent and of the work of His redeeming grace. Although it was a glorious day thus ushered in, yet it was a dreadful day for the ungodly. Take, for example, the awful calamity that befell the Jews because they rejected the Messiah.

But do other prophecies point forward to Christ's first coming as ushering in a day of fire, a day to "burn as an oven"? Thus says the Lord: "Behold, I will send my messenger, and he shall prepare the way before me: and the Lord, whom ye seek, shall suddenly come to his temple, even the messenger of the covenant, whom ye delight in: behold, he shall come, saith the Lord of hosts. But who may abide the day of his coming? and who shall stand when he appeareth? for he is like a refiner's *fire* [which purifies], and like fullers' soap [a chemical solution used in bleaching cloth, along with stomping or beating, to cleanse it]: and he shall sit as a refiner and purifier of silver: and he shall purify the sons of Levi, and purge them as gold and silver, that they may offer unto the Lord an offering in righteousness. Then shall the offering of Judah and Jerusalem be pleasant unto the Lord, as in the days of old, and as in former years. And I will come near to you to judgment; and I will be a swift witness against the sorcerers, and against the adulterers, and against false swearers, and against those that oppress the hireling [worker] in his wages, the widow, and the fatherless, and that turn aside the stranger from his right, and fear not me, saith the Lord of hosts. For I am the Lord, I change not; therefore ye sons of Jacob are not consumed" (Mal. 3:1-6).

"For every battle of the warrior is with confused noise, and garments rolled in blood; but this shall be with *burning and fuel of fire.* For unto us a child is born, unto us a son is given: and the government shall be upon his shoulder: and his name shall be called Wonderful, Counsellor, The mighty God, The everlasting Father, The Prince of Peace. Of the increase of his government and peace there shall be no end, upon the throne of David, and upon his kingdom, to order it, and to establish it with judgment and with justice from henceforth even forever. The zeal of the Lord of hosts will perform this" (Isa. 9:5-7).

Both these texts show that the first coming of Christ was to be "with burning and fuel of fire."

Let us turn to the fulfilment: "And now also the ax is laid unto the root of the trees: therefore every tree which bringeth not forth good fruit is hewn down, and cast into the *fire.* I indeed baptize you with water unto repentance: but he that cometh after me is mightier than I, whose shoes I am not worthy to bear; he shall baptize you with the Holy Ghost, and with *fire*" (Matt. 3:10-11). "I am come to send *fire* on the earth; and what will I, if it be already kindled?" (Luke 12:49). This is not a day of literal fire that literally burns up the wicked, but a day of Holy Spirit fire, a day when the flaming truth consumes the sinners and burns up all the proud and wicked that would attempt to profess among God's people. Under the law,

Moses' church was full of sinners. But under the gospel, Christ established and keeps a pure church by the fire of holiness and truth.

The following scriptures shed light on Mal. 4:1,3, and show in what sense the wicked are burned into ashes: "The sinners in Zion are afraid; fearfulness hath surprised the hypocrites. Who among us shall dwell with the devouring fire? who among us shall dwell with everlasting burnings?" (Isa. 33:14).

"And the prophets shall become wind, and the word is not in them: thus shall it be done unto them. Wherefore thus saith the Lord God of hosts, Because ye speak this word, behold, I will make my words in thy mouth fire, and this people wood, and it shall devour them" (Jer. 5:13-14).

"And I will turn my hand upon thee, and purely purge away thy dross [worthless impurities], and take away all thy tin: and I will restore thy judges as at the first, and thy counsellors as at the beginning: afterward thou shalt be called, The city of righteousness, the faithful city. Zion shall be redeemed with judgment, and her converts with righteousness. And the destruction of the transgressors and of the sinners shall be together, and they that forsake the Lord shall be consumed" (Isa. 1:25-28).

"And it shall come to pass, that he that is left in Zion, and he that remaineth in Jerusalem, shall be called holy, even every one that is written among the living in Jerusalem: when the Lord shall have washed away the filth of the daughters of Zion, and shall have purged the blood of Jerusalem from the midst thereof by the spirit of judgment, and by the spirit of burning. And the Lord will create upon every dwelling place of mount Zion, and upon her assemblies, a cloud and smoke by day, and the shining of a flaming fire by night: for upon all the glory shall be a defense" (Isa. 4:3-5).

Thank God for this day of fire! All the wicked are devoured, consumed, from among the people of God, and the church is kept pure. Instead of this text's applying beyond the judgment, when the righteous will be caught up to heaven and the wicked will be cast into hell, it sets forth the present work of the Holy Spirit and the Word in redeeming to the Lord a pure and holy church, or bride.

The text is a metaphorical expression, figurative language. "All the proud, yea, and all that do wickedly, shall be *stubble*." This cannot be taken literally. Surely no one believes that the wicked will be turned into literal stubble. The language is highly figurative. This fact completely overthrows the doctrine of annihilation founded on this text. No more will the people be turned into literal stubble and be literally burned up than they will be turned into literal wood and literally devoured by God's Word (Jer. 5:14), or the prophets literally turned into wind (Jer. 5:13).

The Bible still teaches that the wicked shall "depart into everlasting fire" and suffer an "everlasting punishment."

THE ETERNAL HOME OF THE REDEEMED

We are told in the Bible that, as "strangers and pilgrims," we are simply "sojourning here" for a time (1 Pet. 2:11; 1:17). This world is not our final destiny; "our conversation [citizenship] is in heaven" (Phil. 3:20). "Knowing in yourselves that ye have in heaven a better and an enduring substance [possession]" (Heb. 10:34). Yes, IN HEAVEN, the place of God's throne and the home of the angels will be our eternal home; therefore "set your affections on things above, not on things on the earth" (Col. 3:2).

All God's people are "born from above" (John 3:3). Their citizenship is in heaven. Their names "are written in heaven" (Luke 10:20). The church of God is "the kingdom of heaven." Thus, all our hopes, our desires, and attractions are heavenward. The mind and heart of the Christian is naturally reaching out unto the eternal world. Earth loses its attraction. Its rubies and diamonds, its silver and gold, lose their luster and brilliancy, as the Christian with an eye of faith sees his riches in heaven. "Thou shalt have treasures in heaven" (Matt. 19:21). The Christian beholds the sparkling jewels, the unsearchable riches of Christ that await him over there, and as he presses forward toward the joy set before him earth's attractions fade away. None but the earthly minded desire to remain here. None but those who are void of spiritual life desire to make this earth their home. "Man is born for a higher destiny than that of earth. There is a realm where the rainbow never fades; where the stars will be spread out before us like islands that slumber upon the ocean; and where the beautiful beings which here pass before us like visions will stay in our presence forever."

The patriarchs and saints of the old dispensation understood this fact and "confessed that they were strangers and pilgrims on the earth" (Heb. 11:13). They understood that this was not their final abode. David, who reigned over Israel and inherited the Promised Land, says, "I am a stranger with thee, and a sojourner, as all my fathers were" (Ps. 39:12). They were strangers even in the land which they received for an inheritance—only pilgrims sojourning here for a short time. The writer of Hebrews says they were seeking a country, "a *better country,* that is, *an heavenly* [one]" (Heb. 11:14, 16). All these scriptures point us away from this earth to "another country." Our short pilgrimage upon earth is compared to a handbreadth, an eagle hastening to his prey, a swift post, a dream, a shadow, a vapor. Life is soon cut down, "and we fly away." That is, "man has gone to his eternal home" (Eccl. 12:5, Septuagint LXX).

That eternal home is not this earth, but is "an house not made with hands, eternal in the heavens" (2 Cor. 5:1). Yes, at the termination of earthly things there remains a future inheritance which is "eternal in the heavens"; "for the things which are seen are temporal; but the things which are not seen are eternal" (2 Cor. 4:18). Paul here speaks of things which are "temporal" (proskaira), for a season or time only; and then he speaks of things "eternal" (aioniou), without end, as the eternal Spirit (Heb. 9:14). The things which we see with our natural eyes are only temporal. They are things which have a short duration, must have an end. "The things which are seen are temporal"—temporary, existing for a time only. The temporal things include this earth and all that pertains to it. All nature teaches this fact. The grass covers this earth with a beautiful and verdant carpet, but soon it withers and molds away [decays and dies]. The leaves which come forth and cheer our hearts in springtime turn to a golden hue when the autumn winds blow and fall to the earth and then decay there. The sturdy oak in whose branches the fowls of the air lodge soon decays and is no more. The same lesson is taught in the animal kingdom.

So also our mortal bodies return to dust, to the earth. Everything around us teaches us "the end of all things" pertaining to earth. The earth itself is one of the things which we see, and Paul positively declares that all we see is temporal—must have an end. The eternal world then, cannot be this one on which we now live. It is the heavenly country.

There is a place called heaven. "The Lord he is God in heaven above" (Deut. 4:39). "The Lord's throne is in heaven" (Ps. 11:4). "The angels of God in heaven" (Matt. 22:30). The Lord Jesus Christ "was received up into heaven, and sat on the right hand of God" (Mark 16:19). "Who is gone into heaven, and is on the right hand of God; angels and authorities and powers being made subject unto him" (1 Pet. 3:22). "For Christ is not entered into the holy places made with hands, which are the figures of the true; but into *heaven itself,* now to appear in the presence of God for us" (Heb. 9:24). It is said of the first Christian martyr—Stephen—that he "looked up steadfastly *into heaven,* and saw the glory of God, and Jesus standing on the right hand of God, and said, Behold, *I see the heavens opened"* (Acts 7:55-56).

Yes, there is a place called heaven, and it will be our eternal home. When time has run its course; when the sun and moon have ceased to shine; when all things pertaining to earth and the earth itself have passed away and have been forgotten and left in the dim past, then, clothed with an immortal and glorified body, we shall dwell in a building of God, a house not made with hands, "ETERNAL IN THE HEAVENS." O my soul, press forward! Pleasures forevermore await you. O world to come, in exchange for the present! O ages, for a moment! A blessed, eternal communion in the holy, blessed, eternal life of God, in exchange for the sacrifices and sufferings of a few short years of earth. For the joy set before me I willingly endure hardness as a good soldier for Christ Jesus. Yes, gladly will I forsake home and loved ones to preach the gospel, and in exchange receive a home in that heavenly and better country.

Since the earth on which we now live will have an end (2 Pet. 3:10), what a consoling thought to know in ourselves that we have in heaven a better and an enduring substance [possession] (Heb. 10:34). This enduring substance is not a literal something upon this earth, as many imagine, but it is "an inheritance incorruptible, and undefiled, and that fadeth not away, reserved in heaven" (1 Pet. 1:4). "Leap for joy; for, behold, great is your reward in heaven" (Matt. 5:12).

Jesus, speaking of that future state said, "In my Father's house are many mansions: if it were not so, I would have told you. I go to prepare a place for you. And if I go and prepare a place for you, I will come again, and receive you unto myself; that where I am, there ye may be also" (John 14:2-3). In the Scriptures we have "Christ's house" and "the Father's house"; Christ's kingdom of grace here, and the Father's kingdom of glory above. The one applies to the earth, the other to heaven. In the passage quoted, Christ speaks of our future hope. By the "Father's house" He means heaven, for that is the Father's dwelling-place. Christ's house is the church here upon earth. By entering the latter we have access to the former, the Father's house. By "mansions," Christ desired to impart to the disciples that heaven, the Father's domain, is large and spacious. He did not wish, as some people believe, to convey the idea that everybody would have a separate house up there; He simply resorted to language that His hearers could understand. He spoke from the standpoint of a literal building so they could comprehend His meaning. Since the Father's house is so spacious, contains many mansions, "I go to prepare a *place for you.*" Christ went into heaven (Luke 24:51). So, in heaven He is preparing our eternal home.

It may be objected that heaven has been prepared from the foundation of the world. The kingdom of heaven, or heaven itself, was prepared from the beginning of the world (Matt. 25:34), but in that kingdom, Christ went to prepare a place for us. Again, Christ was a "Lamb slain from the foundation of the world" (1 Pet. 1:20; Rev. 13:8). Yet in reality, it was fulfilled when He came. So it is also with the place prepared for us. In reality, Christ went to prepare it for us; and the promise is that He will come again, not to remain here upon earth with us, but to receive us to Himself, that where He is there we may be also; that is, He will come back and take His church home to glory, to the world He went to prepare.

When will all this be fulfilled? "For the Lord himself shall descend from heaven with a shout, with the voice of the archangel, and with the trump [trumpet] of God: and the dead in Christ shall rise first: then we which are alive and remain shall be caught up together with them in the clouds, to meet the Lord in the air: and so shall we ever be with the Lord" (1 Thess. 4:16-17). Oh, the beauty of heavenly truth! The church came out of heaven and at last it will all be caught up to heaven and be ever with the Lord.

"But," says one, "did not Jesus teach that the meek 'shall inherit the earth' (Matt. 5:5)? The Psalmist said, 'But the meek shall inherit the earth' (Ps. 37:11). How do I harmonize 1 Thess. 4:16-17, with these scriptures?"

Peter fully explains them. He first shows that in the day of judgment this terrestrial globe, this earth will pass away by being burned up. He foretells its utter destruction: "But the day of the Lord will come as a thief in the night; in the which the heavens shall pass away with a great noise, and the elements shall melt with fervent heat, the earth also and the works that are therein shall be burned up" (2 Pet. 3:10). What then about the promise of Jesus that "the meek shall inherit the earth"? The apostle Peter answers, "We, according to his promise, *look for new heavens and a new earth*" (2 Pet. 3:13), which shall appear after the heavens and the earth composing this globe are "burned up" and "pass away" (2 Pet. 3:7-13). Peter is speaking of that land of light and bliss which Jesus went to prepare.

Also, the Revelator, after describing the judgment-scene, when this earth and its heavens fled away, "and there was found no place for them" (Rev. 20:11-15), says, "I saw a new heaven and a new earth: for the first heaven and the first earth were passed away; and there was no more sea" (Rev. 21:1). He saw the new heaven and the new earth after "the first heaven and the first earth were passed away." The new earth is the "heavenly country," the "better country" (Heb. 11:16).

The new heavens and the new earth will be so much grander than this that the present heavens and earth "shall not be remembered, nor come into mind" (Isa. 65:17); and unlike the present heavens and earth which shall pass away the new heavens and new earth "shall remain" (Isa. 66:22).

"God himself shall be with them, and be their God. And God shall wipe away all tears from their eyes; and there shall be no more death, neither sorrow, nor crying, neither shall there be any more pain: for the former things are passed away" (Rev. 21:3-4). "And they shall see his face; and his name shall be in their foreheads" (Rev. 22:4).

What a beautiful description of the glories of that eternal state. Surely the sufferings of the present time are not to compare with the glory that shall be revealed. "I will give unto him that is athirst [thirsty] of the fountain of the water of life freely" (Rev. 21:6). There the overcomers "shall inherit all things" (Rev. 21:7). "And he showed me a pure river of water of life, clear as crystal, proceeding out of the throne of God and of the Lamb" (Rev. 22:1). John saw this city as "having the glory of God: and her light was like unto a stone most precious, even like a jasper stone, clear as crystal" (Rev. 21:11). "And I saw no temple therein: for the Lord God Almighty and the Lamb are the temple of it. And the city had no need of the sun, neither of the moon, to shine in it: for the glory of God did lighten it, and the Lamb is the light thereof. And the nations of them which are saved shall walk in the light of it...for there shall be no night there" (Rev. 21:22-25). "And there shall be no night there; and they need no candle, neither light of the sun; for the Lord God giveth them light: and they shall reign forever and ever" (Rev. 22:5). "And the building of the wall of it was of jasper: and the city was pure gold, like unto clear glass. And the foundations of the wall of the city were garnished with all manner of precious stones" (Rev. 21:18). "And the twelve gates were twelve pearls; every several [each] gate was of one pearl; and the street of the city was pure gold, as it were transparent glass" (Rev. 21:21). "And he that sat upon the throne said, Behold, I make all things new" (Rev. 21:5). This is the new heavens and the new earth.

In this golden city of the new earth, the King of heaven will have His throne and reign forever and ever. Here the righteous shall "shine forth as the sun in the kingdom of their Father" (Matt. 13:43), yes, "as the stars forever and ever" (Dan. 12:3).

[Editor's note: Amen. Maranatha! Come Lord Jesus!]

THE END

CLOSING ITEMS

GOD, HUMANITY AND SIN

God created the heavens and the earth (Gen. 1); He is Creator of everything (John 1:3; Col. 1:16). He created and breathed life into mankind, through Adam and Eve, in the perfect Garden of Eden (Gen. 2). There was no sin, suffering, or death. Satan, the devil, tempted Eve and Adam to sin and disobey God by eating the fruit of the one forbidden tree of the knowledge of good and evil (Gen. 2:15-17; Gen. 3:1-5). This one act led to the introduction of sin into the world and the fall of humanity (Romans 5:12). Sin separated man from God; God cannot tolerate the presence of sin, due to His unimaginable holiness. God is love (1 John 4:8), but God is also a just God (Isa. 6:8; Deut. 32:4; Ps. 9:7-8), and sin and sinners will be judged and punished (2 Thess. 1:6-9).

Because of sin, we now live in a fallen and cursed world, with Satan as ruler over this world (Gen. 3:6-19; 1 John 5:19; Eph. 2:2). The result of this sin is death (Rom. 6:23), so we need a Savior (Rom. 3:10-18) to redeem us (by paying for and forgiving our sins) so we can be raised up to eternal life with God (Rom. 5:8). So, God, out of His love, sent His one and only begotten Son, Jesus Christ, to be born of a virgin, to live a perfect sinless life as a man, while being both fully man and fully God, and to die on the cross as full payment for our sins (John 3:16; 1 Pet. 1:18-19). God then raised Christ up from the dead after three days to everlasting life, so that all those who believe in Christ and call on His name will also be saved and raised up to eternal life, having their sins forgiven by the payment of the blood of Christ shed on the cross. Christ died for you; Christ took your place.

This forgiveness of sin is a (free) gift of God, obtained only through faith in Jesus Christ, and not by any works anyone can do for themselves (Eph. 2:8-10). The Lord Jesus Christ is God with God the Father and the

Holy Spirit as part of the holy Trinity. God offers this forgiveness of sin and this gift of eternal life freely and willingly to all who choose to receive it, for He wishes that none will perish (2 Pet. 2:9).

Personal note from the editor: If you are like me, you may have many questions, such as: Hey, Adam sinned thousands of years ago, why am I being held accountable for it now? Why did God curse His own creation? If He called creation good, why is there death and animals eating each other? Why is there pain and suffering if God is a loving God? What about evolution and the dinosaurs? Doesn't science, carbon-dating and the "big bang" theory prove that everything evolved billions of years ago from "primordial goo"? Why did God create us knowing we would sin and suffer? Does Satan really exist? If Satan is evil, why did God create him? And why does God allow evil to continue to exist now?

Please deal with your questions head on. Don't ignore them like I did for years, or pretend they don't exist, or let them cause you to stumble and fall, doubt, or worse, not believe in God and in Jesus. For more help on these and other questions, please visit: http://www.eachday.org/.

ACCEPTING JESUS CHRIST

To receive the gift of forgiveness and have eternal life, all you have to do is believe and confess Jesus Christ is your personal Lord and Savior in faith and ask Him to come into your heart and your life, for it is written:

"If you confess with your mouth Jesus as Lord, and believe in your heart that God raised Him from the dead, you will be saved; for with the heart a person believes, resulting in righteousness, and with the mouth he confesses, resulting in salvation" (Rom. 10:9-10).

There is no other way you can be saved! Going to church, being a good person, doing good deeds, performing religious rituals or other man-made schemes will not save you. Such a confession is also accompanied by a genuine sense of repentance (turning away from your sins).

If you want to declare Jesus as your Lord and Savior, below is a simple prayer you can say. Remember, it's not this prayer which saves you, it is your faith! It's what is in your heart that matters to God. You can do this right now, no matter where you are or what you have done in your life.

"God, I realize I'm a sinner and deserve punishment for my sins; please forgive me. I accept Jesus as my personal Lord and Savior. I believe He is Your Son and that He died on the cross as full payment for my sins, and You raised Him up again to eternal life. I place my complete faith, trust and hope in Christ alone for my salvation. Please come into my heart and my life. Thank You for Your awesome love and mercy and this free gift of grace through Christ! In Jesus' name, amen."

Now then, rejoice greatly, new brother or sister in Christ (John 3:1-6)! For God Himself, the Creator of all the universe (Gen. 1:1; Job 38:4), now has a personal relationship with you. Jesus has forgiven you and redeemed you from the dead in sin! You are now born-again (2 Cor. 5:17). You can now abide in Christ, and He in you (John 15:4-9; Gal. 2:20; Col. 3:1-3). Seek Him earnestly each day with daily prayer and Bible reading and He will make your paths straight (Pro. 1:7; Pro. 3:5-6; Ps. 5:3; 1 Thess. 5:16-18; Ps. 23). He will wash you with His righteousness by the blood He shed on the cross, so that on the day of judgment, He will raise you up, and you can stand holy and blameless before God (John 6:40; 1 Thess. 4:16; Matt. 16:27).

How awesome, staggering and stunning! The God of everything, from eternity past to eternity future, cares so much for you and loves you. Now go and be baptized as Jesus commanded (Acts 2:38; Acts 8:12; 1 Pet. 3:21; Acts 8:36-38; Acts 16:31-33), as a public profession of your faith! Hallelujah!

For some suggestions on what to do next in your daily walk (2 Cor. 4:16; Luke 9:23; John 12:25; Lam. 3:22-23) with Jesus Christ, please visit: http://www.eachday.org.

BENEDICTION

"Be still, and know that I am God." – Psalm 46:10

God does not grow tired.
He does not grow weary.
He does not need a day off.
He does not need to call in sick.
He does not need a vacation.
He does not need to stop and rest.
He does not need a timeout.
He does not need to stop and catch His breath.
He does not need to sleep.
He does not give up.
He does not need a second chance to get it right.

He does not "hope He can."
He does not "hope it may."
He does not "hope He might";
He is might.

He does not "wish He could."
He does not "wonder if He will";
It is His will.

He is not surprised.
He is not caught unaware.
He sees all.
He knows all.
He is everywhere.
He is omniscient.
He is omnipresent.

He is omnipotent.
And He will judge all.

He doesn't need to ask permission,
He doesn't need to pay better attention,
He doesn't need to take more classes
He doesn't need to learn anything new.
He doesn't need to wait to see what will happen.
He doesn't depend on mere man for His will to be done.

He is not ignored.
He is not disrespected.
He is not mocked.

He doesn't lie.
He doesn't omit truth.
He doesn't tell half-truths.
He doesn't change His mind.
He doesn't break His promises.
He doesn't forget you.
He cannot forsake you.
Ever, and forever.

He is patient.
He is loving.
He is kind.
He is slow to anger.
He is merciful.
He is righteous.
He is holy.
He is glorious.

He is just.
He just is.

He is who He always was.
He is who He is right now.
He is who He is for all eternity.

He is not overcome.
He will prevail.
He has prevailed.
He is with you this very instant,
Right now, right where you are at.

For He is Creator of all, before all, for all, in all, through all,
upholding all, above all, after all, and all in all.

Rest in the eternal peace of our Lord and Savior Jesus Christ,
today and forevermore. Amen.

BOOKS BY HOLY SPIRIT PRINTS

Visit http://www.eachday.org/

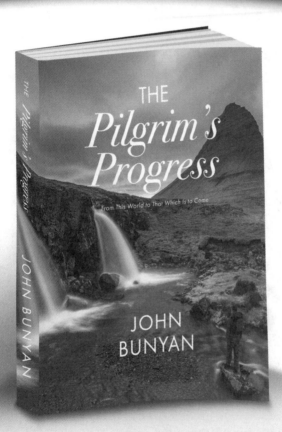

RAYS OF HOPE

Booklet contains 20 tear-out photo & verse cards about hope. Rays of Hope was created to help share the messages of assurance and hope that can be found in the Lord Jesus Christ with those who may find themselves in a lonely, dark, faraway or dangerous place.

His Perfect
STRENGTH...

Booklet contains 20 tear-out photo & verse cards about strength and courage. Created to help share the message of God's holy and perfect strength that can be found in the Lord Jesus Christ with those who may find themselves in a lonely, dark, faraway or dangerous place.

Visit http://www.eachday.org to order

FAITH CARDS

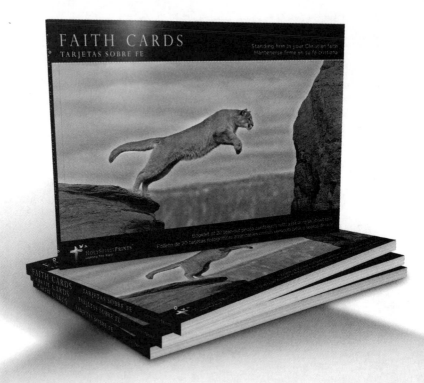

Booklet contains 20 tear-out photo & verse cards about faith. Faith Cards was created to provide simple reminders of the core of Christian faith. Great gift for loved ones in: armed forces, prison/jail, addiction/rehab, recovery centers, or others stranded or posted away from home whose faith is being tested in time of trial or tribulation.

Visit http://www.eachday.org to order

The Heavens
DECLARE...

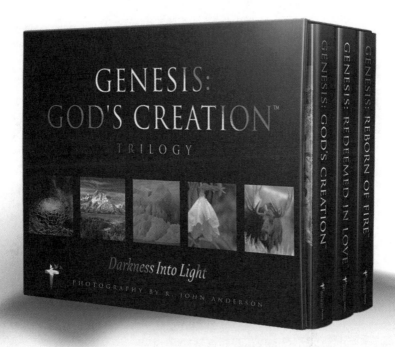

The **Genesis: God's Creation** Trilogy is a beautiful photographic journey through the story of creation as told in the Bible. Celebrate God's creation with your family and loved ones as you follow along from initial created glory, to sin and the fall, to redemption by Christ and back to glory again. The books of the trilogy are: *Genesis: God's Creation, Genesis: Redeemed In Love,* and *Genesis: Reborn Of Fire.*